Raves for
Jen Lancaster

"Jen Lancaster has a sense of humor as sharp as the teeth of those little alligators on her beloved Lacoste shirts."*

Pretty in Plaid

"After three laugh-out-loud memoirs chronicling her adult adventures in unemployment, city living, and weight loss, Lancaster looks back at the poignant moments of her youth and what she was wearing while living them."   —*People*

"Laugh and cry at this hilarious collection of essays that chronicle Jen's fearless fashion faux pas through the ages, her eleven (yup) years of undergrad, and her not so glamorous entry-level jobs. You'll revel in the lessons she gleans from her travails: Primary among them, that the ability to laugh at your mistakes is the best skill you'll ever learn."   —*Redbook*

"She pegs her memories to outfits—a green dotted swiss dress, some stylin' Jordache jeans, crocodile skin pumps—in a way that will win the hearts of all of us who still remember the dusty green of our 1980s-variety Girl Scout uniform (with its fetching beret and knee socks!)."   —*San Antonio Express-News*

"A hilarious look at the poor fashion choices that can, so sadly, define and saddle us with ridicule far beyond our formative years. . . . Lots of readers will find her brown tasseled clogs a disarmingly perfect fit; you can laugh at your own fashion foibles as Lancaster pokes fun at herself."   —*The Sunday Oregonian*

"A powerfully frank mutant strain of chick lit that resonates."

—**The Charlotte Observer*

continued . . .

Such a Pretty Fat

"She's like that friend who always says what you're thinking—just 1,000 times funnier."
—People

"Believe it or not, losing weight can actually be a laugh riot. . . . [Jen Lancaster] mercifully infuses much-needed humor into the life-altering process."
—Chicago Sun-Times

"A surprisingly charming weight-loss odyssey . . . with the winning honesty and humor [Lancaster's] fans have come to expect."
—Publishers Weekly

Bright Lights, Big Ass

"Lessons we've learned from Jen Lancaster: Bitter is the new black; Target is the new Neiman's; pit bulls and surly neighbors are the new Samanthas, Charlottes, and Mirandas; and midday whiskey is always a good idea. *Bright Lights, Big Ass* is a bittersweet treat for anyone who's ever survived the big city (and it's so funny I can almost forgive Jen Lancaster for being a Republican)."
—Jennifer Weiner, author of Best Friends Forever

"Refreshing, hysterical, illuminating! From the title on, *Bright Lights, Big Ass* is an antihaute hoot. In a voice that's charming and snarky, hilarious and human, Jen Lancaster tells the ultraglamorous truth about real big-city living. And it's better than anything on TV. Jen Lancaster does not teeter around on Manolo Blahniks or have lobster for breakfast. She eats pork chops and Lucky Charms. She dreams of shopping sprees at Target. She works temp jobs and spends too much time Googling things online. She wears footie pajamas. In other words, she's a lot like the rest of us. Thank God! And this wonderful, sweet, funny book proves once and for all that Carrie Bradshaw and her *Sex and the City* cronies are big, fat liars. Of course. Of course they are."
—Lori Jakiela, author of Miss New York Has Everything

"Wickedly funny, refreshingly honest, and totally unapologetic."
—Caprice Crane, author of Forget About It

"Jen Lancaster may be one of the few authors around capable of writing her own sitcom; she's smart, wry, and never afraid to point out her own shortcomings while letting us into her uniquely funny world."

—Melanie Lynne Hauser, author of *Jumble Pie*

"Jen Lancaster is the Holy Trinity of funny."

—Nicole Del Sesto, author of *All Encompassing Trip*

"After reading *Bright Lights, Big Ass* I'm convinced Jen Lancaster is the illegitimate love child of Nora Ephron and David Sedaris. She's simply that great—a genetic hybrid of two of America's most loved writers."

—Robert Rave, author of *Spin*

"Jen Lancaster is like David Sedaris with pearls and a supercute handbag."

—Jennifer Coburn, author of *Tales from the Crib*

Bitter Is the New Black

"The woman is nothing if not spunky, and she does have her funny moments, particularly when sticking it to the Man."   —*The Washington Post*

"Carrie Bradshaw meets Barbara Ehrenreich in this memoir about white-collar unemployment after the dot-com bubble burst."   —*Kirkus Reviews*

"She's bitchy and sometimes plain old mean, but she's absolutely hilarious."

—*Chicago Sun-Times*

"Jen Lancaster's confessions should be mandatory reading for the absurdly salaried young smart-arses around town . . . an honest, insightful, and ultimately feelgood handbook for what to do when ruin beckons."

—Deborah Hope of *The Australian*

"A classic story of comeuppance written from real-life experience by the funniest new author from the blogosphere. A strong debut and a must read for any American princess."   —Jessica Cutler, author of *The Washingtonienne*

Pretty in Plaid

A Life, a Witch, and a Wardrobe,
or the Wonder Years Before the
Condescending, Egomaniacal,
Self-Centered Smart-Ass Phase

Jen Lancaster

 NEW AMERICAN LIBRARY

New American Library
Published by New American Library,
a division of Penguin Group (USA) Inc.,
375 Hudson Street, New York, New York 10014, USA
Penguin Group (Canada), 90 Eglinton Avenue East, Suite 700, Toronto,
Ontario M4P 2Y3, Canada (a division of Pearson Penguin Canada Inc.)
Penguin Books Ltd., 80 Strand, London WC2R 0RL, England
Penguin Ireland, 25 St. Stephen's Green, Dublin 2,
Ireland (a division of Penguin Books Ltd.)
Penguin Group (Australia), 250 Camberwell Road, Camberwell,
Victoria 3124, Australia (a division of Pearson Australia Group Pty. Ltd.)
Penguin Books India Pvt. Ltd., 11 Community Centre,
Panchsheel Park, New Delhi - 110 017, India
Penguin Group (NZ), 67 Apollo Drive, Rosedale, North Shore 0632,
New Zealand (a division of Pearson New Zealand Ltd.)
Penguin Books (South Africa) (Pty.) Ltd., 24 Sturdee Avenue,
Rosebank, Johannesburg 2196, South Africa

Penguin Books Ltd., Registered Offices:
80 Strand, London WC2R 0RL, England

Published by New American Library, a division of Penguin Group (USA) Inc.
Previously published in a New American Library hardcover edition.

First New American Library Trade Paperback Printing, May 2010
10 9 8 7 6 5 4 3 2 1

Copyright © Jennifer Lancaster, 2009
Excerpt from *My Fair Lazy* copyright © Jennifer Lancaster, 2010
All rights reserved

NAL REGISTERED TRADEMARK—MARCA REGISTRADA

New American Library Trade Paperback ISBN: 978-0-451-22853-6

Library of Congress Cataloging-in-Publication Data

Lancaster, Jen, 1967–
Pretty in plaid: a life, a witch, and a wardrobe, or the wonder years before the
condescending, egomaniacal, self-centered smart-ass phase/Jen Lancaster.
p. cm.
ISBN 978-0-451-22680-8
1. Lancaster, Jen, 1967—Childhood and youth. 2. Authors, American—
21st century—Biography. 3. Girls—Humor. 4. Clothing and dress—Humor.
I. Title.
PS3612.A54748Z46   2009
814'.54—dc22   200805181897

Set in Bulmer MT • Designed by Elke Sigal

Printed in the United States of America

For the readers, booksellers, and librarians—
you make it all possible!

❖

C·O·N·T·E·N·T·S

❖

Part Two:
The Eighties *81*

Part Three:
The Nineties 227

Epilogue 341

A·U·T·H·O·R'S N·O·T·E

Some characters have been combined for storytelling purposes. In addition, other names and identifying characteristics have been changed for privacy reasons.

The soul of this man is in his clothes.

—WILLIAM SHAKESPEARE

. . . .

Clothes make the man. Naked people have
little or no influence on society.

—MARK TWAIN

. . . .

It has always been the prerogative of children and half-wits
to point out that the emperor has no clothes.
But the half-wit remains a half-wit, and
the emperor remains an emperor.

—NEIL GAIMAN

Pretty in Plaid

November 6, 1974

Dear Mattel,

Your Bella Dancerella Barbie is junk!

Just today the head fell off her. Yesterday, her body fell apart. I do not have any of the pieces to send you because they are junk now.

Maybe you should send me a ~~replac mat riplacemint repleasement~~ another one immediately before I tell all my friends what shoddy products you manufacture.

Your friend,

Jennifer Lancaster

P.S. My Dawn dolls fell apart in the tub when I tried to take them swimming. Please send two Dancerella Barbies to make up for this tragic loss.

October 1, 1976

Hi, Mrs. Cummings,

You don't know me but I am my brother Todd's sister. My mom says Todd is failing your Spanish class. She yelled at him a bunch for getting an F on the test and he was mad. He kept saying "no bueno."

My mom is probably too emotional about Todd's grades to discuss the situation rationally, so you should probably work through me. I am enclosing a blank piece of paper so you can give me a progress report on Todd.

Okay, thank you,

Jennifer Lancaster

P.S. Hola!
P.P.S. Look at me! I'm already bi-lingual!

December 12, 1980

Hello, Brooke Shields!

I'm a big fan even though I'm not allowed to see *The Blue Lagoon*. Plus you're from New Jersey and I used to live in New Jersey and we have the same eyebrows, so it's like we've already kindred spirits.

Anyway, I saw your commercial and I like the Calvin Klein jeans you advertise. I figure you probably have some extra since Mr. Klein likely gave them to you for free.

You're in luck – I happen to need some Calvin Klein jeans and no one will buy them for me so why not solve both our problems and send me some? Seriously, no one in this stupid cow town has Calvins and I'd be the first if you sent me some and I'm pretty sure that would catapult me to instant celebrity.

Your friend,

Jennifer Lancaster

P.S. My auntie says your ads are kitty porn, but that makes no sense because you're totally wearing pants! Also? There are no cats!

February 14, 1981

Brooke,

I am not saying "dear" because you are not dear to me. I ask you for extra pants and you send me back a frigging postcard?

You are NOT COOL.

And I totally pluck my eyebrows now. You should, too.

NOT your friend,

Jennifer Lancaster

P.S. All is forgiven if the pants are in the mail.

January 28, 1984

Principal Stern,

I'm sorry you had to take time out of your busy day of principal-ing to deal with such a trivial matter.

Honestly, I have no idea how or why Justine Moore got the idea that I hated her and that I specifically carried nail scissors around to simulate snip-snip sounds whenever I was behind her in the hallway. And I couldn't begin to tell you who started the rumor about people wanting to hack off a chunk of her ridiculous red hair to punish her for being such a b-i-t, well, you know, female dog.

These allegations against me are hurtful and untrue even though she TOTALLY tried to get with my date by grinding on him when I hit the bathroom at the last school dance. As you can see, she'd have it coming if someone <u>were</u> to give her an unexpected haircut, but it wouldn't be me.

Your student,

Jeni Lancaster

P.S. She has NO proof.

December 15, 2008

Dear Self,

Someday in a fit of nostalgia, or perhaps after watching *Gross Pointe Blank* again, you will be tempted to attend a high school reunion.

Before you load up the CD player with eighties tunes and create a triptych, please read this book and re-familiarize yourself with all the smack you talked about your classmates and hometown.

And then take yourself on a spa weekend instead so you don't accidentally, you know, get lynched.

You can't go home again.

At least not after mocking the prom queen.

Best,

Jen

Prologue

When I was a kid, my mother's mantra was *You are what you eat.*

Considering that I broke the long silence from birth until my thirteenth month of life by uttering the word "cookie," it was safe to say even then that it would not become mine. I knew *I* wasn't a bruised banana pulled from her handbag while waiting on line at the post office, nor was I an unsweetened bowl of Cheerios topped with wheat germ from the foul-smelling hippie health food store. Sure, I'd have happily been a Hershey bar[1] or a bowl of mouth-shredding Crunch Berries, but a poorly boned bowl of homemade chicken soup or a salt-free lentil casserole? No.

Right about the time I was able to cut my own meat and make

------

[1] With almonds.

my own sartorial choices, my Auntie Fanny gave me some of my cousin Stephanie's old clothes. I was instantly enamored; there were colors and styles I'd never seen before.[2]

Instead of the ducky-and-moo-cow tops my mother bought or made by hand, I took first grade by storm in Steph's old purple suede fringe vests and rainbow-striped corduroy bell-bottoms and peace symbol T-shirts. I mean, why would I dress like a baby when I could look like an extra from *Sonny and Cher Show* reruns?

I may not have been able to tie my shoes or spell my last name, but I knew one thing for sure—I was not what I *ate*.

I was what I *wore*.

You never can tell when nostalgia might strike. For many people, it's triggered by a long-forgotten scent, say, the nose on a glass of wine that evokes the aroma of ripe grapes hanging from the arbor in their great-grandmother's backyard. For others, memories come flooding in when a fancy small-plates restaurant conjures up an ironic bread pudding that happens to taste just like the one Mrs. Maguire brought to that block party the day Nixon resigned. For some, it's a snippet of a song: Three bars from Toto's "Africa" broadcast from a passing car and they're no longer swinging a Halliburton briefcase down Michigan Avenue to get to a branding meeting. Instead, they're huddled in their high school commons at lunch, cramming for a fifth-period chemistry test.

And me? Well, more often than not a piece of clothing will spark my memory.

I clearly remember what I had on when I learned the *Chal-*

....

[2] Possibly because they were circa 1966.

lenger exploded,[3] and I know what I was wearing when President Reagan was shot.[4] I saw my husband, Fletch, for the first time when I was waitressing in a pink polo and low-waisted men's green chinos, and a year later when we had our first kiss, I was in a red Ralph Lauren turtleneck, loose sand-colored 501s, and had a red and blue grosgrain band around my watch. I can even tell you the exact gauge of the sweater set I wore the day I made the mistake of carrying a Prada bag to the unemployment office . . . no matter how much I'd like to forget.

The sizes on the tags of my clothing may have changed over the years, but the memories are a constant.

In *Pretty in Plaid*, I recall the outfits (and events) that ultimately made me the kind of condescending, egomaniacal, self-centered smart-ass who would bark orders at waitresses and make assistants cry. My road to hell wasn't paved with good intentions— it was cobbled with gold lavalieres and Gucci purses.

As I examine my life through this book, I can't help but wonder if my mother was right. Maybe I really *was* what I ate. And maybe if she'd let me eat a little more sugar, I'd have come out sweeter.

My parents (and a prom queen or two) might disagree with my recollections and may have entirely different opinions on where and why things got off track.

So maybe it wasn't the sugar. Maybe I'm just naturally an ass.

But, really, who knows? All I can say for sure is that my story begins with kneesocks and a lobster bib. . . .

....

[3] A too-tight pink parka from Lands' End that I couldn't zip over my green wool crew-neck sweater.

[4] A scratchy purple V-neck.

Part One

The Seventies

Sock Lobster

(Navy Knee-Highs)

"I don't need to see a menu; just bring me the lobster, please." I smile beatifically as I return the large plastic multipaged menu to the waitress. I gesture over to the tank by the front door. "Get me the one with the green rubber bands around his claws. He seems like a bully and I don't care for bullies."

Before writing anything on her little spiral pad, the be-smocked waitress gives her golden beehive a quick scratch with the cap of her pen as she seeks my mother's approval. "Is she sure?"

I exhale with angry frustration. "Of course I'm sure; I just told you. And please double-check that I get the Green Meanie. His time has come."

My mom reaches for my clenched hand and in her most soothing tone says, "Jennifer, be reasonable. You don't *really* want lobster, do you? It costs more than ten dollars a pound. How about a juicy steak or a nice cheeseburger with French fries? You can have ice cream afterward."

"Thanks but no. The lobster will be fine." I always get a cheeseburger and fries when we go out to dinner. Steak is acceptable, but only if it's practically burnt and bone-dry. The idea of meat juice touching any other food items, particularly absorbent ones like bread or mashed potatoes, makes me want to hurl.

Besides, today is special and I demand the kind of meal that's commensurate with the occasion. And if what I want is ten dollars a pound, then maybe *someone* should have taken that into consideration when extending the invitation in the first place.

"How about spaghetti or some veal parmesan?" my father suggests. He rubs the bridge of his nose where his aviator frames hit. His new glasses normally make him look like Oscar Goldman from *The Six Million Dollar Man*, but at the moment he appears more tired and aggravated than anything else. I suspect the idea for today's two-hour road trip was not his. "Or how about the hot dog?"

My brother, Todd, makes a face at me from behind his napkin. "You can't have the lobster because you're a *baby*."

I point an accusatory finger at him. "When you stop being afraid of mayonnaise and tomatoes, you let me know, *Toad*." I shift out of striking distance—my brother is famous for his stealthy punches—and my bare legs squeak against the vinyl. My mother wanted me to wear a ridiculous pair of maroon tights today but I balked because my sweater is red and I refuse to clash, particularly on such an auspicious occasion. I compromised by wearing a thick pair of ribbed navy kneesocks, which look far better with my plaid pleated shirt, anyway. Granted, my thighs are freezing, but one must occasionally make sacrifices for fashion.

After I wave off my brother's opinion, I turn my attention to my parents. "You guys didn't drive me all the way to Connecticut for a *hot dog*. No. I want a lobster. You promised me a lobster. It's my birthday and you said I could have a birthday lobster. I mean, when am I going to turn eight again?"

Seriously? Eight is a big deal. Eight's halfway through primary education. Eight means being old enough to stay up and watch *Good Times*. Eight is the new ten. For God's sake, eight means I'm going to be *driving* in a few years.[5]

Best of all, being eight means this is the last year I have to be in the oh-so-lame Brownies with all those little girls. I ask you, what am I supposed to talk about with a six-year-old? *Sesame Street?*[6] I mean, Oscar grosses me out because he's probably sloshing around in the garbage juice that forms in the bottom of the can like when my brother doesn't take it out when he's told, Bert and Ernie are way too confrontational, plus Bert needs to address his unibrow, Big Bird's just plain annoying, and Snuffleupagus is beyond depressing. Can someone please give that beast a hug or a cookie or something?? Personally, I'd rather watch *The Jeffersons* or *Gilligan's Island* or *Bewitched*, except for when Sam's evil cousin Serena is on. All that white skin and black hair creep me out. Girlfriend needs a tan, like, now.

Did I mention I loathe being a Brownie? Number one, I look terrible in that particular shade of brown. Number two, there's an ugly tunic and white gloves involved. Listen, I'm eight—do you

....

[5] Okay, fine, I'll be driving in eight more years. Math is not my strong suit.

[6] Although I do kind of dig *Zoom*, which is on right afterward. That's Boston, Mass—0-2-1-3-4!

know how much dirty stuff I accidentally touch on a daily basis? I'd be way better off in dishwashing gloves. White cotton only serves to highlight my mother's inability to properly add bleach; when she uses too little, they look dingy, and when she uses too much, my hands itch and smell like a pool all day. As for number three, which is wearing a beanie? No.

Plus, no one ever wants to get together and play with Barbies after our meetings. My troop members all prefer those bizarre, big-headed, tiny-bodied, pajama-wearing, pant-wetting baby dolls. One of the girls in the troop named Jodi has this horrible doll that will actually crap its pants after she feeds it this weird green paste. I'm sorry, this is a selling point? I ask you—why would I want to change anyone's diapers when I can change their shoes and hairstyle instead?

The Brownie troop leaders leave much to be desired, too. They're always, *"Oh, let's do crafts!"* Um, *hi*, I'm eight—exactly how many hand-sewn wallets does a girl need, particularly since my Brownie-logo coin purse already hangs from my belt? Besides, it's not like I have any folding money to put in a wallet. And while we're on the topic of crafts, who thought it was a good idea to make Christmas decorations out of the brown paper roll from inside toilet tissue? What am I supposed to say? *"Hey, Jesus! Here's an ornament from me* and *the Charmin Corporation. Enjoy your birthday!"* We haven't actually covered the definition of "sacrilegious" in Sunday school yet, but I'm pretty sure worshipping our savior with ass wipe would qualify.

In our last meeting I had to assemble this hideous pin out of hairy metallic pipe cleaners and then the leaders expected me to just give it to some girl and be all, *"Here's a piece of junk I made in*

Brownies. Wanna wear it and be my friend? Or maybe I could in-
terest you in a hand-sewn wallet?" I bet the cool girls in my class,
like Nancy (with her entire basement full of board games) or Andrea (who has her own tube of tinted lip gloss and pierced ears),
would laugh in my face if I tried to give them a pin.

Now the Junior Girl Scouts on the other hand . . . I'm into
that. I love, love, love Girl Scout uniforms because they are *the*
best shade of green—kind of grassy, kind of mossy, kind of like
the color in a really minty Shamrock Shake. I've discussed mix-
and-match uniform options at length with the two normal
Brownies in my pack. Stacey said she'd be happy with anything,
while my friend Donna plans on going for the whole mod pantsuit look with a white turtleneck and short jumper worn over
flared slacks.

Personally, I've recently become more of a purist after spending my formative years dressed like I was headed to Woodstock. I
now prefer a little more tailoring and would like the printed white
blouse with the longer dress and some simple textured white
tights paired with my wedge school shoes. (Some girls wear the
green tights; I am not one of those girls.) Naturally, I'm a big fan of
the sash and, of course, the beret. How great will a beret look over
my Laura Ingalls Wilder braids? I can't wait![7]

Once I'm a Junior Girl Scout, I'll get to go camping and on
skating outings and to jamborees and stuff. I have no clue what
a jamboree is, but I'm banking on it including cotton candy and
elephant ears.

While I contemplate how fantastic my life as a Girl Scout's

....

[7] Annoyingly, I have to, at least 'til September, when school starts.

going to be, the beehived waitress sets the huge, steaming plate of lobster in front of me.

Um . . . guys?

Someone accidentally left the face on this thing.

Two blank black eyes glare accusingly at me from the end of their googly stalks. And there are all kinds of, I don't know, flippers or gills or testicles or something sticking off its sides.

Here's the thing—I know lobsters start off this way because I've seen them plenty of times before. Last summer at my mom's family's rental house in Maine, I even got to play with them before they were cooked. We raced them and mine was the fastest, of course. But I must have gone to bed before everyone ate because I'd have remembered a gigantic lobster holocaust.

I thought restaurants only served the big meaty tail and maybe the claws with a side of melted butter. At no point did anyone mention I'd receive a soppy dish of steamy sea bug. The polite thing would have been to note this on the menu.

I stare at my dinner.

My dinner stares back.

We appear to be at an impasse.

The waitress returns with a giant plastic bib and secures it around my neck, taking pains to protect my red sweater and most of my plaid lap. Is it just me, or does she seem a little smug right now?

I look at my lobster. My lobster looks at me. I really don't like where this is going.

"Jennifer, eat your dinner before it gets cold," my father admonishes. Yeah, he's definitely still salty about driving to Connecticut. Honestly, I don't know why we came all that way to eat at some cheesy diner, either. Our house in New Jersey is, like, five miles from the bridge into New York City. Surely someone there sells lobsters?

Resigned, but not about to be beaten, I pick it up by the front claw and attempt to take a bite. I figure maybe the shell gets soft during cooking and it turns all tasty like those crabs in Baltimore? I bite down and suddenly fear I may have busted a baby tooth.

"No, stupid, that's not how you eat it! Dummy! You tried to eat the shell! Ha!" my brother crows. Laugh it up, Toad. When your Farrah Fawcett poster[8] gets mysteriously ripped next week, we'll see what's so funny then.

"You have to tear it open. Do it like this." Mom takes her hands and demonstrates what looks like the ultimate Indian burn technique. "Once you've twisted it open, then you tear it apart."

I do as I'm told but I'm surprised by how hard this thing is to twist. Big Mean Green still has some fight left in him. It takes me a couple of tries, but I finally get this bastard turned. Then I pull it apart and . . . *aahhhhhhhhhhhhhh!*

"What is that?!" I scream, pointing at all the tiny horrible pink balls that have come bouncing out of my lobster's body.

"Oh, that's the egg sac. You must have a female. You should eat those, they're delicious!" my mother exclaims. Um, yeah. I would rather kiss a public toilet than bring this stuff within a foot of my mouth.

You'd think after eight years of fighting on all issues dietary and wardrobe-related, she might have some idea about what I do

---

[8] You know, the one where she's smuggling pencil erasers? Frankly, she makes what should be a tasteful one-piece suit look too racy and I don't care for it.

and do not find acceptable. Perfect example? Earlier today I got my present. All I've asked for practically since I turned seven was a Bella Dancerella Barbie. She's got flowing curly blond hair but it's slicked back in a loose ponytail and topped with a crown, so that right there makes her cooler than all the Barbies with stick-straight hair. She's not all rubbery like the other Barbies, either—instead her limbs are firm plastic and her waist is jointed so you can make her do ballet. She can spin and do splits and she comes with toe shoes and a tutu. *A tutu,* I tell you!

So this morning we're eating pancakes[9] and my mom hands me an oblong box and I get all excited because there's only one thing that comes in a box this shape, right? I rip off the paper and come face-to-tear-drop-shaped-head with some messed-up Hallmark-Precious-Moments-Holly-Hobby-nightgown-wearing bullshit doll with a soft shapeless cotton body and a neck that couldn't possibly support her own pumpkin head.

Yeah. I wanted the Dancerella Barbie and instead I got a doll with gigantism and male-pattern baldness.

My mom was all excited so I couldn't even ask, "Why would you give me this?" I had to pretend that I liked it, but I feel guilty every time I look at it because I hate it. I should be grateful, but bad gifts offend me because they say one of two things: either *Even though I've never seen you play with a baby doll and you've made your distaste for them quite clear, I'm going to give you one anyway in an attempt to force you to conform to my idea of how my daughter should be,* or *I bought what was on sale.*

....

[9] Made from lumpy buckwheat and served with but a single drop of faux maple syrup and no butter whatsoever.

Now not only am I stuck with Baby Big Head, but Barbie and I are going to have to call in favors from the stuffed animal brigade in order to send her out on a double date just to ease my guilt . . . and yet this problem pales in comparison to the idea of my birthday dinner containing nothing but reproductive organs.

I twist my lobster again and more horrible parts fall out. I shudder. "The green stuff? What's the oozy green stuff?"

My brother chimes in. "Tomalley, dummy. That's the lobster's liver! You've got lobster liver on your plate! That makes you a lobster liver lover. Ha!"

Jesus Christ, who brings someone a gigantic plate of *liver* and *egg sac*? What kind of messed-up, Draconian diner is this that they would serve such a plate of horrors to a child? On her *birthday*? I mean, I'm only eight! I can't possibly be expected to deal with the trauma of all that's on my plate right now.

"Did you think you'd just get a tail and some claw meat?" my father asks wearily.

I nod. Here's the thing—I wanted Big Mean Green to die for being a jerk to the other lobsters in the tank; I just didn't want his—or I guess *her*—blood on *my* hands. My father takes my plate and gives it to my mom. "Julia, make this less prehistoric for her."

My mom begins to break the lobster down, stealthily stuffing disgusting little bits of entrails into her mouth. My mother is descended from a race of people whose diets primarily consisted of whatever crap they could find washed up on the beach. That part of my ancestry must be recessive.

Minutes later, she returns my plate with nothing but tail and claw meat on it. I nod with approval—this is better. I saw off a part of the white flesh and give it a few generous dunks in the vat of drawn butter. I tentatively place the bite in my mouth and begin to chew.

The lobster is . . . rubbery. Not fishy or crabby or meaty or velvety. It's just rubbery. This tastes like I took a Wham-O Super-Ball, cut it in half, and dipped it in herbed butter. I bet if I threw my lobster tail on the floor it'd bounce around all crazy-like, knocking over coffee cups and spilling soup. I take another bite and chew and chew and chew, but I seem to make no headway. I may as well be nibbling on my dad's new set of Firestones. We drove all the way to Connecticut for *this*?

"What do you think?" my mom asks expectantly, smoothing a hand over her Carol Brady–esque modified mullet.

I contemplate before I answer. "I think I'd like a cheese-burger."

And no, I'm not sorry. If someone would have just saved me one damn bite last summer in Maine at the lobster boil and hadn't greedily wolfed down every scrap themselves, we could have avoided this whole fiasco.

No one gets me a burger[10] so I concentrate on dipping my French fries in the butter sauce. Not bad! I poke a bit more at my lobster and move it around my plate so it looks like I've eaten whatever arbitrary amount is enough to score me ice cream after-ward.

If my dog Samantha were here, I could try to slip her some of the gristly white meat, but she's not much of an accomplice.[11]

....

[10] Fine, just starve me.

[11] Unlike Maisy, the dog I have now. She's so accommodating she'll even eat the napkin.

She's as likely to spit out yucky stuff (e.g., spinach, zucchini, anything my Noni grows in her own garden, which I'm relatively sure she fertilizes, *ahem,* herself) as I am. Chances are if I'm not into it, Sam's not either.

The waitress returns to clear our plates and she's smirking again. Listen up, Flo, at least my hair isn't so big I have to scratch my head with a writing utensil.

"Didn't like it?" She snickers.

"I'm eight; I don't eat that much," I reply. Seriously, I will not be mocked by someone in a *smock.* "However, I've left room for dessert. I shall have pistachio ice cream, please," I tell her officiously.

I'm only guaranteed dessert when we're dining out, so I make sure to order my treat when I select my entrée. (I suspect the waitresses appreciate my efficiency.) The only problem is my mom always dives into whatever confection I receive, which is *so* not fair. She says she doesn't want a whole dessert; she just wants some of mine. I counter by telling her that's unfortunate, because I want *all* of mine and to keep her damn fork away from my pie.

Ninety percent of the trouble I've been in in my life started with dinner in a restaurant.

The waitress tells me, "Comin' right up, hon." And then she winks at my parents, who wink back. What does that mean? Is she in on our at-home no-dessert policy? Is that bitch going to bring the check in lieu of my ice cream?

Before I can figure out what kind of cryptic Morse code is being blinked out by all the adults around the table, I'm descended upon by a crowd of waitresses. They all rush up on me from out of nowhere, their itchy beehives undulating in the wind created by their acceleration. In the center of this huge, hasty group, I notice a giant glowing orb and it's headed straight for me.

Suddenly, I'm enclosed by a wall of flames and smocks and aprons and everyone begins to shout at me at once. I look around and I can't see any of my loved ones, not even Todd. Where are they? What's happening to me?

The noise!

The fire!

The beehives!

The humanity!

The . . . oh, wait.

They're not screaming.

They're singing what sounds like "Happy Birthday." They're trying to celebrate me, not assassinate me.

And yet this still is singly the most terrifying moment of my entire fucking life.

This is probably why we had to drive all the way to the sticks of Connecticut. No quality restaurateur in New York would agree to frighten a child in this manner.

I claw at my thighs because my legs are suddenly covered in raised, itchy red bumps. I rub my scratchy calves together and practically light myself on fire with the friction. I feel like I'm crawling with hundreds of biting ants or like I've caught the chicken pox again times ten.

Seriously?

Stop singing and get me some calamine lotion.

The waitresses finally, mercifully end the song and I make a pledge right here and now that I'm going to go to college and get a good job afterward so I will never be responsible for making a poor little eight-year-old break out into *hives* on her goddamned birthday.

The cake is nice, though.

You Say Extortion
Like It's a Bad Thing

(Green Dotted Swiss Dress)

No one tells you how financially demanding it is being eight. Now that I'm eight, I have the freedom to swing by the candy store when I'm out riding bikes with Donna and Stacey. I'd go there every day, but Swedish Fish aren't free, you know. I also need money to stop in the park and grab a hot dog from the Sabrett guy so I don't have to down as much of my mother's lunchtime culinary abominations.

You think I'm exaggerating? Once she ran out of grape jelly so she gave me peanut butter and lime marmalade on sprouted wheat bread.

Um, yes, thanks, I *would* prefer a spanking to this.

Point? Being eight takes cash and my meager allowance is not cutting it. I *was* able to increase this ration last fall by staging a strike while my dad tried to watch football. I marched around in circles singing "Look for the Union Label" until he promised to increase my weekly allotment from twenty-five to fifty cents. Had I known he'd just come off of six weeks trying to break a union in California and the last thing in the world he wanted was to hear one more word about organized labor, I'd probably have played it a bit more hardball. I bet I could have upped my stipend to a sawbuck.

I still don't have nearly enough capital, so occasionally I will supplement my cash flow by sneaking a single or two out of my father's wallet. I figure it's not really stealing since I'm using the money to buy hot dogs, which provide the kind of sustenance that peanut butter and lime marmalade fail to deliver. I can't swipe currency from my mom, though. She never has more than five dollars in her handbag and knows exactly how many quarters are in her coin purse. She's always complaining how my dad doesn't give her enough money to take care of the household, so her bag is off-limits.

The issue here is I find crime distasteful. I don't like the surge of anxiety I feel when I have to tiptoe into my parents' bedroom, ease open the middle drawer of the dresser, and furtively grab a buck, especially because sometimes I put in all that effort and he doesn't even have any singles. (I can't swipe a five; that's a felony.)

When I offer to start picking up the slack around our house in exchange for goods, services, and cold hard cash, my mom informs me if I'm capable of doing more, then it's my duty to do so and my payment is being provided with food, shelter, and the occasional Girl Scout sash. (FYI, any statement to the tune of *"Yay, you, for providing the bare minimum"* will get you sent to your room posthaste.)

Fortunately, a solution to all my financial woes presents itself in the most unexpected of places—my grandparents' fiftieth anniversary party. To preface, my mother's side of the family is a very festive group. They'll find any reason for an impromptu get-together. My Auntie Virginia and Uncle Kelly are the queen and king of entertaining, and many a pleasant holiday has been spent sleeping on their living room floor, surrounded by snoring cousins, listening to the dulcet tones of Frank Sinatra on the hi-fi and the sound of elder relatives laughing, the smoke from their cigars creating a spicy cloud over the dining room table, where they play pinochle into the wee hours. Last summer my aunt and uncle hosted the Spirit of '76 Fourth of July party, which turned into the Great Watermelon and Marshmallow Fight of '76 when my Auntie Virginia started spitting watermelon seeds down my Auntie Fanny's bathing suit.[12] Although it pained me to waste so many perfectly good marshmallows, the end result of nailing my brother in the face with a wad of wet foodstuff was well worth it.

Because my extended family makes everything a party, when there's an actual event to be celebrated, 'tis a sight to behold. This particular bash boasts a seated dinner for three hundred, a giant dance floor, a live band, an ice sculpture, and an enormous pink mountain of shrimp. There's a vast wall of presents for my

....

[12] Other activities included taking the Pepsi Challenge (I preferred neither) and writing "Happy Birthday, America" on each other's backs in suntan lotion.

grandparents and someone even got President Carter to send my Noni and Grampa an anniversary card.[13]

I'm profoundly enjoying the sparkling apple cider provided for the kids' table when I notice my brother hitting up my dad for a dollar to buy a soda at the cash bar. We don't keep many carbonated beverages in our house except for the undrinkable stuff like tonic water, so having a Coke is a real treat for my brother. I watch as Dad opens his thick brown leather wallet and without a second thought or any kind of negotiation hands my brother a couple of bills.

Hold the phone—Toad got money just for saying he was *thirsty?*

I've got to get in on this action.

"Hi, Daddy," I say, sidling up in such a way as to highlight what a delightful young lady I am in my fabulous mint green dotted Swiss gown with batwing sleeves and my white patent leather Mary Janes. "I'm thirsty and so's cousins Stephanie and Karla. Can I have a couple of dollars to get us all a Coke?"

My dad smiles and whips out a five-dollar bill.

Whoa. Do you know how many times I'd have to wash his car and vacuum the family room to get five bucks?

"You can keep the change," he says, ruffling my hair.

You can bet your ass I will.

I don't actually like soda, so I don't go to the bar at all. Stephanie and Karla are probably swiping champagne off the grown-up tables, anyway.

---

[13] Personally, I was rooting for Ford, having had the opportunity to meet him at a rally in the parking lot of Bloomingdale's. Something about seeing armed guards on top of the mall coupled with the opportunity to skip school for the afternoon seemed *so very right* to me.

I do like five-dollar bills, though. A lot.

I scan the crowd to spot my next victim. "Uncle Tony? I want to get a Seven-Up. Can you give me a dollar, pleeeeease? I can't find my daddy to ask him." Uncle Tony obliges in much the same way my father did, and now I'm up ten dollars. Sweet.

"Hey, cousin Mark? I can't find my father and I want to get a root beer. Can I have a dollar?"

"I'm going to the bar; I'll get you one," he replies kindly.

"*No!*" I exclaim, desperately trying to find a way to spin this. "No, no. You sit, relax. Take it easy. I'll go for you."

He shrugs. "Okay, here's ten bucks—get me and your cousin Steven a Heineken and whatever you want for yourself. Keep the change." Ding, ding, ding, *score*.

Never doubt the power of a little girl in a party dress!

The bartender serves me the two beers—apparently I'm a very mature-looking eight[14]—and I return to Mark's table with his beers and a tidy seven-dollar profit.

I learn pretty quickly to ask only male relatives after a disappointing and potentially disastrous reaction from my aunties. One grilled me about whether my mother knew I was drinking so much sugar and the other told me it was rude to ask anyone for money. They must be immune to the cute overload that is me in dotted Swiss.

In the next half hour, I make almost seventy dollars, but my run of good luck ends when my uncle Jimmy generously throws down a handful of bills and opens the bar.

Damn. Shoulda tapped Uncle Jimmy.

---

[14] It's the batwings.

The next morning my mother finds my bankroll next to my bed and is aghast when she hears where it came from. I try to explain money is "really sort of a gift if you think about it," but she's not hearing any of it. She confiscates my cash and I never see it again.

I suspect she uses it to buy groceries.

God help her if she comes home with any more lime marmalade.

How About a Nice Hawaiian Punch?

(Girl Scout Uniform)

I've waited all year to break free from this pack of losers and this is finally, *finally* my chance. Today's my last Brownie meeting and I'm preparing to fly up to the (attractively uniformed) Girl Scouts. I don't think we actually get to fly, but if we do, I will apologize for so clearly misjudging the Brownies.

I'm on pins and needles all during the Color Guard ceremony. Pledge your allegiance to this flag a little faster, ladies; I'm aging as we speak here.

My friends Donna and Stacey—the *only* Brownies worth knowing—flank me on our spot on the stage in the church auditorium. We're listening to the troop leader drone on about the Brownie Forest and leadership and pride and blah blah blah. All I can hear are my own thoughts and they're saying, *Give me the damn sash already!*

A lot of our parents are in the audience. My mom is toward the back because I'm sure she was late even though we live just down the street. Both Donna's parents are in the front row. Her dad owns a bar and a package store, so he could come because he sets his own hours.[15] My dad isn't here because he's working, and also, I suspect he's about as into the Brownies as I am.

We're standing by what the leader calls a "magic pond," but it's surrounded by plants and we can't see in it. I'm pretty sure there's aluminum foil on it though, and what's more magical than Reynolds Wrap? On the other side of it, there's a bridge festooned with plastic flowers. Each of us is called over individually to give the pledge and we have to recite a verse.

Zzzzzz . . . wake me when it's sash time, won't you?

When my name's called, I repeat the same tired rhyme everyone else has about the twisting and the turning and the showing of elves, and then I look in the water and I see—

Holy shit, that's me! I see me! I see myself! Which rhymes with *elf.*

This pond *is* magic!

How on earth . . .

Oh. Wait. There's a mirror in there. Still, you got me, Brownies. Well played. Perhaps if you'd incorporated a bit more magic or hadn't been quite so stingy when pouring the Hawaiian Punch, I may have been more supportive of your organization.

Pond business complete, I walk across the bridge, which is supposed to be symbolic except I'm pretty sure it was built out of

---

[15] Did you know package stores don't sell packages? Deceptive advertising if you ask me.

an orange crate and I kind of can't get past that fact, especially since it still smells like Florida. Seriously, could we not have, like, enlisted the Boy Scouts to put something together for us? Or spent one less day making wallets and instead learned how to swing a hammer?

We finish up by singing "The Brownie Smile Song" and then do a chorus of "Make New Friends." Yeah, I'll get right on that.

I am deeply disappointed when the ceremony is over and I learn we're not going to receive our uniforms here and now. Rather, my mother will have to go to a supply shop over the summer to purchase the pieces. But I do get a snappy gold Girl Scout insignia pin to go on my sash once my mom buys it and a boss set of embroidered wings.

So that's a start.

"That? Was a pain in the butt," I declare, hands patting the back pockets of my denim Toughskins for emphasis.

My friend Donna's holding her Girl Scout manual and nodding in agreement, her fat black braids bouncing off her back. We're in her sunny L-shaped kitchen, sitting in the rattan chairs by the bay window. We're both exhausted from having just completed the requirement for our cooking badge. Today's experiment involved boiling water, eggs, strained patience on her mother's part, a little bit of screaming, and one first-degree burn. As soon as we finished, Donna's mom took her dad's pack of cigarettes and went outside to smoke, which is kind of odd because she's not a smoker. We can see her from where we're sitting—she's cross-legged on their patio and she keeps puffing and rocking back and forth.

Well, what did she expect when she tried to teach a couple of fourth graders to make egg salad?

Donna and I had to complete an entire litany of tedious steps to earn the embroidered patch. I'd say the effort (and blister) wasn't worth it, but have you *seen* a sash laden with badges and pins? It's glorious! It's like Christmas and Halloween and a birthday, where I don't get a guilt-inducing big-headed doll, all rolled together and then dipped in powdered sugar!

Every time we complete a badge, we bring our page of signatures to our troop leader, Mrs. McCoy. She examines them and orders the respective badge, which we get after a couple of weeks. When they arrive, we have a quick awards ceremony and take our fabulous prizes home, where our mothers sew them on our sashes, or, in my mother's case, pin them on my sash because she's too busy sewing a bunch of other junk that I don't want to wear.

In my opinion, we're not doing nearly enough in our meetings to fill up our sashes. A lot of times Mrs. McCoy veers from the badge-earning part of the manual and wants to teach us lessons about "friendship" and "faith."

Friendship and faith are not going to fill my sash, woman! I don't want to *learn*; I want to *earn*. Let's get with the program already, McCoy! In a perfect world, our scout meetings would morph into little ad hoc badge sweatshops, thirty beret-covered heads bent in concentration and achievement.[16]

My mom volunteered to be one of the assistant troop leaders

---

[16] However, I'm a fan of our refreshment break since it's the only time I'm ever allowed to drink Hawaiian Punch. I'm open to allowing that part to continue.

and she's taking it way too seriously. She's always referring to bits of the Girl Scout code when I don't do exactly what she wants, like if I complain when Todd slinks off and I'm stuck with a sink full of dinner dishes to do by myself, she'll say, "A Girl Scout is friendly and helpful," or if I whisper something in Stacey's ear, she'll be all, "Girl Scouts don't tell secrets." Pfft, they do if they have good dirt on someone! And really? I'm in it for the badges, not some arcane code of ethics.

When I get home from Donna's, I tell my mom about our experiment and she signs off on my badge without question.

Hmm.

This is the first time I've participated in a badge-earning activity without her, and yet she didn't demand an egg salad sandwich as proof. She just blithely believed me.

Hmm, again.

I quickly thumb through my guidebook and catch a glimpse of the badge for art. It looks like a painter's palette covered in little daubs of brightly colored dots. I really, really dig the aesthetics of this badge. And I want it. A lot.

You know . . . Donna and I did color at her house and that is kind of artistic—not today, but one time. At some point. I'm pretty sure. And that kind of satisfies one of the badge requirements, right?

"Hey, Mom?" I ask. "We also did this one today." I point at one of the entries on the page. "Can you sign off?"

"Weren't you the busy little Girl Scout today?" she replies with a trusting smile before scrawling a "JL" in the margin.

"Yes. Yes, I was," I agree, bobbing my head with great sincerity.

Sucker.

From this moment on, every time I'm out of her sight for more than an hour, I return with heroic tales of badge-completing feats. Her signatures begin to rack up on the page and at the next award ceremony, I take home four new embroidered beauties.

I thrill over how these badges feel in my palm and I run my fingers over them all the way home.

However, once I get to my house and we affix them to my sash, I'm less excited. I have only five little badges, which are supposed to be sewn on in rows of three. I don my sash and drag a kitchen chair into the bathroom so I can stand up and see myself in the mirror properly.

Huh.

I turn back and forth, examining myself from all angles. Suddenly, this is a lot less thrilling. My badges don't look symmetrical, despite the fine tailoring of the rest of my uniform. Plus there's a ton of blank green space between where the badges end and the bottom of the sash.

I scowl at my reflection.

No. No, this won't do at all. These badges are a mere thimbleful of water in an ocean of merit. My sash isn't the source of pride that I'd expected it to be. Rather, it's a testament to everything I've yet to accomplish. I see myself in this sash and I feel at loose ends, incomplete, a washed-up ex-hippie at eight.

Then, out of nowhere, I'm struck with divine inspiration. Could it really be that easy? Could I honestly solve my existential angst with a few quick slashes of ink?

I get off my chair and return it to the kitchen. Then I take a pad of paper and a pen and practice writing the initials "JL" over and over again until they're identical to all the other signatures in my manual.

Forgery; the victimless crime.

🎨

Mrs. McCoy seems kind of sad when she hands over my stack of new badges during the ceremony, and later she prattles on about the importance of honesty while we work on yet another stupid hand-sewn wallet. I sip my Hawaiian Punch and do my best to ignore her gimlet gaze. A number of Scouts are sheepish and I take comfort in knowing I'm probably not the only liar of the group.

Besides, I've just scored enough badges to fill up the entire front of my sash. I will no longer be mistaken for some lowly cadet—instead I'm going to look like the colonel of the Girl Scouts! Admiral Lancaster, at your service!

Mrs. McCoy tells us she has a surprise—today we get our order forms because we're going to start selling cookies! A mighty cheer erupts from our group; who *doesn't* love Girl Scout cookies? Is there anything more decadent than the sweet ambrosia of a frozen Thin Mint melting in your mouth while you wash it down with a rich creamy glass of whole milk? Is there anything more comforting than a few Shortbreads served with a golden cup of tea on a snowy afternoon? Or can there be a more perfect pairing than the chocolate and peanut butter in the Tagalong?[17]

I run all the way home after the meeting in order to affix my new badges to my sash. I want to be at my Girl Scouty best when

---

[17] The correct answer is no.

I ring doorbells in the name of my troop. My mom helps me with the safety pins and then lickety-split, I'm out the door with my vibrant sales brochure, depicting all the cookies' deliciousness in full color.

As I head down my street, I feel a swell of pride every time I glance down at my magnificent sash. Yes. This is exactly how I'd hoped it would be. I brush away any niggling thoughts I have about not really earning my badges, as no one knows my dirty little secret.

I knock on my closest neighbors' doors first. Mrs. Schneider across the street obliges with a few boxes of Shortbread—excellent with tea, I remind her—and Mrs. DeGeorge stocks up on the sandwich and chocolate chip varieties. I appreciate her order, but honestly, the chocolate chips are the only clunkers in the bunch. They tend to be dry and the chip-to-cookie ratio is less than desirable. Regardless, I thank her for her patronage and I move on. I get a few more orders and a handful of refusals.

Refusals?

Seriously?

How do you say no to the Girl Scouts? How do you not support an organization that instills such values in young girls? Frankly, I'm appalled when I begin to receive far more nays than yeas.

The afternoon drags on and I'm discouraged by my results after the initial few sales to friends and neighbors. Honestly? I'm ready to call it quits. I've moved an adequate amount and have more than satisfied any sales requirements. Besides, I'm tired, and after all this cookie talk, I'm getting really hungry. Granted, my mother will tell me to have an apple, but even fruit would be better than the rumbling going on down there right now. I'm going to make one more stop and that will be it.

I'm at the gray house with black shutters on the crest of the hill that leads down the street and into the rich neighborhood one block over. I don't know these folks, but their landscaping is lovely. When I walk Samantha, I'm mindful to never let her drop a bomb on their lawn.

I knock and a middle-aged lady I've never seen before opens the door. She's wearing a sweat suit and a big gold cross around her neck. I give her my whole pitch and she's totally into it, nodding and smiling. But before I get her to commit to any boxes, she begins to ask me about my sash, because, really, who wouldn't? I'm talking *glorious* here, people.

The lady points to a badge on the third row, second one in. "That's a pretty badge. What does it stand for?"

Primarily red and purple, this badge depicts people doing . . . something. Archery maybe? "Um . . . ," I stammer. "I kind of forget."

"Oh. Well, then, how about that one?" She gestures toward a sunny yellow one at the bottom of the sash. There's a cup on it with steam rising out of it.

"Tea making?" This comes out as a question and not a statement.

She scrunches up her forehead and her hand idly adjusts her necklace. "And this one with the flag?"

I scramble to come up with a reasonable-sounding answer. "I, um, got that one because I love America."

"What about this one with the boiling cauldron?" Her lips begin to flatten into a straight line.

I draw a total blank. A cauldron? I've got a merit badge with a *cauldron* on it? Think, self, think. When would someone use a cauldron? I mentally snap my Hawaiian Punch–stained fingers. I've got it. "Witchcraft!"

Her friendliness begins to dissipate. "I see."

Desperate to change the direction of this conversation, which is so clearly getting away from me, I ask, "Which cookies would you like?"

She hesitates before answering. "I'm going to pass today." She thanks me for stopping by and then quietly closes the door.

As I retreat down her driveway, my sash begins to feel a lot less impressive. It feels . . . heavy, kind of like it's pulling down my neck and shoulders with the weight of all those new badges. And suddenly those small pangs of guilt I'd been able to sweep into the corner of my mind come to the forefront. The guilt's now too big to push aside with a broom. It sits there right in the center of my mind and my chest, immobile as a boulder.

I feel like a fraud and there's nothing I can do to change that.

Or is there?

Could redemption really be an option?

I stand there with the chilly New Jersey wind whipping the hem of my dress up and nudging my beret out of place. Yes, I believe I *could* fix this, but I'd have to commit to putting in the work. Am I willing? Am I able? Would it even be worth it?

A current of air lifts my sash practically to eye level. I might only be eight, but damn it, I know when fate is trying to get my attention. So I square my shoulders and tuck my order sheet under my arm. My mission is clear. I adjust my beret and begin to march down the hill toward the wealthy neighborhood. Maybe I didn't earn all these badges legitimately.

But it's not too late to make up for them.

When I receive my next badge at our scout meeting, I demand my mother sew it on properly. I wear it like a medal of honor. When anyone asks what the big brown patch on the back of my sash is for, I gladly tell them it's for selling more cookies than anyone else in the region. I win!

I canvassed the rich people one block over, hounding them mercilessly until their names filled every blank on my order sheet. I was far more aggressive than any bill collector or repo man. I didn't even care that it was going to take me ages and ages to deliver all those cookies when the time came.

Because I know that I legitimately earned that patch on the back of my sash. And I am proud.

The Green Badge of Courage

(Kelly Green Speedo Tank Suit)

Donna and I are at our Tuesday night swimming lesson at the YWCA. She's working on getting her Athletics badge. Technically, I already have one, but I'm going through all the steps anyway. I don't have to; I want to.

Besides, I love swimming lessons! I dig everything about them—carpooling with Donna and her sister, smelling the chlorine on my stretchy green Speedo bathing suit[18] later when I get home, watching the steam form at the top of the natatorium where the air meets the freezing cold glass, floating along in warm water even though it's the middle of winter, and best of all, hitting the vending machine after the lesson.

....

[18] I have a delightful Pucci-inspired bikini but I simply cannot execute a perfect swan dive in it without losing my bottoms.

Every week I bring a quarter to buy ice cream from the machine. My mother monitors my coin situation because she realizes that given the opportunity, I would eat dessert until I collapsed on myself like a dying star.

Usually I choose an ice cream sandwich because I can never properly wipe all the Fudgsicle residue from the corners of my mouth. I'm not a huge fan of the vanilla stuff covered in a thin chocolate layer, either. One bite and the coating falls on the ground, and five-second rule or not, I won't eat a treat off of a place where ten thousand bare feet have trod.

I insert my quarter and hold my breath, exhaling when I open the trap door to find one sandwich. Once earlier this winter I put in a quarter and got *two* ice cream sandwiches, so I'm perpetually hopeful.

We had a great lesson tonight. We worked on backstroke so I got in plenty of quality ceiling-viewing time. I particularly like when the water surrounds everything but my face and how muffled and muted all the gleeful screaming and splashing becomes. Maybe I'm getting more mature now that I'm nine, but I'm beginning to recognize and appreciate these small moments of Zen. Plus, I'm the fastest at backstroking and nothing pleases me more than beating the Speedos off everyone else.

Donna, her sister Leslie, and I are all dry and dressed after our lesson, my wet suit stuffed in a plastic bread bag inside my satchel. We've got our towels wrapped around our damp heads and we sit in companionable silence on a bench in the front entrance, enjoying the last of our ice cream as we wait for their dad to pick us up. My favorite bit of this ritual is when the sandwich melts into my fingers, leaving just enough bonus ice cream and cookie shell to lick off afterward.

"Hey, look, Tony's here!" Leslie exclaims.

"Who's Tony?" I ask.

"He's a friend of my daddy's," Leslie tells me. "He hangs out in his bar."

"He's real nice," Donna adds. "Hi, Tony. What are you doing here?"

"Hey, girls! Your dad asked me to come and get you."

"All right, let's go!" They grab their stuff and begin to follow Tony. I am none too thrilled to be riding with someone I don't know, but Leslie and Donna seem comfortable so I grudgingly toss my wrapper in the trash and pick up my tote bag. I would simply call my mother but I only had the one quarter and obviously I just used it.

We ride to Donna's house and I position myself next to the door, just in case. I figure if anything weird goes down, I can get out first. My rationale is I don't have to be faster than Tony; I only have to be faster than Donna and Leslie.

I'm not quite sure why we don't just swing by my house first because it's closer to the Y, but all my worrying is for naught when we arrive at Donna's house minutes later. Both her parents are there and all the grown-ups greet each other and then go downstairs to their rec room. It's still kind of early, so Donna and I head into her parents' bedroom and watch some of *The Man from Atlantis.*

Half an hour later during a commercial break, I tell Donna's mom I should probably go home, to which she replies, "Great! I'll let Tony know."

"Excuse me?" I ask.

"Tony's going to leave so I can have him drive you to your house."

Um, hi, I'm only nine,[19] and even I know this is the worst plan ever to be uttered out loud by an actual adult. She wants me to catch a ride in the dark alone with some guy who hangs out at her husband's bar?

Is she crazy? (Or is this payback for the egg salad?)

I gawp at Donna's mom for what seems like an hour before I finally reply, "No."

She bends toward me like she didn't hear me. "I'm sorry?"

I fold my arms and raise my chin in defiance. I'm not going to be bullied into doing something that makes me uncomfortable. "I said no. I'm not riding with him. He may be your family friend, but he's not mine. My parents have never met him and I don't know his last name."

She sighs. "Jennifer, his last name is—"

I interrupt. "I don't care what his name is or that it's just three blocks. I'm not getting in a car with that *stranger* by myself. If you don't want to drive me, then call my mom and she can come get me. Or else I'm staying here."

Resigned, Donna's mom gets her keys and silently leads me out to her little gold Toyota wagon. Donna and Leslie tag along, too, and the atmosphere is festive as we drive up the hill to my house. I arrive home safe, sound, and in plenty of time to see the end of the show.[20]

I tell my mother what happened and she makes a quick,

....

[19] Got a Barbie Dream House, woo!

[20] I'm a tremendous fan of Patrick Duffy's entire body of work.

heated call to Donna's house. Later, as she tucks me in and kisses me good night, my mom tells me I just earned an unofficial merit badge in courage.

What I don't tell her is that I knew if I'd taken that ride, anything could have happened, and none of it good.

And that would have ruined ice cream sandwiches for me forever.

Miss New Jersey Has Everything

(Brown Tasseled Clogs)

Today I'm taking the shortcut home. Often I go the long way so I can stop in the park and pay a visit to the swing set (or hot dog stand), but this afternoon is not about dawdling (or sauerkraut). My dad's finally home after his extended business trip to Indiana and I suspect there's a present in his suitcase with my name on it.

(Dear God, please let it be candy!)

My friend Beth and I make a beeline through the woods across from school. Her house is on the cul-de-sac right by the tree line on the other side and mine is a couple of blocks past that. Beth's house is kind of famous because the Prudential Insurance people once picked it to be in a commercial. At the last minute, Beth's mom decided she didn't want a film crew crashing a tree through her big living room window even if they promised to fix it right afterward, so the director used the house next door. We got to be there for the filming anyway. I loved when they used that snappy black slate thing and shouted "Action!"[21] When the commercial ran during *Happy Days* a few months later, we could see Beth's garage in the shot.

I'm delighted by my friendship with Beth because she used to not like me. Hers was the first birthday party I attended right after we moved here from Boston in third grade, and my mom made me give her a Mrs. Beasley doll for a present.

Mrs. Beasley. From the uber-creepy show *Family Affair.*[22]

And what little girl doesn't want to play with an astigmatic senior citizen doll outfitted in a bib and an apron? Oh, wait. All of them. Had I not been so utterly charming when we went on our first Girl Scout camping trip in fourth grade, Beth would have never given me a second chance, and who could blame her?

However, we're close friends now, especially since my bestie Stacey moved to Arizona last summer. Walking home together has only improved our bond. We haven't been able to cut through the woods for the past few months because the ground was squishy and I didn't want to get my clogs muddy. Granted, all those people in Holland wear wooden shoes because it's damp, but I assume theirs aren't adorned with jaunty leather tassels and hammered brass tacks. Considering I had to get straight As on my report card in order to convince my parents to buy them for me, I'm loath to put them in any mortal danger.

....

[21] Unfortunately, the director rejected my suggestion he put a charming little brown-haired girl in the shot. Their loss. I could move some property and casualty insurance, yo.

[22] You can't name a boy Jodi! It's simply not done!

Beth and I scurry down the dry wooded path, recounting our Field Day victory last week. We were on the red team and I had the genius idea to get a red T-shirt with the word "Red" spelled out on it in iron-on letters. I wore white jogging shorts with red trim and I snagged a pair of Todd's red-striped tube socks and I tied a red bandanna around my pigtailed hair. Seriously, when I showed up to school that day? I pretty much blew everyone's mind. My theory is the blue team was so astounded by my fashion savvy that it weakened their defenses and we were able to pull off the win. Or possibly they thought the whole competition was dumb and didn't try terribly hard. Either way, we won.

The best part is that I was recognized as one of the most outstanding students in the fifth grade after the competition. The principal called all my favorite people in class—Donna, Beth, Tracey, Andrea, who's let me use her lip gloss on more than one occasion, Nancy, who in addition to having a basement full of games also sports a Dorothy Hamill haircut, Joe Major, who I would totally have a crush on if boys weren't yucky, and George, who wears shiny silk shirts and lets me borrow his pink marker.

Anyway, I was worried for a second as I watched the elite members of the fifth grade claim their spots onstage, but thankfully the last name the principal called was mine. Donna and I were so thrilled to both be part of the group that we were hugging and jumping up and down! Afterward, Nancy invited me over to play board games in her basement[23] and Tracey decided that I simply *must* try out for cheerleading with her. Without a doubt,

....

[23] I kick so much ass at Mystery Date!

it was the best day of my life so far, even surpassing the time I found a giant box of sixties Barbie dolls and girls' books in the neighbor's garbage.

We get to Beth's house and I say good-bye. I yank up my striped socks (with individual toe slots!), adjust my Mickey Mouse backpack, and hike up the hill.

"Good afternoon, Miss Jennifer! How's this fine day treatin' my favorite granddaughter?" calls Mike, the sweet old Irish crossing guard who's been working this corner ever since he retired from the New York City police force. Last year we had to do a Girl Scout project with a grandparent, so I asked him to be my adopted grandfather since my Noni and Grampa live in Boston and my Nanny and Gaga had passed away.

"Hi, Mike! I'm great! I got an A on my spelling test and my dad's home today!"

"You'd best hurry on home to see him then! But not too fast, m'dear—I don't want you to twist an ankle." He points at my clogs. The heel's not even an inch high, yet every time I put them on I feel as glamorous as Kristy McNichol.

"Okay, I'll see you later, Granddad!"

I know he's not really my grandfather, but sometimes it's nice to pretend.

I stroll down Prospect Avenue, enjoying the feel of the June sun on my face. Our street is quiet, so every time my wooden heel hits the asphalt it sounds like the clip-clop of horses' hooves. I've only gotten to ride a horse a couple of times in my life, but I love them so much. I want to pet their glossy fur and scratch their broad muzzles and hug them around their strong necks and braid their manes. (One time my cousin Stephanie was mounting a horse at camp and it stepped on her thigh. She had a bruise the size of a watermelon. I don't really want that.)

I always get in trouble for handing in my homework with horses drawn in the margins of my notebook paper. Plus, *National Velvet* is my favorite movie and I've read *Misty of Chincoteague* ten times already. Recently my Girl Scout troop went to Washington, D.C., and on the way we spent one night camping in Assateague.[24] I created an elaborate plan to sneak up on one of the wild ponies (preferably black with a white patch between his eyes) and tame it and make him my own just like the Beebe family. Mrs. McCoy promised me before we left that if I caught one, she'd transport it back to New Jersey in her station wagon. She was totally on board.

I grudgingly accept that she was humoring me, as all the shaggy ponies bolted when I got within a hundred yards of them. I guess Girl Scouts aren't ninjas, after all, particularly when clog-clad.

You know what? Even without my own horse or pony, my life is pretty great. Our neighbor works for a dairy and he's been giving us these fantastic fruit-on-the-bottom yogurts, which are almost like ice cream, but healthy so I'm allowed to help myself. (I put them on a plate and flip over the container so it comes out looking like an ice cream sundae.) And lately, Dad's been generous with spare change every time we pass the Carvel.

Since Toad got involved with after-school sports like football, he's had an outlet other than me for his aggression and our hand-to-hand combat has greatly diminished.

....

[24] Is it just me or is that a funny word?

My grades are good, my friends are excellent, and my Girl Scout troop has five overnight excursions planned for next year. Can they top the outstanding adventures we've already had in our nation's capital and at Rutgers ballgames and in a deluxe lodge in upstate New York, where we shoveled off a bit of the lake for our own private skating rink and made maple syrup candy in the fresh snow? My guess is yes!

How lucky am I to already have my life so figured out? I mean, we'll probably spend the summer in my grandparents' old place up in New Hampshire again and I can go to the beach every day, and when my dad comes up on Saturday, he'll take me to the bookstore to buy some paper dolls. Then, next fall I already know I'm assigned to Mr. Lockwood's class, as are Donna, Beth, and Tracey, and there's an excellent chance I'm going to make cheerleader, considering Tracey's stepmom is the coach. Then I cheer through junior high and high school, go to college at Pepperdine so I can be there when they film *Battle of the Network Stars*, which will allow me to meet Henry Winkler and thus become Mrs. Arthur Fonzarelli. Perfect!

In the immortal words of both Laverne and Shirley, nothing's going to stop me now.

Even though he didn't bring me any candy, I'm still glad to see my dad. He's been in Indiana for weeks at a time off and on for the past year. He's out there so much his company even rented him an apartment, where we visited him over spring break. We flew out of New York, and when we got into Indiana airspace I was shocked to see nothing but a massive expanse of white when I peeked out the window. Where were all the big buildings? Where were all the people? And what was up with those enormously empty snow-covered fields?

After spending a week in Cow Town, Indiana—the highlight being attending a high school basketball game[25]—I put Indiana on the *States I've Visited* list with the notation "I see no reason to ever return."

When Todd gets home from baseball practice, my parents call both of us down to the rec room. Our rec room is in the basement, which is the most interesting part of our house. The upstairs is all cramped and tiny. Only one person fits in our kitchen at a time and you have to walk through my parents' bed-room to get to the backyard. However, our basement is ridicu-lously, luxuriously expansive. We've got a rec room with a whole separate bar area at the end of it, another room where we keep our pool table, and an entire second kitchen, which is way big-ger than the kitchen upstairs. (Don't ask me why we don't just use that one.)

The basement's where our color TV and cable box live, too. It gives a girl a comforting feeling to return from a taxing day of fifth grade and know she has enough channels to find *The Brady Bunch* any time she wants to watch. Sometimes if my parents aren't paying attention, I can sneak glimpses of R-rated movies on Home Box Office, too!

So we're all in the basement for a family meeting. I'm intrigued because we've never had a family meeting before. Normally, if my

---

[25] On my last school field trip we toured the CBS studios in New York and screened a television pilot. You need to incorporate a little more Hollywood if you want to im-press me.

parents have something to say, they just say it. No need for pomp and/or circumstance.

My dad slips behind the bar to fix himself a small glass of something brown over ice while my brother and I spin around on our bar stools. My mom doesn't yell at us for "wrecking the seats" by twirling in them, also another first. And she doesn't even shoot me a look when I accidentally kick the bar with my wooden clog. Huh.

Then, without any warning or warm-up, my father looks us in the eyes and says, "I fired the man running the distribution center and now I have to take over. We're moving to Indiana."

To which I reply, "Pfft. Maybe you're moving to Indiana, but I'm not."

I'll spare you the details of my clichéd expressions of grief— the rending of garments, the wailing, the gnashing of teeth, the kicking of the bar really fucking hard with wooden clogs, etc. Trust me—I made my displeasure known.

I'm about to call my favorite librarian at the Bergen County Public Library to have her locate a book that will tell me how a ten-year-old can legally emancipate herself when I'm struck with a thought.

"Hey . . . ," I begin. "If I agree to move to Indiana, will you buy me a horse? We could live in an actual farmhouse and have a barn."

My parents exchange glances and then my dad answers, "Absolutely. I will absolutely buy you a horse."

"Then I'm in," I agree. "How soon can we leave?"

❖

FYI? My father is a *liar*.[26] And the Cow Town public librarian is less than helpful when I request she find me a book on how I might go about suing my parents for breach of contract.

Today's the first day of school in Cow Town. I haven't really met any kids in my new neighborhood yet because as soon as we moved in, I came down with pneumonia and had to spend a week in the hospital.[27] After I was released, I was stuck on bed rest for quite a while. Were we still living in civilization, after I recovered I'd have had plenty of time to invite neighbor kids over to enjoy my new pool because I wouldn't have to start school until next month. But because this system's calendar is based *on the planting season*—hi, is it 1870 all of a sudden?—I'm stuck beginning classes in early August.

Back in Bergenfield, the first day of school is a huge deal and all the kids break out their very best bits of back-to-school wear. The girls wear pretty wrap skirts and flowered sundresses and the boys don khakis and oxfords. Things get more casual later in the week, but the first few days are all about putting on a show.

I decide to make my Northwest Elementary School debut in a longish plaid skirt and matching shawl that our old neighbor Mrs. Schneider sent me when she heard I was in the hospital. I'm pairing it with a creamy ruffled blouse and, of course, my clogs. I try

---

[26] Years later he told me he had no intention of ever buying me a horse. He simply refused to negotiate with a ten-year-old.

[27] Diagnosed by the same physician who later treated me for hepatitis when actually I just had mono.

to convince my mom to let me borrow a pair of her nylons, but she's not having it, so I just wear regular knee-highs.

My house is close to the end of the bus route, so when it stops to get me almost all the seats are full of kids from neighboring farms. Just like one of those E. F. Hutton commercials, the second I step on the bus and attempt to find a place, all conversation stops and everyone stares at me. Sure, it's nice to be noticed, but not like this. No one speaks to me. They just stare. Jaws hang slack. Frankly, I wouldn't be surprised to hear dueling banjos at this point.[28]

School is five miles away in the middle of a soybean field and I count seven different kinds of livestock en route.[29] The school bus is a virtual oven and I can feel a bead of sweat roll between my shoulder blades, so I stuff the shawl in my book bag. The heat magnifies every odor and there's a sickly-sweet smell coming from the floor. I try to open a window but the dirty kid next to me tells me I'm not allowed to touch them while the bus is in motion. Sure. Great. I'll just breathe through my shawl, shall I?

My mom registered me last week, so I know where I'm supposed to go. I make my way to the sixth-grade classroom and take a seat. All the desks in the back are full, so I wind up in the front row. When the bell rings, my new teacher Mr. Hauenstein welcomes us to sixth grade and mentions he sees new faces and he asks me to introduce myself to the class first.

I stand up and turn around, assessing the students for the first time, and I realize I'm the only person not in jeans or some variety of T-shirt. A few of the kids are even wearing their barn boots

....

[28] No one tells me I've got a real pretty mouth, though. So there's that.

[29] I admit my pulse quickened a bit when I saw a whole paddock full of horses.

because they came to school directly after feeding their livestock. Guess that explains why the bus smelled like poop.

The kids in the class look me up and down. I shift in my clogs, adjust my shawl, and begin. "Hi, I'm Jennifah Lancastah and we just moved heah from Bergenfield, New Jersey, which is right outsiddah New Yawk City."

A few giggles erupt in the back of the room.

Did I just say something funny? I turn to Mr. Hauenstein for guidance and he encourages me to tell the class more about myself.

"Um, I've been a Girl Scout for a coupla yeahs and I also usta play violin in the orchestrah." The tittering gets louder and I see kids using their hands to cover their mouths. "My ballet teachah was a membah of a real New Yawk ballet company and took the train from the city fuh class every week. Right befowah we moved, we wah gettin ready to do powint wahk in toe shoes."

I fear I may be losing the room for some reason. Then it occurs to me there are no orchestras or principal dancers with the American Ballet Theatre here in Cow Town and I've got to do something quick to be more relatable. I decide to end my introduction with the statement I'm sure will turn all these farm kids toward my side. "And I like hawses!"

What feels like several years later, the laughter in the room finally stops. Red-faced and shaking, I take my seat. As I do, I hear a kid in the back row mumble, "Hey, New Joisey, nice clawwwwghs," and then the giggling starts again.

Yeah?

We'll see how funny these clogs are when I use them to kick you in the jimmies at recess.

❖

I manage to make it through the first week of school without stomping on anyone's spleen, but not without effort. There's another new kid in my class, too. My dad brought his dad out here from Boston to help run his distribution center. The other new kid also has an accent, and every time he speaks he gets the same treatment as I do. How is his saying "idear" instead of "idea" any more weird than when local kids talk about the "crick" that runs behind their houses or how George "Warshington" was our first president?

Regardless, I've been studying the newscasters on the Fort Wayne 21 Alive! ABC affiliate and trying to make myself sound like them. Yes, I'd like to stand out, but for cool stuff like my shoes and not because of how I sound. I'm finding if I try really hard and pay attention to every word that comes out of my mouth, I can approximate the regional dialect. I look forward to it coming naturally someday.

I've joined the Cow Town chapter of the Girl Scouts and I'm surprised by how unpopular the organization is. In New Jersey, there were a ton of troops and I had my choice. Pretty much if I want to be a Scout here, there's only one option. Point? I plan to practice my new and improved non-accent this evening at my meeting when I pledge to "help people at all (and not awuall) times."

After trading in my shirts and clogs for jeans and T-shirts, I've pretty much stayed under the radar here until this morning. Since it's meeting day, I wore my full uniform. I expected classmates to crow over my now legitimately earned badges and to admire the jaunty tilt of my beret, but instead they just laughed again. Apparently the only thing less cool than joining a Girl Scout troop is actually wearing the uniform. And yet no one makes a peep when kids crowd on the bus wearing their 4-H[30] regalia, which . . . pfft! They don't even have sashes!

My mom drops me off at our meeting place, which is an empty activity room in the elementary school. Not only do we not have access to a kitchen or a stage like we did in New Jersey, we don't even have tables or chairs! We're forced to sit on the cold tile floor and the rivets from my clogs dig into the sides of my feet when I cross my legs.

Mrs. Bissell, our new neighbor up the street, welcomes me to the troop and asks what kind of stuff we used to do in New Jersey.

"Oh, boy, we did so much neat stuff!" I exclaim. "We'd go camping—sometimes we'd stay in regular tents on the ground, sometimes in those permanent tents with wooden floors in real campgrounds, a few times we stayed in big lodges, and we slept in a dorm when we went to Washington. We also took a lot of day trips and went ice skating in Rockefeller Plaza in New York and we saw the Rockettes perform and one time we even toured a McDonald's and afterward they gave us all the free cheeseburgahs we could eat! So whadda youse guys do heah?"[31]

Mrs. Bissell seems to have lost the color in her skin while I'm recounting all of my adventures. She looks around at the suddenly expectant faces of all the other Girl Scouts in the room.

....

[30] A youth organization created by the Department of Agriculture.

[31] To this day, my accent will creep back in when I'm excited. (Or drinking.)

After a long pause, she clears her throat and finally says, "Well, tonight we're making hand-sewn wallets."

Wallets.

Of course we're making *wallets*. And this troop doesn't do refreshments so we're not even having Hawaiian Punch.

I am seriously going to die in this town.

I hope someone remembers to bury me in my clogs.

A Series of Unfortunate (Pant) Events

(Bloomingdale's Underwear)

This is *not* a vacation.

I am supposed to be on Mackinac Island in Michigan right now riding around in carriages and eating candy. I am *not* supposed to be wedged into the overstuffed backseat of an Oldsmobile for the fourteenth consecutive hour. Nor am I supposed to be wrestling with my brother over who can catch and eat the fruit flies flitting around back here since they're our only source of sustenance.

My father's been going on and on about Mackinac Island ever since we moved to Indiana and he's been looking forward to this trip for a year. I wasn't sure I wanted to go to Michigan because I prefer the ocean to some random lake, no matter how "great" everyone says it is. The second Dad told me tourists get around the island on bikes and horses, I was intrigued. And the minute he talked about it having the most homemade fudge shops per capita, I was sold, as was my brother. *Say Yes to Michigan*, as the state's ad campaign implored? Our pleasure!

The only person not excited about our pending vacation was my mother. She didn't want to go to Michigan; she wanted to go back to Boston and see her family. However, my father was resolute, saying he didn't want to spend his entire vacation in the car. (The more likely excuse is he can't stand most of her relatives.[32])

When the Michigan plans were finalized, there was much yelling and stomping of feet and slamming of doors, and no, not by those of us awed by promises of fresh fudge.

Last night, Dad rounded up all our alarm clocks, saying we wouldn't need them. He woke us up after what seemed like an hour in bed and Todd and I staggered into our shared bath, brushing teeth and washing faces in our dual matching avocado green sinks, feet squashing into the shaggy gold carpeting.[33]

I was still bleary as I ate my banana and wheat toast and was surprised to see how dark it is at seven a.m. Dad told me that because he lets me sleep in until the ungodly hour of eight a.m. during the summer, I've never noticed this. As Todd and I shuffled our groggy selves into the backseat, loaded up with pillows and blankets, we learned the truth when Dad flipped on the radio. It was actually four a.m. Todd and I both laughed that Dad fooled

....

[32] Except for Auntie Virginia and a couple of my mom's sisters' husbands. I suspect this is why he's taken every opportunity to move farther and farther away from them. I bet we live in Alaska by the time I graduate.

[33] I'd ask who the genius was that thought carpet in the bathroom was a good idea. But I imagine it's the same person who put it there to match the gold butterflies in the wallpaper.

us, but my mother just seethed because she wasn't let in on the plan. Um . . . wanna bet that was intentional, Mrs. Half an Hour Late for Everything?

Dad told us it would be about a six-hour drive and Todd and I high-fived each other in anticipation. My brother and I put our differences aside every time we go on vacation. More often than not, these little road trips start to take on the feeling of a hostage situation due to the lack of access to food, water, and toilet facilities— Dad believes rest stops are for amateurs—and also because of the hostility emanating from the front seat. My mother never wants to drive, contenting herself with misreading maps and providing constructive criticism on all the ways my father could improve his performance on the road. On trips like this, often all Todd and I have is each other, and so we assume a truce.

I spent the first few hours in the car daydreaming about all the fudge I'd buy—rocky road and chocolate chip and vanilla and butter pecan. I imagined rolling it on my tongue, the piece getting all smooth and melted, eventually leaving nothing but the crunchy nuts. If I'm really lucky, they'll have peanut butter fudge like our next-door neighbor makes me every time I shovel her driveway without asking. There's something about the combination of salty and sweet that's so very, very right.

After I mentally exhausted my taste buds, I started dreaming about all the horses I'd see up there. Shortly after we moved to Indiana my allergies got worse—apparently living in the middle of a cornfield is problematic—and I had to go through a battery of tests. I learned that I'm desperately allergic to pollen and mold and dust mites, and somewhat to cats, dogs, and horses. I get weekly shots and I have no problems around our dog or our neighbors' cats, but my mom decided she'd keep me safe by not allowing me to take riding lessons. But if there are horses all over this island, she can't keep me from hugging at least one of them!

The miles were rolling by and my dad decided to play Frank Sinatra on his snappy new cassette player because we all like him, but when my mom insisted on harmonizing, he snapped Frank out of the stereo and turned on talk radio.

Drive, drive, drive. I caught a nap and when I woke up I was taken aback by how little the scenery had changed. I guess I thought northern Michigan would be more woody, more picturesque . . . more hills, more moose, perhaps a black bear or two? Instead, it looked flat and open and dull. Honestly, it reminded me of Ohio. Also? It had been six hours—weren't we there yet?

When I started seeing signs for Scranton, Pennsylvania, ten hours into the trip, I began to suspect something had gone awry. And getting stuck in traffic outside of Albany, New York, was also a clue that we may have veered from our intended path.

My mother launched into such hysterics when she saw the *Michigan, Stay Left; East Coast, Veer Right* road sign that my father apparently decided he'd rather drive seventeen hours straight[34] than listen to her wailing for the next four days while the rest of us tried to *Say Yes to Michigan*. So *she's* the one who throws a fit, yet *I'm* the one who suddenly loses fudge and horses? I'm sorry; was divorce not an option?

Presently we're in Connecticut, mired in some heavy Friday night traffic, only made worse by construction. My dad intends to push on through so we haven't had anything to eat since brunch.

....

[34] Or possibly into an abutment.

We were allowed five minutes to attend to any biological needs when we got gas four hours ago and now I'm cursing myself for not spending my fudge money on vending machine fare. My mother has a few sticky prunes in her bag—most likely the origin of the fruit flies—but I suspect I'll never be *that* hungry.

Our intended destination is my grandparents' house in the Boston suburbs, but the traffic is too snarled. We move something like twenty feet in an hour. Eventually my father gives up and heads toward my Auntie Virginia's house not far from where we're stuck. I'm delighted with this development. Not only do Auntie Virginia and Uncle Kelly have a springboard on their pool, but they have HBO! As soon as we moved from Jersey, we lost access to cable service. Because we live in a subdivision in the middle of the sticks, we're told it will be years before we get cable.[35]

If I can be honest without sounding like the worst grandkid ever? I really hate staying with my Noni and Grampa. Don't get me wrong—I adore hearing my Noni's stories about a very stupid little Sicilian boy named Giovah who's always doing wacky stuff. Like there's the one when his mom tells him to not stop watching the door when he has to babysit his little brother? So he simply takes the door off its hinges and brings it with him to go out and play, leaving his brother alone to drown in the tub. And then there's the one where Giovah's parents commit a crime and Giovah sees it. He may be slow but he's honest, so his parents hatch a plot to make him look crazy by throwing dried fruit off the roof.

....

[35] I am in college before someone finally strings a cable line from town onto our street. By the time I got my MTV, I was ready for VH1.

That way, if the *polizia* interrogate him, he'll say, "Yes, they did it the day it rained figs and raisins."

I assume these are parables, but I'm never quite sure what lessons I'm supposed to take from them.

As for my grampa, he's gruff but sweet, and if I'm well behaved I get to go to his shoe repair store and try on all the unclaimed footwear.[36] I don't ever get to keep them, even though some of these things have been there since the fifties when he opened the store. I suspect no one's coming back to claim their old saddle shoes.

So, spending time with my grandparents? Yes, absolutely! Just please not in their enormously creepy, dirty house.

All my aunties have tried to make the house less creepy and dirty, but my grandmother violently refuses their help. I'm told Noni is very stubborn about her home because she was born and raised in poverty on the other side of the world. Then she got to America only to live through the Depression. She married my grampa, who had a compulsive gambling habit until he joined Gamblers Anonymous a few years ago.

Suffice it to say she's beyond thrifty. Even though she lives a few miles from downtown Boston, she's converted her whole side yard into a vegetable garden, much to the neighbors' dismay. (According to the neighborhood association, it's fine for her to have a few tomatoes and maybe some basil. They're less forgiving when she plants a quarter acre of corn all the way up to the sidewalk.)

Noni won't throw anything away, either. Ever. Her basement

---

[36] And smell the horse glue that he keeps in pots at the edge of his workbench.

is so full of weird old stuff that I'm afraid to go down there.[37] In her kitchen alone, there's one useless dryer and two hulking, dead refrigerators.

They've been there my entire life.

There's a third refrigerator in the back of the pantry that they can actually use, but it was made before the advent of freezer technology. So if we ever go out for ice cream with them, we have to eat it all because we can't save it. Although once someone forgot and put a pint in the fridge anyway. I substituted the melted vanilla for milk the next morning on my Kix cereal and it was a little bowl of heaven.

Even though they live in a huge house, there's only one bathroom and it is *scary*. There's a wobbly, chipped claw-foot tub in the middle of the room and they keep a bucket behind the toilet because it runs all the time. Their mean Rottweiler-Lab mix Edwina uses it as a water bowl.

Once my Noni decided she'd redo the walls because she found a bucket of paint on the street. While hard at work, she accidentally slopped a little white on the red-and-black-checked floor tiles. Instead of wiping it off, she decided to make the rest of the floor match, so it looks like a bag of cotton balls spilled. It's weird.

The worst part of the bathroom situation is that everyone goes in and out of there while other people are using it and this is *very wrong*. My dad and I are the only ones who not only shut but also lock the door when we're in there.

When we stay at the house, I'm assigned to sleep in the airless

----

[37] Todd, a couple of cousins, and I finally ventured down there after my grandfather's funeral in the late eighties. We formed a human daisy chain and made it four feet into the underbelly of the house before we got spooked and ran back upstairs.

back bedroom, which gives me asthma attacks because Noni won't throw out her old horsehair mattresses. How is it not okay for me to ride a pony for half an hour, but to spare my grandmother's feelings I must sleep on a bed that's so full of old horsehair and dust mites that it's been responsible for me having to go to the emergency room twice?

I seriously hate that house.

Sometimes I can talk my parents into letting me stay with my Auntie Fanny and Uncle Tony in Cambridge, a few minutes away. They have a big, nice, clean house with a huge deck off the second floor. I get to stay in cousin Stephanie's room and try on the toe shoes she has hanging from one of the posts on her canopy bed. On the third floor, their sink is painted porcelain and their faucets are swans and when you turn the water on it looks like the biggest swan is throwing up—it's so beautiful! But because this visit will be both brief and unplanned, I doubt I'll get to stay there when we get to Boston.

After a delightful evening of late-night swimming and an uncensored Robert Redford movie,[38] I sleep like an angel on Auntie Virginia's green velvet couch. Then I get ready in her private guest bathroom with its pink tub and shelves lined with every product Avon's ever manufactured.[39]

Before we leave Connecticut, I convince my Auntie Virginia to send me off with a care package. She's the world's best cook,

....

[38] He swore a lot!

[39] Auntie Virginia gave me a lot of Avon products as presents. Mom wouldn't let me throw the boxes away because she told me they were valuable, so I spent my entire adolescence with only one usable bathroom drawer because the rest were filled with old packaging.

and because of her, I enjoy exotic stuff rarely touched by other eleven-year-olds, like shrimp scampi and roasted peppers . . . but only if she makes it. Auntie Virginia loads me up with meatball sandwiches, macaroni salads, and sweet amaretto cookies studded with pine nuts. I hug the Tupperware containers to me all the way to Boston.

The other downside of staying with my grandparents is the food. Noni's scrappiness extends to her cooking and she uses bizarre, greasy, gristly pieces of meat in her sauce that I'm pretty sure were originally earmarked to make couches and dog food.[40] Once, after a string of particularly horrible family meals, my father whipped out a McDonald's bag when the Sunday gravy was served. This happened before I was born but my Noni's still pissed off about it.

When we finally arrive in Boston a full thirty hours after we left Indiana, we pull up in the driveway and my mom dashes out and knocks on the front door, expecting to receive the conquering hero's welcome.

Except no one's home.

So we go across town to visit my dad's gracious old Aunt Arabella in her immaculate Cape Cod–style home, which is full of porcelain bulldogs draped in Union Jacks. She says I can play with them, but my mom won't let me touch them. My Auntie Abba never had any kids because she had a big career as an orthopedic nurse. Rumor has it she used to work with Dr. Salk, the guy who invented the Marco Polio vaccine, but this has never been confirmed. My

----

[40] A few years later when their dog Edwina finally passed away, there was a lot of speculation as to whatever happened to her body. I kind of don't want to know.

Gaga, her late brother, is the one who told us this, but he used to tell us all kinds of outrageous lies. For years I actually believed that Moon Island was a real place, housing the contents of every flushed toilet. And alligators. Lots and lots of alligators.

Auntie Abba has kind, crinkly blue eyes, and when she kisses us there's a vaguely scratchy feeling above her lip, but it's not weird. Actually, it's kind of comforting. She's also got these huge earlobes, which are supposed to be a sign of the aristocracy from which she's descended. Her dad was an earl but he left his title to marry a commoner. My mom thinks that was such a romantic gesture. I say he should have kept the title and lived in sin.

Anyway, my auntie is so happy to see us! She serves us hot tea with sugar cubes and a crystal dish of bridge mix while my mother frantically paces to the kitchen to dial and redial her parents' house. We don't stay long and Auntie Abba tears up when we go. My heart hurts as she stands in the doorway waving good-bye to us.

We finally hook up with my grandparents and go to their house, where my lungs promptly protest, allowing me a cocktail straw's worth of air each time I breathe. Perfect.

On our second morning in Boston, my mother realizes she hasn't got enough underwear, probably because she packed in a snit. (I do not actually offer this opinion. But it's totally true.)

Having been a Girl Scout, I am *Always Prepared* and brought almost a dozen pair of underpants with me. This over-preparation in no way should be interpreted as a desire to share my bounty with my mother, even though I'm now as tall as she is and we fit into the same size. But since there's no functional dryer in my grandparents' house, she doesn't have the option to wash her own and I am forced to open the coffers.

She wears my favorite pair of underpants and snags my cute terry-cloth top, too. Let's just say I am less than gracious about the whole matter, but I comply. I do, however, put my foot down when she tries to snag my super-short *Three's Company*-esque jogging shorts.[41]

My father takes uncharacteristic sympathy on me and gives Mom some money to buy me school clothes. And then he runs off to hang out with his friends from childhood. I've seen him for maybe ten minutes since we've gotten here. (He's no fan of the facilities, either.)

We take Todd and Grampa to the shop, where they'll spend the day talking about the Red Sox and the Patriots, and Mom, Auntie Pammie, and I drive my grandfather's white Thunderbird (with red leather interior!) to Marshalls.

My mom picks out for me white pants cut like jeans and a brown pair made from some space-age material. I suspect they were the cheapest items on the rack and I don't want them. Auntie Pammie intervenes, assuring me they make me look like Debbie Harry, which is excellent because I really love Blondie.

For good measure, I use my candy cash to purchase a pair of underwear that say "Bloomie's" across the butt in dark, bouncy letters. Auntie Pammie says it's lucky to find stuff from Bloomingdale's at Marshalls. Auntie Pammie works in the city and dresses like the women in *Glamour* magazine, so she's a credible source.

When we get back to my grandparents' house, I roll my great prize into a ball and stuff it into a sneaker. Maybe my mom can

---

[41] Lady, after two kids? No.

seize my horse-and-fudge vacation . . . but she's not taking my first status symbol.

All my friends in the neighborhood are my age but they're a grade younger than I am and still in elementary school. Because I was born in Massachusetts and I was right on the age cutoff, my parents had the option of sending me to kindergarten at four. Mom figured I'd be fine starting early because I was tall. Not mature, not advanced for my age, not a prodigy in any way, just tall. However, rules are different in Indiana, and a lot of kids didn't begin kindergarten until they were close to six. Not only am I the youngest person in my class, but now that I've started junior high, I'm the youngest person in the whole school. But what's really scary is that I'm the youngest person on the junior high–high school bus.

I spend the first few weeks trying to be very small and innocuous. I get on the bus and open a textbook to make it look like I'm doing homework. But I'm in seventh grade and I don't have that much work to do outside of school. My dad says this is problematic and precisely why Indiana ranks so low nationally in regard to education. He also says I'm never going to learn what I need to gain admission to an Ivy League college, but if I can't talk him into getting me a pair of Gloria Vanderbilt jeans, I'm guessing his paying for Dartmouth isn't an option. (By the way, ask me how many shades of purple he turned when my English teacher made the following notation on my Edgar Allan Poe essay: "This sentence needs fixed.")

The problem is I get tired of pretending to do homework so I start to read on the bus. And apparently people who read for pleasure are *stupid*, at least according to the ninth graders Jodi and Kari.

Now that I've caught their attention, they won't leave me alone. They make fun of my hair[42] and they call me Fang because one of my front teeth is chipped. Seriously? My minor dental imperfection offends them? I mean, Jodi's hair is a giant, Roseanne Roseannadanna bush and she always has bits of sandwich caught in her braces and dried spittle in the corners of her cracked lips. Kari's not perfect, either. She has some weird skin condition that's left her with huge Palomino pony patches up and down her arms and on her neck. But I'm polite and don't mention it (out loud).

My mom says appearances don't matter and that no one's judging anyone based on her looks. She says that grooming is silly and vain for a girl my age. She says deep down Jodi and Kari really want to be my friends and that the best course of action is to simply ignore them until they come around.

Excuse me, but when has ignoring a bully ever actually worked? If I try to ignore them, they're going to roll over me like Germany did Poland back in World War II.[43]

So I do what's worked so far in my life—I fight back.

"Nice garbage bag!" Jodi taunts the minute I leave the safety of the bus.

"Same to you!" I retort.

"That doesn't make sense. She's not wearing a garbage bag; you are," Kari snarls.

---

[42] Wavy, brown, parted in the middle, just like every other girl on the bus.

[43] *Summer of My German Solider* starring Kristy McNichol—entertaining *and* educational!

"I'm not wearing a *garbage bag*. I'm wearing cool space-age pants just like Debbie Harry. And they came from Boston. Where are your pants from? Fort Wayne?"

Check and mate, bitches.

They're silent for a minute and then Jodi barks, "Debbie Harry? More like Dirty Harry! Ha! Ha, ha!" They both start guffawing and slapping each other on the back.

I contemplate this. "So, you're saying my pants make me look like a middle-aged, hard-living homicide detective?"

They're immediately silenced. Of course they are. My debating skills were formed in the highly superior New Jersey school system, and they've only had access to what barely passes for public education in this cow town.

Both their faces harden. Kari squinches up her eyes and Jodi narrows her cracking lips and starts breathing out of her mouth really loudly.

Oh. I guess I accidentally said that last part out loud.

You know, sometimes it's appropriate to stand and fight.

And sometimes you should just fucking run.

As I dash down the hallway I can hear them both chanting "Plastic pants! Plastic pants!" when I duck into first period. Fortunately, I have my allergy shot this afternoon and I won't have to ride the bus.

But there's always tomorrow.

I'm wearing my new lightweight white pants today because it's eighty degrees out and we're not allowed to wear shorts to school. I manage to secure a seat up close to the driver, thus assuring myself an unmolested ride to school. Of course, there's that brief intermission between arrival and being allowed to enter the school at first bell. And that's when Kari and Jodi strike, catching me on the steps by the front door.

"Nice pants, jerkface!" Kari hisses.

"Yeah, they're from Boston, too," I smugly reply.

"So what? You're not allowed to wear them. It's after Labor Day. *Duh.*" Jodi laughs.

Now wait a minute, if Crestview Junior High suddenly has a dress code based on national holidays, why was I not informed? Seriously, I'm a compulsive rule follower. If this is now law, shouldn't someone have sent a note home?

The girls don't get any more time to tease me because the bell rings. I dash to the bulletin board in the main hallway to see if there's something written up about wearing white, but there's only a poster advising me to have a safe and happy holiday weekend. What the hell?

Kari and Jodi quickly come up behind me and then they really start cackling. When I got dressed this morning, I grabbed the first pair of white underwear I found. Unfortunately, they were the ones with "Bloomie's" stenciled on the backside . . . which is totally visible through my sheer slacks.

They stay behind me, shrieking and pointing and calling people over to look at my pants. My brother's asshole friend Criss follows me all the way to the third floor, saying, "Hey? What do your pants say? What do your pants say?" Even though I have some friends at school, no one helps me. No one defends me. I'm on my own.

Gym class, which I normally hate, can't come soon enough,

because I just happen to have an extra pair of underwear in my gym bag. Like I said, I am *Always Prepared*. They're pale pink and you can sort of see the color through the pant fabric but it's *way* better than advertising a department store back there, no matter how upscale.

Today we're square dancing, which according to my dad is absolutely the best use of his educational tax dollars. He says perhaps someone can also teach me to run a cash register and load a truck since that's all anyone will be qualified to do after graduating from this lousy school. I make the mistake of repeating this to a classmate and my gym teacher hears me and takes me aside to yell at me for having a bad attitude.[44]

I'm already feeling kind of raw today and when Miss Franklin shouts at me, the only way I keep from crying is by focusing on her hair, which is frosted with white tips. She looks like she stuck her head in a snow bank. I mean, I may only be eleven and have committed the fashion faux pas of wearing white pants after Labor Day, but even *I* know that basing your hairstyle on inclement weather is a *Glamour* Don't.

As we do-si-do and promenade, it occurs to me that my mom is wrong. Appearances *do* matter. Clothes count. Grooming is important. And the right look may well give me the power to stop bullies.

I don't know how to fix myself yet.

But I'm going to find out.

❖

[44] This is neither the first nor last time someone will have this conversation with me.

Part Two

The Eighties

Take a Picture, It Lasts Longer

(Jordache Jeans, Part One)

"**Y**ou look *way awesome*."

With a wink and a lopsided grin, photographer Mike Matthews confirms what I already know. Hella-yes, I look awesome!

But . . . perhaps I'd better check again, just to be sure?

I glance in the mirror of my slim brown Cover Girl compact. The iridescent blue liner I carefully applied on the inner rims of my eyelids is staying in place nicely and my navy mascara hasn't smudged a bit. The three shades of purple shadow I use totally complement the plaid of my lavender oxford as well as the fuchsia Izod I'm wearing underneath it. (Asking if my collar is popped is like asking if Michael Jackson can moonwalk. I mean, *duh*.)

My lips are coated in the sparkly pink-gold "Italian Sunrise" gloss I bought at Spencer's Gifts and it makes my pout totally kiss-able.[45] My hair's just the right amount of poufy and feathered nicely, even though I can't quite get it to meet in two symmetrical wings in the back like my neighbor Sara Smyth can. I'd love to know how that bitch manages to get her hair so perfect every day. A lot of times I sit behind her on the bus and just stare at her head, trying to figure out her secret. Hot rollers? Aqua Net? The devil magic that comes from listening to Iron Maiden and Judas Priest? Rumor has it she gets up at four thirty every morning to get ready for school.[46] Whatever, it doesn't matter because I look *so* Phoebe Cates right now.

Satisfied with my reflection, I snap the compact shut and a puff of Noxzema-scented air escapes as I attempt to wedge it back into my hip pocket.

Seriously, though? Even without verifying the current state of my hair, makeup, and wardrobe? I'm *not* being conceited when I say I look awesome.

How am I so sure?

Because I'm wearing the size-five Jordache jeans my friend Sissy Anderson gave me. You're automatically hot when you wear size five; it's, like, written in the Constitution or *Vogue* mag-azine or something. Plus, the jeans themselves are extra rad— they're really dark blue and the denim is superthick and they've got a big panting horse embroidered all swirly on the back right pocket in white thread. They flatten my front and enhance my

---

[45] Or it would, if I had a boyfriend . . . and if that boyfriend enjoyed viscous cotton candy flavor.

[46] Then again, I don't have her childbearing hips, so I don't need to overcompensate with, like, utterly flawless hair.

butt and they make my legs look totally long . . . even if they do accidentally cleave my girly parts into two denim hemispheres.

If Princess Diana wore jeans? I'm pretty sure these are the ones she'd choose.

The only thing is I suspect my Jordache are supposed to be a little baggy, yet I kind of fill up every available inch of space within them. When I take them off, my thighs are deeply indented where the seams hit and sometimes I need to punch my legs to regain feeling in them. I'm often forced to lie on the floor and use a rat-tail comb to properly zip them.[47] Also, there was that one time in world history class when I almost blacked out after sneezing. But, what*ever* . . . if I can stuff myself into them, then I *am* a size five and thus can't *not* look good. These jeans are like that old joke: What do you call the guy who graduates last in his class in medical school? *Doctor.* A size five is a size five, no matter how snug. So there.

You know what? These jeans are totally lucky, too. I was wearing them when Kyle Eckert (*quel* stud!) said hi to me for the first time in typing class and also when my nemesis Justine Moore[48] got busted for smoking in the girls' bathroom during lunch. *C'est magnifique!*

Not only are my Jordache a completely excellent brand, I got them for free. While on the bus to a speech meet last fall, I complained to Sissy that my cheap-o-rama parents think designer jeans are a waste of funds. My dad's always babbling on about

---

[47] They're so tight around the crotch region that I technically may not be a virgin anymore.

[48] Like, it's my fault her grody boyfriend asked me to dance?

stupid investments and stocks and bondage and how he doesn't want to piss away his hard-earned money on silly status symbols like a pair of Calvin Kleins. Hey says he'd rather send money to the IRA.

I *so* don't get it.

Why would he support those guys who are always bombing London?

Sympathetic to my plight, Sissy generously offered up her prized pair of Jordache, telling me they hadn't fit her since she quit smoking.

What she neglected to mention was she stopped smoking because she was pregnant. And all that semester I'd wondered why her weight centralized itself into a beach ball on her midsection. My best friend Carol suspected something was up, but I was totally taken by surprise. I just assumed all those times Sissy wanted to go to McDonald's after school meant she was finally over her eating disorder. So maybe these jeans are only good luck for me?[49]

"If you girls were any hotter, you'd melt the film," Mike tells us.

I beam with quiet confidence and reply, *"Mais oui!"* and Robyn squeals, "Oh, my God, you're totally scamming on us!" Mike pinches me and I give him a playful shove as we all proceed down the hall.

We're currently in search of the perfect bank of lockers to climb so Mike can photograph us on top of them for our high school newspaper. My picture's going to be in the next edition of the *Campus*. I'm the editor of the features page and I'm planning on running the photo with the headline JENI TO VACATION IN

---

[49] I mean, as long as I keep them on.

EUROPE. I've budgeted most of the page for the picture and the story because I'm going to print my whole itinerary. I'm going to visit the Eiffel Towel and the Palace of Versailles and the Louvre and Notre Dame, which is apparently not just a college! I'm cruising down the Rhine River on a boat in Germany! Who *wouldn't* want to know every detail of all these exciting destinations?

Mr. H., my journalism teacher, suggested the story include a variety of students' vacation plans, but who really gives a crap if Kerry Clark will be visiting her ailing aunt in Cleveland? Ohio may be the one place on earth more *tres ennuyeux* than Indiana. Or am I supposed to do an article on Jamie Peachtree, who's traveling to Decatur for a 4-H soil judging dealie? When Mr. H. told me about this, I was all, *"Really, he's headed out of town to look at dirt? Fascinating! I'll stop the presses for sure."* And how uneventful will Marina Perez's trip to Guatemala be? She's going to be building a church with her youth group, not cavorting with cute local boys on a big sandy beach, drinking fruity rum punch. Yawn!

Seriously, I'm going to *Europe*, people! I'm seeing the cradle of civilization and not some big, dumb dirt box. Not only am I going to Germany and France, but I'm hitting Switzerland and Belgium, too! I bet my classmates couldn't even find Belgium on a map! Okay, maybe I couldn't either, but Belgium's got to be close to Germany, France, and Switzerland.[50]

When my tour group got together last weekend for a pre-trip meeting, the advisor said something about passing through Luxembourg, but I can't worry about every single town we'll visit. I'm

---

[50] I could absolutely pick it out if given a multiple choice quiz.

only concerned with the countries, especially France. I cannot *wait* to get there and show off how *bien* I speak the language!

Heather Mueller, one of the seriously popular cheerleaders in my school, got all pissed off when she heard about the French leg of my itinerary. She was like, *"You know, I was born in Paris."* Um, if your dad was stationed at an air force base there, that doesn't make you French or your Ramstein-born sister German, you *spaz*. That makes you a military brat, not a soon-to-be world traveler such as me.

Besides, Heather's dad was transferred out of Paris weeks after she was born. It's not like she can tell me about all the cool museums and shops, or even if European chocolate actually is more smooth and rich than the American kind.

Granted, it would help my social status if she and I were buddies, but she hasn't been nice to me since we moved here from New Jersey because I stole all her *I-was-born-in-Paris* thunder, simply by virtue of having spent time somewhere interesting while not *in utero*. Our friendship? A total lost cause.

Anyway, the only thing that matters right now is being *tres jolie* in this picture. Robyn and I decided we'd look extra-foxy if we posed sitting with our backs to each other, each hugging one of our knees. Robyn's not actually going to Europe with me, but she's my friend, she wanted to get out of journalism class early, too, and she totally will enhance how good I'll look in this photo. Seriously, this is the first rule in my handbook.

The Official PRETTY Handbook:

❖

Jeni's Comprehensive Guide to Outstanding Awesomeness

❖ *Rule One*—If possible, pose with other girls when being photographed. It's like if one pretty girl is good, more than one is exponentially better. (And if you're having a bad hair day, they'll totally deflect it for you.)

❖ *Rule Two*—Wear the smallest size you can squeeze into. You can worry about comfort when you're old. And if you buy jeans with the size label displayed on the outside back right hip, use thin black marker to change it. If someone on the school bus is going to look at your butt when you walk by, let it tell the story you want them to read.

❖ *Rule Three*—There's no such thing as too much eyeliner.

❖ *Rule Four*—Ditto on hairspray.

❖ *Rule Five*—Make boys think you're dumb. That way you can trick them into doing all kinds of stuff, like buying you a pie.

❖ *Rule Six*—Your brother doesn't realize his friends are cute. Try to position yourself in the vicinity of his room when the guys are over. If you can do so in a bathing suit, all the better. (This only works if you have a pool. Try to get a pool if you don't have one.)

❖ *Rule Seven*—No matter how hot they might look, the guys who hang out in the computer math lab at lunch are going to grow up to be total losers who can't get jobs. Avoid them.

❖ *Rule Eight*—If you're a brunette, Sun-In is not your friend, regardless of how great the results appear on stupid naturally blond Sara Smyth's head. And it takes over a year for all the orange pieces to grow out.

❖ *Rule Nine*—Double-pierced ears are adorable. Triple-pierce them and you may as well find yourself some clear heels and a stripper pole.

❖ *Rule Ten*—Plaid is always cute. ALWAYS.

After much debate, we finally pick the right spot to take the photograph. There's *beaucoup* light coming in from the atrium across the hallway so we'll be lit perfectly! Robyn wrinkles her nose and I realize we must be close to Mary Jean O'Halloran's locker. Despite the school custodian's best efforts, it still smells vaguely of the manure Charlie Shuttlecock stuffed into it when he found out she cheated on him.

You see? *That's* how messed up rural Indiana is. People don't express their anger with words; they say it with horseshit.

Robyn is able to vault on top of the lockers in one fluid movement because she was gymnastics star in junior high.[51] Years of hoisting myself out of the pool have made me strong enough to lift my own weight, but my jeans are so tight I can't swing my leg up to take hold so I fall backward.

I try again, jumping up first, but I don't have enough momentum behind me. I completely biff it and land so solidly on the flat soles of my stupid Gloria Vanderbilt riding boots that the shock radiates all the way up my spine. I try a third time with similar results and a thin line of perspiration begins to bead on my forehead. *Merde!*

"C'mere, babe, I'll give you a boost," Mike says. He puts his newspaper-issued camera down and makes a foothold out of his clasped hands, steadying them on his knee. He lifts me up so quickly[52] I almost bite it again, but luckily Robyn grabs my arm to steady me. He laughs while I scramble to right myself. "You'll never make it onto the squad if you can't master a simple lift."

Ouch, *burn*! The fact that I'm not a cheerleader is a blight on my would-be idyllic high school existence and Mike totally knows it. We've discussed this at length when we talk in the darkroom every day after school. I'm an honor student, my teachers are nice, and I'm in all the best activities like newspaper and speech team and school musicals. So it's not that I'm not known or liked—I'm just *drama club* popular, not *Heather Mueller-cheerleader* popular. And how am I going to snag a boyfriend if

---

[51] Why do all the boys in my class think being a gymnast is so hot? What's so erotic about a balance beam?

[52] Wait, did he just touch my butt? And did I like it?

I'm not cheerleader popular? Yeah, I've got a ton of guy friends from theater, but none of them have ever made a move on me.[53]

I tried to be a cheerleader when we moved here. I had excellent enthusiasm and decent moves, but I also had the stigma of being "different" so no one voted for me. Now if anyone ever asks, I simply say there's no way I'd enjoy standing around some loud, drafty ballgame, being ogled by a stadium full of pervy fathers.

The truth is I don't actually want to do the work it takes to lead cheers at games. I just want the outfit. There's something magical about our cheerleaders' uniforms—buffed black-and-white saddle shoes with slouchy socks, pleated red skirts that show hidden black panels every time someone jumps or spins, and sweetly demure, yet form-fitting, black vests embroidered with a Vikings logo. The vests are paired with thick white turtlenecks in the winter and worn alone in the spring. Something about this outfit turns plain girls pretty and pretty girls stunning and it draws the attention of every person in the room. Even though I have no desire to do a split in front of a bunch of panting strangers, I believe in the power of clothing, so obviously I'd want to wear that which possesses mystical qualities.

Whatever, I'll be cheerleader popular when everyone reads the article about my fabulous European tour. I'm not going to ruminate on what I don't have for the moment.

Mike's grinning when I peer down at him from my new perch atop the locker. I tell him, "Oh, my God, you're so *gay!*"

Except that he's not, as evidenced by how he moons over me in journalism. Mike's on the swim team so his hair has those

[53] I suspect it's because I'm a terrible singer. Sigh.

superglossy blond streaks and his shoulders are borderline dreamy. When he wears his stylish checkered Vans, a Journey concert T-shirt with contrasting baseball-jersey sleeves, and a white bandana around his neck, lots of girls find him handsome. (And last week, when he had to go to the dentist and his mom made him wear an oxford and an Izod vest, I almost got swoony before I realized it was him.)

The thing is, he's a *sophomore*. He flirts with me all the time, which makes it such a pity that no junior girl would ever date an underclassman. (*C'est so* robbing the cradle.)

Oh, well. Maybe I'll find a cute age-appropriate guy in France and he'll fall madly in love with me because I can conjugate over five hundred French verbs. I'm, like, totally fluent. "*Parlez-vous français?*" he'll ask. "*Mais bien sur!*" I'll reply.

And how radical would it be if I met some kind of minor European prince at, like, a disco and he was all hot for me because of my sexy American jeans and boss French accent? I'd return to the States ultratan (because he took me to his palace on the Riviera, naturally) and totally thin because we were always dancing and eating exotic French fruit on the beach and my Jordache would practically hang off my hips instead of constricting me so much that lunch[54] is never an option. Then when I got back to school, I'd be way continental and I'd kiss Heather Mueller on both cheeks and tell her, "*That's* Princess *Jeni to you.*" Then she'd really be envious and I'd laugh about how sorry she was for never letting me onto her precious cheerleading squad.

I'm realistic enough to understand my royal plans might not

---

[54] Or, for that matter, bending.

work out, so I've come up with Plan B. I've got my eye on this one boy I met at our trip advisor's house last weekend. His name is Tom and he's a senior from Fort Wayne![55] He seemed kind of quiet while our tour group went through our Institute for Foreign Study *Get Ready, Get Set, GO!* brochures, but maybe he's a total party animal when he's not shoved into a tiny love seat next to his mother? (And how adorable was it that he kept his arm around her the whole time?) I can't wait to go on our trip so I can get to know him better.

But until I meet my prince—or get Tom to notice me—I guess I'll be content with how popular I'll be after my feature runs.

---

[55] It's the Paris of Indiana.

Plan B

(Jordache Jeans, Part Two)

*H*ey, wanna know what *doesn't* make you instantly more popular?

Using a campus-wide publication to inform your classmates that your cheap-o-rama parents have the means to send you across the Atlantic for spring break while everyone else is going to a dirt rodeo. Maybe I should have mentioned in the article that most of the trip is covered by the scholarship I received because we hosted a foreign exchange student for three years?[56] But if I had, I wouldn't have had the column inches to include my photo. You can see my dilemma.

I can't fathom how a trip to Europe is cause for teasing, but today felt like seventh grade all over again, like all the hard work

---

[56] Yet I stand by my decision not to feature the soil judging competition.

I put in with vent brushes and cosmetics and *Seventeen* magazine was for naught.

How is it that a few mean comments can make me feel all chip-toothed again? Suddenly, instead of strolling along in my brother's supercute fraternity letter sweatshirt, Izod shirt with a flippy collar, and excellent jeans on my way to world history, I feel like I'm on the back of the bus in seventh grade, being grilled by Kari and Jodi before I discovered contact lenses and vent brushes and they left me alone.

Anyway, today Justine Moore was the worst out of everyone and I had a total flashback. She cornered me after English class, saying I was going to stop shaving my pits like all the Frenchies.

My response? "Yeah, well, your boyfriend doesn't seem to mind."

So maybe I've learned a couple of things since seventh grade.[57]

All that school unpleasantness is behind me because I'm going to Europe! My mom takes me to the meeting point in a McDonald's parking lot and I convene with the trip chaperones and the other kids from area high schools. We're traveling by van to the airport in Chicago, then we fly to New York to meet up with students from Houston, then we all go to Germany as a group. I'm so excited it doesn't even occur to me to grab some fries or a shake for the road.

....

[57] By the way? Last I heard Kari was doing nails for a living in a little shop down by the jail. *Who's laughing now?*

Normally Mom would be sniffly and sad I was leaving, but tomorrow she and Dad are using his frequent flier miles to vacation in Hawaii for the first time. I feel more than a little liberated knowing we're going to be on opposite ends of the globe for a whole week. (I wonder if Mom isn't equally excited, because she almost burned rubber leaving the parking lot.)

I ride up to Chicago next to a girl named Sandy. She's wearing a coordinated teal green warm-up suit and it's wicked cute! She compliments my taste in jeans—Jordache are her favorite, and she brought a pair, too—and by the time we reach O'Hare we're complete soul sisters. Sandy goes to school with Tom, so while we're waiting for our chaperones to check us into the flight, I take the opportunity to grill her about him.

"Do you have any classes together?" I ask, rifling through my carry-on to find my passport.

"We both have advanced placement English with Miss Hoffman during fourth period." Sandy grabs her passport and we hand them over to one of our chaperones.

"Uh-huh, yeah, and?" I'm sitting cross-legged on the floor of the terminal, which has only been made possible by changing into a different pair of pants. My mom insisted I'd be uncomfortable not being able to bend during the ten-hour flight, so I'm clad in a comfy pair of khakis. Oh, but trust me, I *will* break out the Jordache the second we hit foreign soil.

"And what? I'm not sure what you want to know. He's really quiet. He always has the right answer when he's called on, though."

"So he's smart and not arrogant about it—I like that. Tell me more!" I say, nodding eagerly.

Sandy looks up at the ceiling, concentrating. "Um, once he did a book report on the life of Oscar Wilde."

I shrug. "Never heard of him. But I love Kim Wilde. Her 'Kids in America' song is one of my faves. I wonder if they're related?" If so, this is yet another way the universe is telling me we're made for each other. "What else? Does he play football? Basketball? Maybe he's a swimmer? I kinda like swimmers for some reason."

"No . . . nope, um . . ." Sandy snaps her fingers. "He's in the marching band, though!"

I mull this over for a moment. "Band *could* be cool—does he play the drums?"

"Negatory. The guy who plays drums lives on my street."

"Bummer. So . . . what kind of girls does he date?"

Sandy begins to gather her things and stand because our group is moving to the gate. "That's the funny thing—I can't think of one girl in our school he's ever dated."

I gasp. "Do you know what that means?"

Sandy's eyes open wide and she leans in close. "Tell me!"

I look around to make sure no one else is listening in. "It means he likes girls who live out of town!"

Even though I'm sure to meet a European prince because of my *parfait français*, Tom is still my Plan B.

We sit behind Tom and this dweeby guy Brian on the flight to New York. I love how Tom looks right into Brian's eyes while they speak—he's so intense! I wonder what they're talking about— maybe me?? Sandy and I can't hear them over the roar of the jet engines. Instead of eavesdropping, we amuse ourselves by creating barf bag puppets of our dream boyfriends—Sandy makes Boy George and I make Freddie Mercury. *J'adore!*

As soon as we get to JFK, I hit the ladies' room. Sandy went to buy a New York T-shirt from the gift shop and I'm by myself. I wonder if we're in the international terminal because everyone here is chattering in languages I've never heard before. Two ultrastylish girls all done up in wrapped scarves, skinny pants, and shortie boots are washing their hands at the sink. I notice their Air France bags and really take a listen to what they're saying.

Sacre bleu, they're speaking *French!* My first authentic French people! I totally have to talk to them and show them my brilliant language skills! I run my hands over my khakis to smooth them out, adjust all the buttons with clever sayings[58] on my jean jacket, and finally sidle up to the girls, employing my most authentic accent.

"*Bonjour, mon nom est Jennifer! Je parle le français! J'aime vos chaussures! Je vais en France! Peut-être je*, um, will buy *vos chaussures!*"[59]

The girls look at each other with their elegant raised European brows, then give me the once-over, their eyes lingering on my pants. Ahh! I *knew* these stupid khakis were a mistake! They

[58] My favorite one reads "My mother thinks I'm at the movies." Although, unfortunately, I probably *am* at the movies.

[59] Hi! My name is Jennifer! I speak French! I like your shoes! I'm going to France! Maybe I will buy your shoes!

finally respond in rapid-fire French, and to me? It sounds exactly like this:

"Blah blah blah blah blah blah blah. Blah blah blah. Blah blah blah blah blah blah blah. Blah blah bete blah blah blah."

I stand there and nod pretend-knowingly.

Um, what just happened here? This is *not* the kind of French we speak in Miss Knipp's class.

The girls appraise me once more, snicker, and walk away. It takes me a second to realize I actually recognize one of the words they've said.

Bete.

They said *bete* and gestured at me.

Bete is French for "stupid."

So much for my cunning linguistics.

I slump against the wall of the washroom. I guess this means even if I do meet Prince EuropeGuy, I won't know what he's saying to me. I'll probably be all, *I love you, too,* when in fact he's trying to tell me I have toilet paper on my shoe. If I can't communicate with him (which I can't because apparently I speak Miss-Knipp-Cow-Town-Indiana-style French and not real French), how will I ever have the verbal dexterity needed to trick him into buying me a pie? Or a tiara? Or a castle?

Plan A is over, which means so is my chance of becoming cheerleader popular.

I wash my hands hard to scrub off the sting of failure. I stare at my reflection for a long time and it occurs to me that I'm only sixteen and it's possible this won't be the worst thing that ever happens to me. So I square my shoulders and try to march out of the bathroom with confidence. Even if I don't feel it, I have enough theater training to fake it.

As I shuffle toward the gate, I make the conscious decision to move on to Plan B. And now I'm off to figure out how to maneuver myself into the seat next to Tom on the flight to Germany. Although, I notice Tom brought a clarinet in his carry-on baggage. Is it just me, or is that kind of queer?

❖

Gay Paree

(Jordache Jeans, Part Three)

The woman who organized this trip is a dour older lady named Norma. She's got steely gray hair and her eyes are narrowed into angry little slits, untouched by my good friend Max Factor. She holds her lips like she's perpetually smelling Mary Jean O'Halloran's locker. She works for the Institute for Foreign Study and she and my mother met during choir practice at the Baptist church. Mom joined that particular ministry because the pastor visited her in the hospital when she had some minor surgery when we first moved here. We've been in Indiana six years now and I've yet to figure out how one quick bedside visit can turn her from mellow, moderate Methodist to Bible-beating Baptist. Shoot, *I* visited her in the hospital . . . I don't see her worshipping at the Holy House of Jeni.

I completely loathe the Baptist church, yet I'm forced to

attend and it is sooo eerie, particularly since a lot of the members pray out loud. Like, you can hear all the bad stuff they've done while they're asking God for forgiveness. Say what you will about the Methodists, but they have the good sense to keep their sins a little closer to the vest.

When we were Methodist, we talked a lot about Jesus and all the neat stuff He did for other people—it was shiny, happy Christianity. The Methodists made me feel like Jesus was my friend and, like, He'd be cool if I asked to borrow some lunch money because I forgot my purse at home or if I accidentally got my p-e-r-i-o-d on His white leather car seats. Jesus wouldn't be all agro if I ever bailed on Him at the last minute because my crush finally asked me to the movies. And if I had cramps or a sinus headache, He'd lay a finger on my head and be all *Dude, it's totally handled*. The Methodist Jesus would be just all right with me, exactly as the Doobie Brothers promised.

At the Baptist church, it's nothing but hellfire and damnation and 666 and the mark of the beast. I'm all, *"You guys? The Exorcist? Was fiction. And Damien isn't real either!"*

My Baptist Sunday school teacher spent an entire month telling us about how the Rapture was coming and that the righteous would be spirited up to Heaven immediately and how those who didn't believe would be left to fester on the earth. He'd show us these freaky films where all of a sudden people would just vanish, leaving nothing but running cars and spinning office chair seats.

Really? I had enough trouble worrying about Kari and Jodi. The *last* thing I needed was some fundamentalist zealot attempting to scare the wits out of me in the name of the Lord. I remember thinking, *If you're indicative of who's going to be in Heaven, I choose earthly festering, thanks.*

What's really ironic is the church inadvertently helped me figure out how to get Kari and Jodi off my back. We were in a pew one Sunday morning and a sad woman was standing next to me, quietly pleading for God to bring her husband back. Being a small congregation, it was common knowledge that her rotten husband had dumped her for someone younger and thinner. The more she begged God to fix everything by making her skinnier, the more I realized that He isn't a Maytag repairman, ready to make a house call at a moment's notice. He's not going to come down, reach into his tool box, and wave a magic wand to make her pounds disappear. But I bet if she looked around, she'd find the tools He provided so she could help herself . . . and not so she could get that cheating bastard back, but so she could find a way to be happy in herself.

Then I had my own epiphany- -the same rules applied to me. If I wanted to stop being teased, I couldn't just pray for Him to give Kari and Jodi laryngitis. (Or get hit by a bus, no matter how much fun it was to imagine.) I had to take responsibility for myself by assuming an active role in eliminating that which was mockable. I started showering and drying my hair before school, rather than taking a bath before bed and throwing my wet locks up into a ponytail. I put aside my fear of the dentist and finally got the chip in my tooth fixed. I asked for contact lenses for Christmas and I began studying *Seventeen* magazine for fashion tips and makeup tips.

I figured out how to reinvent myself, making my appearance work for me, not against me.

Of course, there's a chance I may have overcompensated.

Anyway, because my mother is anxious to impress Baptist Norma, she didn't sign the permission slip allowing me to drink alcohol while I'm in Europe . . . which is bogus. Mom had no problem when I slugged down all those sombreros[60] at my cousin Debbie's wedding. Not only was I in eighth grade at the time, but I went back to Auntie Virginia's house and barfed on her green velvet couch. And once when we went to a vineyard in the Hudson River Valley, she and my dad *laughed* when they caught me swilling wine out of tasters' abandoned cups.

I was *seven*, for Christ's sake.

If they try to make alcohol all mystifying for me now, I'm probably going to lose my mind when I go to college.

Anyway, even though I've only tasted liquor twice in my life before, I'm pretty sure I know what it feels like to *need* a drink. We've been in Germany for eight hours and I'm ready to either get plowed or go home. Norma and the rest of the chaperones have taken to "treating" each other at every meal, picking up tabs for various food and beverages. But it's not really treating—Norma's got an accounting system that would put the Internal Revenue Service to shame. Each time we've eaten, it's taken an extra twenty minutes to settle up because Chaperone A owes Chaperone B the German equivalent of thirty-seven cents because Chaperone A got a large coffee when Chaperone B was paying and Chaperone B had a small one when A paid, which . . . *Aarrggh!!* Do! Not! Care!! Shouldn't we be seeing some culture and shit right now?

All of us kids have to wait on the tour bus while the grown-

---

[60] Kahlua or other coffee-flavored brandy and cream. *Yum.* I will have these again.

ups arm-wrestle each other over what's really a few pennies. They finally work out the tab—for now—and we motor to our first hotel.

Correction.

We motor to the hotel where we students are staying and we find out the chaperones—you know, the ones who our parents trusted to watch over and protect us and keep us out of bars—are staying at a nicer hotel down the street.

Norma just fucked up.

And this trip suddenly got interesting.

$$\mathsf{\underline{Y}}$$

"A pub!" Sandy shouts from our tiny bath, where she's busy massaging a whole can of mousse into her tightly permed hair. "I want to go to a pub!"

"No, no!" I argue. "A disco! Let's hit a disco!" So I'm not quite ready to let go of my European prince fantasy.

"How about a beer garden? Germany is famous for beer gardens. *Gehen wir zum Biergarten!*" exclaims Curtis, one of our new best friends from Houston. He's lying on Sandy's bed with his legs kicked up in the air, propped against the wall, darling argyle socks peeking out from under his jeans. He's totally cute in a Michael J. Fox kind of way, all tidy and pink and shiny and tucked in.

Sandy pops out, her ringlets glistening with moisture. "Is that German for 'order me a cold brew'?"

"Y'all, I think pubs, discos, and beer gardens are the same thing over here," replies Steph, Curtis's classmate and platonic[61]

....

[61] For now, she hopes!

best friend. She idly picks at her cuticles. She's way more organized than us and has been ready for the last twenty minutes.
She's sitting on my bed, tapping out a staccato beat with her sensible ballerina flat. "Let's stop debating and just *go* already."

"Steph, relax. We'll be ready in a few," Sandy scoffs, wiping
her hands on a scratchy towel.

Curtis turns to Steph. "Honey, unclench, please."

"I can't help it if I think we need a plan," Steph snaps.

Curtis sits up and shoots the cuffs on his perfectly pressed
button-down shirt. "How about this—how about we venture out
and hit the first place we see with a neon bottle in the window?
Neon's the international sign for 'drinks served here.'"

"Everyone cool with that?" I ask and Sandy and Steph nod.
"Alrighty, let me just go tell Tom and Brian the plan. Which room
are they in?"

Sandy tells me, "Four doors down to the right."

"Sweet! Hey . . . know what I just thought? Maybe if Tom
gets some liquid courage tonight, he'll make a move on me!"

Curtis snorts and lies back on the bed. "Yeah, good luck with
that, darlin'."

"What do you mean?" I ask. I paw through my luggage to
find my hottest outfit.

He gives me a knowing look. "You'll see."

I make Curtis stand in the hallway while I put on my least
modest blouse, buttoned almost low enough to see cleavage. I paint
my jeans back on and slide into the pair of Nine West pumps that
I swiped from my mom and then I saunter down to Tom and Brian's
room. I bang on their door and it takes them a few minutes to answer. "Hey, you guys! We're going out for beers! Come with us!"

Brian answers the door in his pajamas. I don't see Tom in the tiny room, so he must be in the washroom down the hall. We girls got so lucky to score an en suite bath! "I can't," says Brian. "My mom wouldn't sign the permission slip."

"Um, *dude*? Your mom is in Fort Wayne and your chaperones are in another hotel. Pretty sure you can have a brew if you want one," I tell him.

"No, thanks." He seems resolute. Or, like, jet-lagged or something.

"Oh-kaaay. Tomorrow then, totally," I say with no sincerity. Like I care if *he* joins us, anyway. "What about Tom?"

"What about me?" Tom materializes right behind Brian. What, was he hiding behind the door?

"We're going out for beer. Come with us!"

Tom shakes his head. "I can't."

"Oh, don't give me that permission slip bullcrap, too. No one's here! No one will know! What happens in Europe stays in Europe!"[62]

"It's not that—it's . . ." He hesitates. I try to look at him all understanding-like. It's okay, handsome! You can tell me! "It's . . . it's just that I promised my grandmother that I'd send her postcards every night. Also, I'm supposed to practice my clarinet."

"Ha! That's hilarious!" I reply, giving him a quick shove. "Get dressed and let's go."

Tom shifts uncomfortably against the door and glances back at Brian. "Sorry, I've got plans here."

"Seriously, come on." I tug his hand and he stands stock-still.

....

[62] Las Vegas Tourism Board, you totally owe me.

"Wait, you're not kidding? What are you saying?" Um, did I suddenly lose all my cute the minute we crossed the pond? How can that be? I followed every rule on my list . . . except wearing plaid. Damn.

"I can't." No. *No.* How are we going to share our first German kiss if your stupid lips are wrapped around a clarinet?

I decide to change tactics. Perhaps goading him will work. "Are you saying you'd rather send a *postcard* to your *grandma* than go out for drinks?"

No go on the goad. Tom shrugs sadly, says good night, and gently closes the door behind me.

I stomp down the hall in my pinchy shoes. My God, how can he not want to go out with a bunch of girls (and Curtis) whose inhibitions have been greatly lowered by first-time consumption of alcohol?

Who'd say *no* to that invitation?

What kind of huge, huge nerd doesn't like tipsy chicks, especially on a whole 'nother continent?

Weird.

"Here's one! Here's one!" We've been dashing up and down the cobblestone hills for twenty minutes now and we're all a bit bitchy. Who knew it would be so hard to find someplace that serves beer in Germany? That's like not finding pineapples in Hawaii. Or oaks in Oklahoma! We had to go through a darkened passage to get to this place, and even then we only found it by accident when one of Sandy's bracelets fell off and bounced down the alley.

We appoint Sandy as our leader because her accessories brought us here, so she's the one in charge of throwing open the front door. She confidently takes four steps into the bar, and we follow, hoping to make our big entrance just in case there are any European princes there. (I'm not the only one who wants to be more popular in school.) But then Sandy stops abruptly, causing Steph, Curtis, and me to slam into her. We all go down and wind up tangled in a giant pile of American denim.[63]

Any chance of dignity already shot, we brush ourselves off and grab a table on the periphery of the bar. The whole place is really dark and smoky and our eyes have yet to adjust. *"A bar!"* we exclaim in stage whispers. *"Oh, my God, we are in a* bar*! If only all the kids at home could see us now!* How radical are we??"

Curtis is the only one of us who takes German so it's up to him to tell us what to order. However, he can't figure out the menu and throws his hands up in frustration. Everything listed is foreign to him. Like, even though he can pronounce the word "Gewürztraminer," he doesn't know what it might possibly mean. Is it delicious? Is it swill? Is it *liquor*? We're clueless.

We head up to the bar en masse and I order a dry white wine. And here's a language lesson I didn't know. The German word for "three" sounds just like English word "dry," so when I place my order, we're served three glasses. We don't want to let on like we're not, you know, *cool*, so Curtis, Steph, and I grab the goblets. Sandy's on her own so she orders a Becks because she once saw a commercial for it during *Friday Night Videos*.

We're so busy trying to work out how I screwed up the drinks,

....

[63] And false bravado.

it takes us a few minutes to figure out we're the only girls (except Curtis) in this bar.

"Do you believe in miracles—*Yes!*" I squeal. "There's got to be two dozen guys in here!"

"We are going to meet so many men!" Sandy shrieks.

"A lot of them are nice-looking," Steph reluctantly agrees, glancing at Curtis to see if her statement causes a reaction.

"They're *ours*," I agree. The proximity to boys has definitely lightened our moods. "You guys, they're ours for the taking! And, gosh, they *are* cute! And they're dancing! I love when guys are confident enough to dance by themselves!"

Curtis just sits there with a wry lemon-twist smile on his face, soaking in the atmosphere.

"What's with you?" I ask.

"Nothing." He giggles.

Sandy inquires, "Then why are you smirking?"

He replies, "Y'all are going to have a big, stupid, American flash of realization here in three . . . two . . . one . . ." He turns his head to gaze at two men all dressed up in matchy-matchy motorcycle jackets. And their leather pants? How deliciously European! "Wait for it . . . and, now." The men's heads begin to move closer and closer and then . . . *Holy shit!*

Sandy yelps, "*Ahhh!* We've got to haul ass out of here right now! We're in a gay bar! Ohmigod, ohmigod, ohmigod!!" She shoots straight up out of her chair, knocking it over and spilling half her beer.

"Come on, come on, we've got to go!" I agree, grabbing my coat and purse. "Hustle! Hustle!"

Curtis sits there calmly, crossing his legs. "Stop."

"What? We can't stop—Curtis, we need to leave this place right this second!" All of Steph's anxiousness is back, and then some.

Nonplussed, Curtis replies, "*Why* do we have to run out of here? Ponder for a minute, won't you? Y'all are worried they're going to give you *gay cootie*s or something?"

Sandy pauses by her upset chair. "Well . . . no."

He continues, "And does preferring boys to girls really make them any different from you? Does it make 'em bad people?"

I volunteer the next answer, "I guess not, right?"[64]

Steph cocks her head and peers at Curtis like it's the first time she's ever really looked at him. "Are . . . are you trying to tell us something?"

Curtis sighs and takes a delicate pull on his glass of wine. "Y'all are about the slowest people I ever did meet."

Three sets of overly mascaraed eyes blink for about a minute before any of us speak.

"Wait, *you're* gay? As in you prefer men to women?" Sandy asks.

"Mmm hmm," he replies.

"*No way!* I don't believe it." How can this be? I wonder. I didn't see any of the signs!

Curtis nods. "Believe it." Steph appears to be crestfallen. "Is this a huge shock to you?" he asks, placing his hand over hers.

"You mean . . . you're not secretly in love with me and you weren't waiting to get me alone in Europe to make a pass at me?" Steph wails.

....

[64] The Methodist church I went to used to be pretty clear on the notion of loving and accepting everyone. Their Jesus would totally have gay friends. The Baptists? Maybe not so much.

He shudders. "Jesus, no."

"Oh. Will you still go to prom with me?" She sniffs.

"Couldn't stop me."

Steph gives him a wan smile and then chugs her entire glass of wine. Then she holds the glass up and waves it at the bartender. Fortunately, he's fluent in the international language of disappointment and begins to open another bottle of wine.

Meanwhile, lightbulbs begin to go off over my head. "No *wonder* Tom didn't want to go barhopping with us. He's gay, too?"

"Nope. He's not playing for my team."

"Then what's his problem?" I ask.

Curtis grins. "He's just a huge nerd."

Sandy sits heavily back down into her chair. "Now what?"

"Girl," he says, motioning for the bartender, "now we drink."

We spend the evening doing just what I'd imagined I'd do in a German beer hall—linking arms with gorgeous European boys and belting out songs. But instead of singing folk songs, we shout our way through all the American music on the jukebox. You know what? *Everyone* speaks Madonna. None of us gets a date (except for Curtis), and that's okay. We dance and laugh and drink sour beer and bitter wine and choke while trying to smoke filterless German cigarettes.[65]

After Curtis's confession, we all get a lot more real with each other. We open up and share the kind of confidences we couldn't

---

[65] Even now, almost twenty-five years later, it remains one of the greatest nights of my life.

admit to our friends at home. I feel like for the first time I see who I am inside, and realize I'm more than just a collection of artfully blended eye shadow and neatly trimmed bangs and skinny jeans.

The rest of the trip passes in a similarly alcohol- and pastry-fueled unchaperoned haze. I climb the Eiffel Tower—there's more vomit on the observation deck than I might have imagined. I see the *Mona Lisa*—it's smaller than I thought. I narrowly avoid eating horsemeat, but I make up for it by wolfing down a dozen éclairs. I am summarily mocked by a border guard in Luxembourg. Apparently, I'm wrong. It is a country or at least the guard seemed to think so. I struggle to explain to a French pharmacist that my friend needs to buy mini-pads because she has a "red river in her pants." And I learn that my French is fantastic after six glasses of champagne.

I never do have my big European romance. But in the course of opening my mind to new possibilities, I figure out there's someone I really like and that person's been there the entire time and I never even noticed.

Wanna know who it is?

It's *me*. I found out that I really like *me*.

I'm sitting on the plane bound for New York and all of the kids on my tour are passed out in the seats around me. We had a huge all-night party in the hotel on our final day in Belgium. We even convinced Tom and Brian to drink a bottle of Stella Artois with us! They both practically gagged when they took their first sips and *then* asked for water, but hey, it's a start.

I should be sleeping right now, but I can't. My pants are too tight. And these aren't my jeans; they're my khakis. Every pair I packed seems to be a little smaller. Somehow all the cheese and wine and croissants with extra butter have had an effect on my waistline. Living the high life? Has its price. When I get home, I'm probably going to have to retire my Jordache jeans for good.

But that's okay. Being on this trip has given me more confidence, like, *real* confidence and not just the kind that comes from perfectly feathered bangs.

And you know what?

I bet maybe, just *maybe* the world won't end if I go out with a sophomore.

❖

Clipped Wings

(Pfft, Who Cares Because I May as Well Be in Prison Stripes)

Jennifer –

Here's the ten dollars you requested for gas. In return, the following tasks will be complete when I get home from work:

Vacuum pool and clean out filters. Bag up debris and place in trash—do not dump cricket carcasses on the cement again. Use metal brush to scrub algae from steps.

Cut grass in front and back and bag clippings. The lawn is already healthy and does not need to be "mulched" again.

Wash station wagon and vacuum interior.

Dust and mop family room.

Bring trash barrels back into garage.

Unload and load dishwasher.

—Your Father

Hey, Dad,

Why not just have me hook a plow around my shoulders and till the field beyond our fence while you're at it?

By the way, I bet the Department of Labor would be <u>very interested</u> in seeing the amount of work you expect a seventeen-year-old to accomplish for ten measly dollars.

I shall be calling their offices the moment I locate their number.

—Your Daughter[66]

[66] So. Very. Grounded.

"Jeni?"

"Jeni?"

"Jeni."

"Jeni Lancaster! Are you even with us today?" My advanced placement teacher snaps me out of my reverie by tapping me on the shoulder. I respond by practically jumping out of my skin.

Instead of listening, I've been gazing out at the atrium across the hall. Winter's finally over and tulips have come out and the spindly gray trees are leafy and green. I can't help but admire the metamorphosis—spring's putting on quite the Hollywood production. It's almost like Mother Nature knows what a big deal this year is for me and she's pulling out all the stops.

Normally I'm more attentive because this is my favorite class, but given the weather and my looming graduation, I have to wonder why we're even bothering with *Macbeth.* I already got into the college of my choice[67] and I tested out of my English requirement. At this point, I couldn't care less whether or not Lady Macbeth removes all the crud from her hands. Jesus, Lady, why don't you try some lemon juice and quit being such a drama queen already?

"I'm sorry, Mrs. H., I was looking at the flowers. Aren't they beautiful?" I gesture toward the tree covered in blossoms. "What is that pink one, like a magnolia or cherry tree or something?"

"My prom dress is that same color!" exclaims Rachel from the second row.

For God's sake, Rachel, enough about your dress already.

Everyone in here knows about your dress. The janitor knows

---

[67] Dad said I had a choice of Purdue or IU.

about your dress. The lunch lady won't look you in the eye for fear of hearing about your dress. You've talked about nothing but prom for the past two months. I'm not sure who in this class can say what the Three Witches represent, but all of us can describe how your boyfriend Ty's already reserved a white tux with a pink ruffled shirt and a boutonnière with a pink-dipped white carnation surrounded by a small but tasteful array of baby's breath, which he will wear to a pre-prom dinner at the Wharf in Fort Wayne, where you will order the rainbow trout because sometimes Ty fishes for trout with his dad when they go on vacation, which is so cool that he has a nice relationship with his father because that means his dad trusts Ty enough to loan him his fully restored antique white Ford truck, which is awesome because Ty's planning to lay a blanket down in the back so when the after-prom is over and before you go to Nick's Café for biscuits and gravy (on which you prefer extra pepper), you'll drive out to the woods by the reservoir, where you will allow him to go to third base if and only if you are elected to prom court, which you won't be because everyone hates you and your incessant prom chatter so damn much right now.

Or maybe I'm just mad because I've been shopping for dresses for a month and I've yet to find one that fits?

Without even turning toward the atrium, Mrs. H. returns to her own desk at the front of the room and sits down heavily. Very slowly, clearly enunciating every word, she says, "Miss Lancaster, that would be a germane question if this were a botany class. However—"

Stupid show-off Ray Harper in the front row corrects her. "Actually, Mrs. H., botany is the study of *plants*. Dendrology is the study of *trees*. If you want to get technical, dendrology is the study of *all* wooden plants including shrubs and lianas." No one says anything, but all of us are thinking, *Lianas? This is exactly why you're flying solo to the prom, nerd-o.* "The difference between dendrology, and, say, simple plant taxonomy is—"

Mrs. H. interrupts, "The question I originally posed, *Jeni*, was about Macduff attempting to dethrone Macbeth. What was his motivation?"

Julie sits next to me. Sometimes I eat lunch with her and our mutual friend Mary when my boyfriend's absent. We girls are partial to the bread sticks at Noble Romans.[68] We have an open campus at lunch, so we can eat anywhere within walking distance. We used to be able to drive during lunch but too many kids were coming back the second half of the day drunk or pregnant. If we stay in the cafeteria, I'll normally have Boston cream pie or an ice cream sandwich. (My mother thinks I'm having salad. *Ha!*)

Julie lives on a farm but totally plans to leave this cow town and dance in MTV videos during her summers away from agriculture school. She interjects, "Hey, wouldn't Macduff be an awesome name for a band?"

"Ooh, or one of those dogs with the really hairy faces?" I add.

"Yes!" Christy exclaims from her seat next to the windows. "You could call him Duffy for short—how cute is that?" Christy and I have recently become friendly because we're going to be in the Miss Cow Town pageant together. She and I do an across-the-classroom high five.

....

[68] And really, what's more Roman than salty white bread dipped in nacho cheese?

Mrs. H. removes her glasses and rubs her eyes. She places her fingers on her temples and stays that way until the bell rings a couple of minutes later. I respect Mrs. H. for at least trying to engage us seniors these last few weeks of school. The rest of my teachers started showing filmstrips days ago.

While we shuffle out of the classroom, Julie slips me a quiz scratched on a ratty piece of loose-leaf paper.[69] "Do this in astronomy and then pass it to Mary before seventh period."

I settle into a seat in the farthest reaches of the planetarium, and as soon as the lights go down I unfold the quiz. It's full of all the usual questions—e.g., Who's your favorite band?[70] and What's your favorite show?[71] The quiz is kind of boring because who really cares if I like croutons or bacon more? (Maybe I don't even *want* a salad, you know?)

What surprises me, though, is when asked to choose between Scarlett O'Hara and Marilyn Monroe, no one else has selected Scarlett. I'm not surprised that Julie picked Marilyn. When the "Material Girl" video came out, she taught herself every single one of Madonna's moves. (She wanted to buy Madonna's BOY TOY belt at Merry-Go-Round but her mom wouldn't let her.) So Julie's a little obsessed, but I don't understand how everyone else could choose Marilyn. That's insane!

Come on, Scarlett fought to keep her land and stole from dead soldiers and made a set of curtains look fierce! All Marilyn did was

---

[69] In my day, we didn't have Internet memes! We had paper quizzes! And we answered them in longhand! Uphill! In the snow!

[70] Wham, naturally.

[71] *Facts of Life.* I *so* want to be Blair Warner. Were *Gossip Girl* around at this time, I'd have wanted to be Blair Waldorf.

stand over a subway grate, show her underpants, and make out with the president—and look where it got her. Granted, one time I was doing a quiz and the question was what famous person would I like to meet and I chose Marilyn, but only because I thought she needed a friend who'd give her good advice. I'd be all, *Why don't you get back with that guy Arthur? He seemed supernice. And lower your voice, you sound kind of dumb. Also, blond hair and black eyebrows? Oh, honey, no.*

I'm still grumbling about the Marilyn/Scarlett conundrum when I arrive at my locker after seventh period. My boyfriend Jimmy is already waiting for me, holding my jean jacket. Jimmy is kind of awesome . . . and not just because he does whatever I tell him, even though sometimes when we go to Baskin-Robbins I make him buy me a whole Grasshopper pie. (He has to order his own sundae, because that pie is *mine*.) I might marry him, but not until I'm at least thirty because I want to finish college and become an anchorperson in one of the major markets first. I'm thinking New York or LA, but Boston would do in a pinch.

I wanted to be an actor for a long time, mostly because I could so see myself on TV. I decided to consider newscasting, though, after my drama coach explained to me that I couldn't sing, like, at all, despite being "one of the better thespians" in our school. Not "the best," just "one of the better." I figured that was grown-up talk for "don't quit your day job," so television broadcasting/telecommunications became my Plan B. I've been conducting interviews in the bathroom mirror ever since I was tall enough to see myself in it, so it is kind of the ideal career for me. When that camera finally rolls, I'll be so ready!

I got into college at both Purdue and Indiana, but all year

long I've been gearing up to attend IU because of their excellent telecommunications program. Or I was, until I spent the weekend in my brother's fraternity house at Purdue for Grand Prix. The way I look at it, I can be a telecom major anywhere; I only already know a fraternity house full of guys on one campus.[72]

Jimmy isn't pleased about my attending Purdue because he wasn't accepted. I keep telling him not to worry about it because I totally love him and we're never going to break up. The thing is, I'd be a bad girlfriend if I didn't remind him that if he was going to be so serious about college, then maybe he shouldn't have cut all those classes and gotten himself kicked out of Catholic school last year. I'd like to date a guy in a fraternity, so not only will he need to find a college, like, now, he should make sure he gets in somewhere with a strong Greek system. But whatever, I'm confident we're meant to be together, like Maddie and David on *Moonlighting*. Everything's going to work out fine and in thirteen years or so we'll get married and I'll be Mrs. Jeni Lancaster. (I'm keeping my name—it sounds more broadcasty.)

Jimmy tries to kiss me when I approach but I stop him. "Marilyn Monroe or Scarlett O'Hara?"

"Who and what?"

Okay, if he's my soul mate and we're going to be together forever, he's going to have to get a little better at interpreting what I say on the first go. "I said, *Marilyn Monroe* or *Scarlett O'Hara?*"

....

[72] Late that night, my brother locked my friend Mary and me in his room. He said nothing good happens in a fraternity house after three a.m. But from the sounds of the party in the hallway, he was all wrong.

"To do what?"

I glower at him. "To take to prom."

"I'm going to prom with you." Sigh. Sometimes I worry about him not being so smart, but then he buys me pie and I forget.

I grab my jacket from him, slam the locker, and wave the quiz at him. "Would you rather the very blond, breathy, vapid Marilyn or the ass-kicking, frankly-my-dear-you-*do*-give-a-damn Scarlett?"

Without hesitation, he replies, "Marilyn. Definitely Marilyn."

Oh no.

This may well be a breach no pie can fill.

"Let's get the peach one," I say.

"Jennifer, you haven't even tried that one on. Stop being ridiculous," clucks my mother.

Whenever I disagree with anyone in my family I'm not wrong, I'm *ridiculous*. I'm being ridiculous when I beg not to have to clean the pool until my brother's finished mowing even though he freely admits to aiming the clippings toward open water. When he plows the strip right by the diving board, he can actually bank half a bagful into the deep end; I've watched him do it.

And apparently I'm *not* a savvy young entrepreneur when I take the ten dollars I earn for washing the car and run the car through the five-dollar car wash. Honestly, the car wash is far more thorough than I could ever be with just a hose, bucket, and bottle of dish detergent. The car's spotless, I turn a five-dollar profit, and can spend the two hours I save working on my tan.[73]

----

[73] It's called outsourcing and American businesses should totally look into it.

Ridiculous?

Yeah, ridiculous like a fox.

According to my mother, I was being *ridiculous* when I argued against driving hours out of our way to pass through Knoxville on our way home from spring break in 1982. Why waste time gawking at a world's fair that wasn't set to open for months? We were all tired and I had to go back to school the next day, so voluntarily adding time to the trip seemed dumb. *I* wasn't ridiculous—the whole enterprise was. I drilled her as we loaded up our station wagon, *What are we going to do there, interview the construction workers? Are we going to have them tell us about all the exhilarating rides and fascinating attractions and delicious carnival-type treats we aren't going to experience because we're two months early? Why do we want to see a closed, half-built amusement park?*

But I was thirteen, and thus not a credible source. Plus I was already grounded for when we got home because I refused to eat the travel snacks my mother had packed. (Hey, I can't help it if the combination of onion rolls and marshmallow fluff makes me queasy.) We headed to the fair anyway, driving hours out of the way to pass by a closed, half-built amusement park full of construction trailers and men in hard hats. It was precisely as much fun as I predicted.

I am decidedly *not* being ridiculous right now. But if I engage my mother in an argument, chances are I'll end up with no prom dress at all and nothing to do on prom night but watch TV with my parents. So I counter with the most benign argument I can muster. "The shiny white fabric washes me out. I'm all pasty."

I try to make my point with a smile in my voice. I have to do my best not to be a smart-ass because my mother says only cheap girls have sassy mouths. My dad hates when I'm sarcastic and takes every opportunity to quash my burgeoning cynicism. He drove this message home particularly hard during the Great Michael Jackson Debate.

"Sissy's mom will take us up there and drive us back as soon as it's over. I'm not going to be joyriding with a bunch of teenagers—I'll be with a parent. What's the big deal?" I reasoned.

"You're not going out of town," my father said.

"Sissy is cheap," my mother added. Anyone who wears black eyeliner is cheap, in my mother's opinion.

"Come on! The concert's supposed to be legendary! This is the Victory Tour—Michael's gonna be doing songs from the Jackson Five plus performing stuff off the *Thriller* album. 'ABC' and 'Beat It'? 'Billie Jean' and 'Never Can Say Goodbye'? Performed on the same stage? I'm talking the greatest show ever by the greatest group ever."

My father waved his hand dismissively. "Elvis Presley was a great singer. Michael Jackson sounds like a little girl."

My dad saw one of Elvis's first shows in California. He still talks about how crazy the audience went and how random girls stood on his shoulders without even asking permission. Come on, *I* could be a shoulder girl at the concert! Then maybe someday an old Michael Jackson fan can tell his daughters about how *I* jumped on his back. Surely my dad understands the magic of being part of the crowd. The show will be just like Woodstock, only, you know, more explodey. "History's going to be made on this tour. Don't you want me to be a part of history?"

Dad shook his head and opened his newspaper. "No."

"I saw Sissy smoking the last time I picked you up after school. I don't like you being around smokers." Then she mouthed the word "hard." In my mom's book, being hard is even worse than being cheap.

I may or may not have stomped my foot at this point. "Every single person in your entire extended family smokes," I argued. "Should I not be around my aunts and uncles and Grampa? Are they cheap? Are they hard?"

"Jennifer, you're being ridiculous." *No, really, how is it different?*

"I have the money to pay for my ticket. I won't need anything from you. You can meet Sissy's mom—she's really nice. She's a mom, so she's automatically responsible," I pleaded.

My mother cleared her throat and raised a knowing eyebrow at my dad. "She's a *divorcee*."

That did it. I hate when my mother gets all judgmental and officious about people she's never even met based on superficial criteria. Come on, do they judge her because of her peculiar penchant for ponchos?[74] "You don't even know her!" I shouted. "How can you write her off just for getting a divorce?"

My dad calmly closed his paper. "Jennifer, you are not going to the concert. It's nonnegotiable. Say one more word and you're grounded."

Ever see those old Warner Bros. cartoons where Elmer Fudd is hunting Daffy Duck? To draw Daffy out of his bunker in the hollow tree, Elmer only needs to tap out "Shave and a haircut"

....

[74] Well, maybe. I mean, dude, the seventies are over.

because he just knows Daffy can't leave the knock unfinished. No matter the consequences, something compels Daffy to meet the challenge. And even though Daffy's well aware that if he pokes his head out and sings, "Two bits!" he's surely going to get his beak blown off?

Yet he can't resist?

Yeah, me, too.

I glared at my father. "Word!"

And then he blew my beak off. I spent the next two months on lockdown while the dulcet-toned man with one sparkly glove went on to thrill audiences without me.

No way I'm about to miss prom because of my own big mouth, though, so I continue to press my point in a nonconfrontational manner. "I feel like all the white makes me look waxen. Pallid, even. I'm practically cadaverous."

My mother smirks. "Someone's been paying attention in advanced placement."[75]

Mom and I are standing in the Juniors department at Hudson's. I'm presently wearing the full-length white Gunne Sax gown that I saw in *Seventeen* magazine. Originally, I'd torn out the ad because the dress caught my eye. However, I've since realized it was way more flattering on the model, not because she's thinner than me but because she has no b-r-e-a-s-t-s.

The dress is shiny and white with a tight bodice and a long A-line bottom. The top is divided into two pieces—there's a binding strip of fabric that hits about midchest and then there's an overlaying piece that comes up in a U shape, forming a white satin

----

[75] Yet she wonders why I'm a smart-ass.

canyon or possibly a moat. The gap is large enough that someone could store her lipstick or a compact in there.[76] For a flat-chested girl, the cut would add volume. For those of us who don't need the help, it's . . . *breastacular.*

I started to "develop" in fourth grade, and by sixth I wore a B cup. I stopped getting taller in seventh grade, but that's the only place my, um, expansion was stunted. Now I'm close to a D and have a strict *don't ask, don't tell* relationship with my chest. The deal is I wear binding bras and loose alligator shirts and they comply by making themselves scarce. One time last summer my friend Veronica came over to swim and she couldn't get over the way I filled out my bathing suit. She kept calling me "stacked" and swatted me in the chest, asking, "Where the hell did these come from?" I spent the rest of the day with a T-shirt over my suit.

The idea of a garment that not only informs the rest of the world I have b-r-e-a-s-t-s but in fact squeezes them together so much they form an ass-crack's worth of cleavage[77] makes me extraordinarily self-conscious. Plus, if we purchase this dress, I'll spend all of prom night grasping the top of the bodice, trying to lift it up past my lips because it rides at about half-mast. This won't work at all.

"I love you in white. You'll look so beautiful on your wedding day! I can't wait to walk you down the aisle!" my mother coos. Well, you're pretty much going to have to wait. Really, would Joan Lunden have gotten her gig on *Good Morning America* if she were a child bride? I think not.

....

[76] If it weren't weird to do so, I mean.

[77] And thrusts them up so high I could rest my cheek on them.

Why's she so anxious to see me married, anyway? I only recently packed away my Barbies, and that's just because Jimmy thought it was weird for me to have them. The only way I'm getting married any time soon is via gunpoint. Also? If my mother sends me off to the dance n-a-k-e-d from the waist up, I won't make it through the night intact, let alone through college. Seriously, I've extorted enough pie out of my long-suffering boyfriend. At some point, he's going to demand it in return.

I scowl at my pasty, busty reflection. And that's when I notice what might be my salvation. Two thick, floor-length black satin strips of fabric are sewn right underneath my ass rack. I bet I could take them and tie them around my neck like a halter, providing lots more coverage and support. I grab the strips and begin to pull them up and around until my mom stops me. "Jennifer, you're being ridiculous. Let go." I release the fabric and watch as my mother fashions the ribbons into an enormous saggy bow that detracts from my chest almost as much as a big neon sign blinking *Tits! Tits! Tits!* might. Perfect.

My heart in my throat,[78] I retreat to the dressing room. I tear off the gross white one and don the peach-colored dress whose ad I also admired.

Now *this* is a dress! The top only shows my collarbones and smashes everything else down nicely. And check out how wide the skirt is! I bet this wouldn't even fit into a car! Shoot, I barely fit in this dressing room! Remember how in *A Christmas Carol* one of the ghosts-of-Christmas-whatever had those mini-wraiths hiding in her petticoats? I could totally stuff them under here! (Not that

....

[78] And my boobs in my ears.

I'm planning to smuggle any child-ghosts into prom under my skirt, but it's nice to have the option, you know?) I love this! I'm like a fabulous Barbie birthday cake or a really pretty embroidered toilet-paper topper. Better yet, with all the ruffles and the giant hoop, I'm a complete ringer for Scarlett O'Hara! Fiddle-dee-dee!

I strut over to my mother, proudly displaying the skirt's twelve-foot diameter. I spin and accidentally take out an entire purse display.

While we place all the handbags back on the stand, I say, "What do you think? So much better, right? I can even wear a bra under this one."

She takes a step back and assesses me with a critical eye. She touches the lace draping from the portrait collar and fluffs out the ruffles. "I agree, it's nice, but you can't wear this for the pageant. Take it off before you get it dirty." With that, my mother helps me with the zipper and sends me back to the fitting room.

Shit. With all the end-of-high-school stuff happening, I keep forgetting about the stupid beauty pageant. Oh, wait, excuse me, I mean *scholarship* pageant. (In which we will be judged based on our beauty.) I begin to ruminate as I wedge my way out of all the lacy layers. My mom saw the pageant notice in the paper a couple of months ago and convinced me to sign up. I can't believe I let her talk me into it. Sure, I like the *idea* of being in a beauty pageant, but I imagine the reality will suck. I've already gotten my preliminary schedule and there's stuff on it like dance classes and etiquette lessons. I hate dancing and I'm totally already polite. I chew with my mouth closed and usually remember to say thank you—what's left to learn?

The pageant information pack also contained information on

wardrobe requirements. The director was pretty specific about not picking anything promlike for the evening wear competition.

Damn.

Wait—brainstorm! Sure, I'll have to go all Marilyn for the pageant, but I can still be Scarlett for the dance. I'll simply get *both* dresses! This is a genius solution—why didn't I come up with it sooner?

I meet my mother at the counter with the gowns under my arms. "We'll get this one for the pageant and this one for the prom."

My mother snorts. "Wrong."

"What do you mean?"

"You're not getting two dresses."

"I need them both." If I have to wear the white one to prom, Jimmy will have to bring three corsages—one for me and two for my friends.

"Jennifer, you're being ridiculous. You're getting one dress."

"Okay, I want this." I place the Southern belle dress and its eight thousand yards of intricate peach lace and taffeta on the counter.

"You can't wear this in the pageant. You have to get the white one. That's final." My mom hands her credit card and the white dress to the cashier.

The problem isn't that my mother's being unreasonable. It's that these are the only two dresses we've found in all our shopping expeditions that fit me. Today is our very last chance for me to find something that isn't an Izod to wear. Nothing is cut for my figure—I've spent weeks trying to squeeze my top half into size thirteen/fourteen dresses, while the rest of me completely drowns in fabric. I suppose I *could* have something tailored, but I'm opposed to wearing a size thirteen/fourteen dress on principle.

"How about this? How about I just quit the pageant?"

"You really want to quit before you even try? Doesn't sound like you."

Again, she's right. I don't want to quit, because I'm confident I can win. Most of the score is based on an interview, which, again, hello, I've been preparing for my whole life. Plus talent weighs heavily—I'm planning to do a dramatic interpretation. I might not be the best actress in the school, but I guarantee I'll be the best in the pageant. Plus, how great will I look in a crown?

Grudgingly, I give in. "Okay, okay, you win. I do the pageant and I wear the white dress."

As the cashier completes the transaction and wraps the gown in plastic, my mother tries to make me feel better. "You know the white dress will serve so many purposes. Not only will you wear it to the pageant and dance, but you'll have it for college formals. Really, this is almost like a bridesmaid's dress—cut it off and you can wear it again and again." I ignore this last bit of advice because it comes from a woman who incorporated enormous magenta fur muffs into her wedding party garb. Bet she told her bridesmaids they could reuse their muffs, too.

We leave Hudson's and we're strolling by the ice rink when my mom slaps herself on the head. "I almost forgot! We have to get you a bathing suit while we're up here."

"For what? Both my suits from last year are still good."

"No, for the swimsuit competition."

And that's when I realize I'm a month away from standing in front of an entire auditorium with nothing between me, my naked chest, and the audience but a millimeter of Lycra.

Suddenly the white dress seems delightfully conservative.

❖

This is the prom?

This is what all those cheesy songs and overwrought John Hughes movies were about?

This is what I've been building up to during my last twelve years of public education?

This?

Most magical night of my life, my ass.

Listen, I can accept that we're not having our prom in a big hotel ballroom like every other school in the universe. The closest nice place is in Fort Wayne and we already have the drinking-est, driving-est senior class in years,[79] so obviously making everyone travel thirty Night Train–fueled miles each way is a bad idea. And it's not like we could hold the prom in the small conference room of the LK Motel, where my dad attends his Rotary Club meetings on the first Thursday of every month. I understand the only logical place to host a dance for five hundred seniors and their dates is our gym—but does it have to look like a ballgame could break out any second now? For Christ's sake, I can see the nets! The scoreboard is visible! People are dancing on the goddamned three-point line!

The junior class is responsible for throwing the prom. Last year my class spent nine months turning the basketball court into One Fucking Enchanted Evening Under the Sea. We had people walking around in scuba suits and mermaid costumes and we created a sandy beach area where kids could kick their shoes off and dance barefoot. Anything vaguely sports-related was draped

....

[79] We've had more DUIs than acceptances to Notre Dame.

in fishing nets and strewn with seashells. We made giant Neptune-y pieces out of papier-mâché. We did *not* get together a week beforehand to blow up balloons, string some streamers, and hang a half-assed banner painted with some child's interpretation of how the French Quarter would look if it were one-dimensional and located next to the concession stand in a gymnasium.

Instead of decorating the entire gym, our lame juniors only created enough artwork to fill a small portion of it. They built a stage for the band, but there's nothing behind it but two-thirds of open court. Also? I'm curious—is the French Quarter supposed to smell like sweat socks? You'd have thought they'd at least put out some candles or potpourri.

There's not enough room for everyone to dance—prom's sole purpose—so most of us are stuck in the bleachers or at the rented wrought-iron tables. Actually, I'm okay with this. Jimmy and I got up for the first Journey song and I quickly realized I should not lift my arms past my shoulders if I don't want to flash the entire senior class. (At least I didn't find this out while doing the victory walk-'n'-wave at the pageant.)

For the first time I'm glad I'm not in the lacy peach gown because a bunch of other girls keep getting their dresses tangled up in the chairs' grillwork. I spend much of my night watching classmates trying to mend rips while crying off all their mascara. Their dates awkwardly attempt to comfort them—fail—and the chaperones are frantically breaking into the Home Ec room to procure thread, needles, and safety pins. And the junior class members are doing their best to hide from the seniors, who are shrieking, *"This is all your fault!"* Honestly? *Carrie* had a better time at prom.

When it finally comes to its merciful end, we only have half an hour to change and make it back to the gym before after-prom begins. I live about ten miles from school, so we go to Jimmy's house in town. I've been planning my post-prom outfit for weeks. I settle on some turquoise capri pants and a baby pink cotton sweater cut in the shape of a polo shirt. I've got a big asymmetrical white leather belt that hangs low on my hips and loads of white bangles to stack up my arms. I have three pairs of white shoes to choose from and an enormous palette of every color eye shadow Maybelline manufactures.

Yet as I unpack my bag I realize I brought everything except for the most important piece—a bra. I spend fifteen minutes just working up the courage to ask Jimmy's mom for one. Which isn't embarrassing. At all. We get back to the gym moments before the door closes and they lock us in for the next four hours.

The lock-in is supposed to keep us from drinking and d-o-i-n-g it tonight and it's an effective strategy . . . for those of us who make it back in time. Those who get locked out end up going to the woods by the reservoir for a big party.[80] Jimmy's been begging me to ditch after-prom, but I'm not about to make out with anyone while wearing his mother's bra—there's simply not enough pie. Besides, the junior class is holding a raffle and what if they give away a ten-speed bike and I'm not there to claim it? Not that I want a dumb old bike—I just don't want anyone else to have it if it's supposed to be mine.

The post-prom event ends at five a.m. and I go right home (sadly, bike-free) and crawl into bed. My mother wakes me up at

---

[80] I blame all of tonight's accidental teen pregnancies on the juniors, too.

seven a.m. to hear all about the night then blows a gasket when I ask her to please get out and let me sleep for a while. My sarcastic (exhausted) mouth gets me grounded for the next two weeks.

An hour later, my dad makes me get up to wash the car. Since I'm grounded, I can't even take it to the car wash.

Ridiculous.

Judge Not, Lest Ye Be Singing a Billy Ocean Song

(White Satin Gown)

"Say cheese!"

I don't want to say cheese. I want to *eat* cheese. Unfortunately, that's been off the menu in the weeks I've been getting ready for this stupid pageant.

I lean back against the tree and give a three-quarter smile. Three-quarters is the perfect amount for a photograph. Grin too big and you're nothing but teeth, gums, and unattractive forehead wrinkles. Too small and you look like a sourpuss.

It's superbright out here and I squint until a second before the photo's snapped—that way my eyes are wide open in the shot and I don't get blinded while I wait.

I applied Clinique bronzing gel to create contours on my face. I used navy liner to make my eyes brighter and cool-toned dark lipstick to make my teeth appear whiter. In person I'm a tad drag queeny, but I should look great on film.

"All right, one more time and . . . you're done." The photographer waves me off and then begins to monkey with his camera.

"Are you sure? Don't you want to take some more?" I ask. I'm here in the park with the rest of the Miss Cow Town contestants. Our pageant is part of the city's Ancestry Days festival and our photographs will be included in the newspaper's special circular that comes out a week beforehand. I'm slightly aggravated because all the other contestants have posed for dozens of pictures but the photographer only takes, like, three of me.

"No, I'm good," he replies. He calls contestant Lee over and I return to sit at the picnic table with Christy.

"That was quick," she observes.

"Wasn't it?" I ask.

"Did you make him mad or something? Why didn't he have you pose by the water and on the ledge like everyone else?" She uses a vent brush to puff up her hair, then smoothes on some cream blush.

"That's an excellent question."

I wonder if it has something to do with my mother's feud with the local paper? A while ago, the paper ran an article about a woman in town who'd found a letter Abraham Lincoln had written in a box of her grandmother's things. The paper was so excited to have a local item of historical significance, they devoted half the front page[81] to the discovery. The second my mom read the article, she knew the letter sounded familiar . . . mostly because we'd al-

---

[81] Above the fold!

ready seen the same exact letter on a Girl Scout outing to the National Archives in Washington, D.C. She called the paper and informed them of their error, and they were duly mortified.

The paper printed a tiny retraction days later, but there's been bad blood between my mother and the editor ever since. I suspect this has less to do with her discovery and more to do with her suggestion that they write an article on *her* since she's in possession of a gift shop copy of the Declaration of Independence.[82]

Christy asks, "Who's up after Lee?"

"Heather Mueller."

"Then I may as well get comfortable."

We both roll our eyes. Heather's got a boyfriend now so she's a little nicer to people than she used to be. Regardless, we're still not fans. Buffy, our pageant director, has taken a shine to her because she's a great singer. (Or maybe she's just impressed that Heather was born in Paris?)

Buffy's been transparent in her belief that Heather has the most potential in the Miss Indiana pageant[83] so she's been personally coaching her on everything. She even gave her a different dress for the evening wear competition. Now, instead of having a fullish satin gown like the rest of us, Heather's set to compete in a skintight, straight silk sheath covered in a million rhinestones. With one extra-sparkly dress, Heather's been transformed into s-e-x on a stick. And the rest of us resemble a pack of debutantes. Gee, I wonder what the judges will prefer?

....

[82] Also, every time I get a high mark on a composition, she sends it to them. I imagine they're a bit tired of reading my English homework, too.

[83] Despite her penchant for frosty white eyeliner.

Buffy's pretty neutral about me and Christy. We aren't her favorites, but she's also not openly hostile toward us. She *despises* Lee and Dee, Lee because she lives in sin with her boyfriend, and Dee for having uneven eyes and a twisted spine that gives her kind of a lurching walk. Sin and spine notwithstanding, both these girls dance way better than Christy or me, yet they're stuck in the very back for our production number. Plus, Buffy wouldn't approve either of their bathing suits and made Dee cry by criticizing her singing in the talent rehearsal. (Yet she brought in a vocal coach to work with the already-perfect Heather. No favoritism here!) Also, Lee and Dee got stuck with the worst sponsors—the lube shop and the oil refinery. I'm totally appalled by the preferential treatment. I'd expect this kind of behavior in a bigger city, but we're in a tiny little burg and we're competing for $500 scholarships. Seriously, who's got that much stake in a meaningless local pageant?

Just as Lee finishes her session with the photographer, Buffy swoops in out of nowhere and personally directs Heather's shoot for the next half an hour.

Aarrgh.

My picture runs in the paper on Sunday and by Wednesday's pageant rehearsal, I've already determined that I'm going to win Miss Photogenic.

How do I know?

Because I'm the only contestant who receives letters from prisoners in the local jail.

Three cheers for me! Three cheers for my drag queen makeup!

And three cheers for the paper's decision to print our home addresses![84]

❖

The pageant is tonight so today's chock-full of activities. Our first order of business is the Cow Town Ancestry Days parade.[85] I'd assumed we'd all ride on a float, and I'm sorely disappointed when I find out that's not the case. Instead of building a flashy, exciting float and having us appear all together in pageanty solidarity, Buffy recruits the local Corvette club to drive us separately.[86] And really, what's more festive than watching a person ride by really slowly in a car?

We're supposed to perch on the trunk with our legs hanging in the backseat. This wouldn't be scary if (a) our parade route weren't hilly and (b) I weren't in a very short skirt. Complicating matters, I have to ride with my nemesis Justine Moore, whose dad is president of the Corvette club. She drives the entire parade route in fits and stops and by the time it's over, I deserve a goddamned crown just for hanging on. And a trophy for not showing my underpants.

I'm windblown and crabby when we get to the high school for the interview portion of the pageant, but it's fine because I'm totally going to ace this part. Put Heather in all the shimmery dresses you want, Buffy, but you can't keep the judges from seeing my shapely brain!

....

[84] P.S. No, I don't care to be your pen pal.

[85] Not sure what "ancestry" we're celebrating—our town's unofficial fondness for racism? Having the highest rate of cardiovascular disease in the state?

[86] Try and guess who's in the lead car. Hint: not me.

I enter the room, trying to recall all the poise lessons we learned in practice. The only bit I remember is not to sit all the way back in the chair, which . . . why? Why is that impolite? I'm concentrating so hard on not touching the back of the chair that when I go to sit I almost miss landing on the front. Nice. Bonus points for me.

One of the judges, the local undertaker, says, "Jennifer, your bio says that you want to be a journalist."

Am I supposed to be doing something with my hands? I've been told not to gesture, which is like asking me not to speak at all. Should they hang by my sides? That looks weird, like I'm waiting for the guards to strap them down so I can be electrocuted. They must go in my lap—should they be folded? Not folded? And what does hand folding entail anyway? Fingers linked? Unlinked? Stacked on top of each other like a set of flapjacks? Ooh, flapjacks—buttery, fluffy, maple syrup covered . . .

The judge interrupts my inner monologue. "Jeni?"

"Huh?" I snap to attention, deciding on the palms-down flapjack stack. "Yes, hi. I'm Jeni." I give them a three-quarter smile. Stunning!

The undertaker cuts a sideways glance at the Realtor to his left. "Yes, you introduced yourself already. I asked you a question."

"Oh, sorry, I was looking at my hands. It's very hard for me to talk without them but Buffy says it's rude, but . . . whatever. What'd you want to know?" I flash another grin. My lip easily slides past my teeth because I put Vaseline on them. Actually, I put too much Vaseline on them and it looked like I'd eaten a piece of wax fruit so I had to floss the excess out with a folded note card.

"I asked what your thoughts were about the journalists who were kidnapped in Beirut. If you were in that situation, what would you do?"

"Oh, that's easy! I wouldn't get into that situation. I don't want to be *that kind* of journalist. I want to be a television journalist who sits on a couch and has coffee with famous people. I imagine the set of *Good Morning America* is supersafe. Unless it's, like, the day the people from the zoo come? And there are tigers on the set? Although I bet there's a guy there with a tranq gun because there's no way Joan Lunden is going to let some big cat slash up her face and mess with her moneymaker. Or wait, has that ever happened on *Good Morning America*? Or am I thinking of Johnny Carson? He's always got snakes from the San Diego Zoo trying to climb into his pants, doesn't he? But they probably aren't poisonous so I'm sure it's fine." Buffy coached us to be honest and bubbly. I'm so effervescent right now I may well float off my chair.

"I . . . um, wow. Moving on, can you tell us about your platform?"

"Come again?"

"Your platform." I smile and blink. Oh, no! Buffy specifically told us we didn't need to pick a platform until the Miss Indiana pageant. "Your cause." I mentally scramble to come up with something. The judges interpret my silence as misunderstanding. "The issue you feel strongly about. For example, Heather's platform was touching children with music." Okay, number one, eww . . . touching kids with anything sounds totally pervy, and number two, why does she have a fucking platform and no one else does?

Funny seems to be my only option here. "Heh"—I giggle

nervously— "I'd say my platform is not getting kidnapped by the *Beirutians*! Heh!"

"I assume by *Beirutian* you mean the Lebanese?"

So . . . yeah. I might not have the verbal ability upon which I'd been banking. Possibly I should brush up on my interview skills before my first day at *Good Morning America*? Or, like, consult a map? Oh, well, I'll do better in the swimsuit portion.

After all, I'm the only girl who doesn't have to pad her suit.

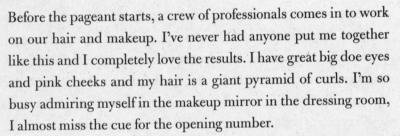

Before the pageant starts, a crew of professionals comes in to work on our hair and makeup. I've never had anyone put me together like this and I completely love the results. I have great big doe eyes and pink cheeks and my hair is a giant pyramid of curls. I'm so busy admiring myself in the makeup mirror in the dressing room, I almost miss the cue for the opening number.

Our first competition is swimsuit and we go onstage one by one. While we mug for the judges, the emcee reads our bios. "Jeni Lancaster is seventeen years old and plans to attend Purdue University in the fall, where she'll major in communications. She weighs in at one hundred and twenty-five pounds[87] and is five feet nine inches tall.[88] She enjoys swimming and doing aerobics."[89]

I come out from behind the curtain and strut around the stage. This goes well until I look into the audience and see all those people checking me out in my swimsuit. I linger in front of

---

[87] Lie. I'm more like 135–140.

[88] Lie. I'm more like five feet seven.

[89] Lie. She enjoys reading a book by the pool and eating candy.

the judges for a fraction of a second instead of the requisite ten, and then practically run back to the safety of the dressing room.

Perhaps my strength lies in the talent portion?

We get disqualified if we go over three minutes in the talent portion. I'm doing a dramatic reading and I'm worried because whenever I've timed myself, I'm right on the three-minute mark. Before I go onstage again, I decide to speak a little faster for safety's sake. I mean, I can't win if I'm disqualified. And I'm banking on doing well here to make up for the interview and swimsuit rounds.

I get onstage and act my heart out. And I do a fabulous job.

In less than two minutes.

I wonder if I sped things up a little too much?

Regardless, the evening gown competition awaits!

Unless the judges are looking for a contestant who steps on the hem of her dress, inadvertently yanks the bodice up to her chin, all while sweating and dropping f-bombs under her breath, I'm probably not going to be Miss Cow Town.

That's right, I'm Miss Photogenic, *bitches!*

Naturally Heather wins the pageant. She's so faux sincere and mock surprised when accepting her crown that I want to punch her spangles off. Instead, I stand there and graciously congratulate her.

Even though I don't win or get runner-up, I'm pleased. After all, Miss Photogenic's picture goes on the front page of the newspaper. None of the runners-up even get featured at all. Landing on the front page is like one step closer to being on television.

Lee, Dee, and Christy are all crying backstage because they didn't win anything and they gave up eating sugar and butter for nothing. I feel terrible for them. They each tried really hard and it's so unfair their efforts went unrecognized because some bitchy Realtor wanted to relive her high school days by ingratiating herself with the only cheerleader in the competition.

By the way, you know how when you watch Miss America and you see the losers crowding around the winner, covering her with smeary-lipstick kisses? And it totally looks unintentional?

Trust me; it's not.

I lend the girls my bloodred lipstick and instruct them on offering Heather "gracious congratulations" before she poses for her winner pictures.

With each graciously congratulatory kiss, they feel better. And when they're done, we make a date to go out for donuts.

Later, Mom tells me that in the middle of Heather's talent portion, my father sighed loudly and announced, "This is the last amateur performance you drag me to."

That more than makes up for missing Michael Jackson.

They're Quite Aware of What They're Going Through

(Bass Weejun Penny Loafers)

I've been dreading all summer saying good-bye to Jimmy. My brother, my best friend Carol, and Jimmy have driven me here to campus. I insisted my parents not take me, and my mother insisted I was being ridiculous. Thankfully, my dad saw this as an opportunity to play golf and not carry heavy things, so he was fine with my decision. He was kind enough to stand in the driveway the whole time I was loading up the station wagon, telling me I was packing wrong.

We're at my dorm and it turns out I don't have a room assignment yet. Since I turned my acceptance letter in late, I have to wait a day or so to find out which room is mine. In the interim, I have to move all my things into my dorm's guest apartment. There's a bedroom, a huge living room, a kitchen, a dining area, and a full bath. *Sweet.* I kind of hope I never get an assignment.

I say good-bye to Carol and Todd and they leave me alone with Jimmy. I cry a million tears and cling to him as he walks out the door of my (sweet) temporary housing. "Good-bye, Jimmy! I love you!" I call after him.

I sit on the bed in my (sweet) room and feel sorry for myself. I miss Jimmy.

I miss my pool.

I miss my dog.

I miss my parents.

I even miss my brother. He was supposed to be here this semester but he and a couple of his fraternity brothers decided they'd have a better time road-tripping to the Kentucky Derby than studying for finals. He flunked out and won't be back on campus until spring. I'm totally on my own.

This was a mistake. I shouldn't have gone away to school. I should have stayed home and gone to the Purdue extension in Fort Wayne. Or I should have gone to IU because I wouldn't be starting until next week and Carol would be there to help me past all the scary parts.

I should call my parents.

I should have them come get me.

My mom totally would. It's not too late to change my mind. Classes haven't started yet. I should get my calling card out of my purse and find a phone.

Ooh, hey, there's one in here! Sweet!

As I pick up the receiver, it occurs to me that I should . . . I should maybe get a fucking grip.

I should not be so quick to throw in the towel.

I should not quit before I even begin.

I should . . . I should put on my favorite madras plaid shorts, a white oxford, and my perfectly broken-in Bass Weejun penny loafers and maybe say hello to the boys I know at my brother's fraternity house.

When I get back from hanging out with a dozen cute Delta Sigs— possibly my best idea ever, thanks—I check in at the dorm's front desk. My permanent room has been assigned! I gather up my stuff, swipe a couple of the brownies someone was storing in the fridge, say good-bye to my private bathroom, and make my way up to the fourth floor.

I'm told to find the resident advisor and she's located directly across from the water fountain. I knock on her door and introduce myself. She's modeling a new pleated skirt and I show her how you have to undo the basting at the bottom in order to make it extra-twirly. Manufacturers only leave them sewn up so the pleats don't get messed up while on the rack. My RA was unaware and almost went to the resident advisors' dinner looking like a dumbass. I suspect I just bought myself one look-the-other-way pass.

While we chat, a very cheerful, very bouncy blond girl comes flying out of the room next door.

"Are you Jen?"

Technically, I'm Jeni, but as soon as she says this, I realize the *i* is superfluous. "Um, yeah," I say. "I'm Jen." Jen. *Jen*. Hey, I like how that sounds.

"I'm so excited to meet you! I'm Joanna! Welcome, roomie!"

She quickly throws her arms around me and then starts grabbing my suitcases while the RA helps me maneuver the rolling rack containing my wicker headboard and flip-and-fold chair. Once we get everything into the room, Joanna exclaims, "I wrote to you this summer!"

"You're kidding—I never got your letter. What did you say?"

"I wanted to know if we should get matching comforters and stuff. I figured we could get together and shop since I live in one of your suburbs."

Cow Town has suburbs? How can that be? Cow Town has more livestock than people.

"Are you sure you wrote to *me*?" I ask.

"Aren't you Jennifer Malloy?"

"No, I'm Jeni Lancaster. I mean, *Jen* Lancaster. I didn't have housing until this afternoon, so Jennifer Malloy must have backed out or something."

"Oh, well, her loss!" Joanna bounces over to her pink and blue tulip-sprigged bed and launches herself onto it. She folds up into lotus position and insists, "Tell me everything about yourself!"

We talk while I unpack and sort all my stuff. When I pull out my loafers, she squeals and rushes to her closet—she has the exact same pair! I notice she's wearing white Keds with slouchy white socks. No one wore them in Cow Town so I never gave that look a thought, but now that I see how cute they are with shorts and polos, I reconsider.[90]

---

[90] This is a trend I embrace for almost the next twenty years.

I brought basically everything I own because I didn't know what I'd need and also I am *Always Prepared*. Putting my junk away takes a couple of hours, particularly since we stop and discuss each item. We compare our musical tastes—she has more new wave music than I do, but not because I don't like it; I've just not had the chance to hear much of it. The Fort Wayne stations play nothing but Van Halen, AC/DC, and Journey.[91] My only exposure to other kinds of music is via *Friday Night Videos* or glimpses of MTV caught when we travel out of town.

Although we weren't in contact when we were packing, you'd never suspect it. She didn't bring anything to put on the walls and I brought lots of cool posters of Paris and Germany. (We listen to them falling off the walls every night for a week until I finally agree to take them out of the packaging and simply stick them straight to the cinder block.)

I brought a black-and-white TV and she brought a jam box. (I'd planned to listen to my music on my Walkman.) I brought a hot pot and canned soups, she brought bowls and spoons. Our synchronicity surprises us both and I realize we have all the makings of a lovely friendship.

As I unzip my third suitcase, I pull out my white satin gown.

"Ooh, is that your prom dress?" Joanna asks.

"Uh-huh. I'm planning to get it cut off so I can wear it to dances."

"My gosh, that's such a good idea! Let me show you mine."

----

[91] This is a trend they embrace for almost the next twenty years.

She bounds off her bed and leaps to grab a framed photo on her desk. "Here." She thrusts it at me.

I look at the photo—she's in a darling pink silk drop-waist dress, posing with a goofy kid who looks like Gilligan. "Hey, how come you're wearing a crown?"

She gets sheepish for a second. "Oh . . . that's because I was prom queen."

Of course she was prom queen.

Of course she was.

I don't ask if she was a cheerleader. I sort of don't want to know. I quickly change subjects. "Do you want to go to a fraternity party tonight?" I might not be queen of anything and I never actually earned a crown, but I do know some boys and I can bring parties to the table.

"No, thanks. I can't. I've got to get ready for bed." She grabs her shower caddy and heads to the bathroom.

I sit back on my freshly made bed, smoothing out the wrinkles from the packaging. So I'm living with the prom queen *and* she won't go to parties? Fabulous. All those positive feelings I've started to develop for this charming girl fly right out the yet-to-be-curtained window.

Just then, she pokes her head back in the room. "But I can go tomorrow!"

Hmm. There may be hope for her yet.

I have my first opportunity to re-wear my white satin gown to a fraternity pledge dance fall semester. The campus dry cleaner hems it for fifteen dollars. My date is in my brother's fraternity. He's a junior and he's really popular and he's from a big city, so at first glance I'd worry he's a bit out of my league. But we're in the same French class and we both have a penchant for loafers. As class progresses, I help tutor him and we become friends. When I mention how much fun the dance sounds, he surprises me by asking me to be his date. And, seriously? He owns his own tux. *How cool is that?*

We're supposed to ride down to Indianapolis on the bus with all the other members, but my date gets tied up during a philan-thropic activity[92] and returns to campus late. We end up driving down ourselves. We're not planning to stay over, but if my date drinks too much, then the plan is to crash on the floor in my fra-ternity big bro Andy's room.

I use Andy's bathroom to change out of my khakis and loaf-ers and into my dress. I've gained a few pounds since I wore this last due to drinks and fatty cafeteria food and not having my mother stand over me like the Butter Nazi. All the weight's gone straight to my chest and . . . it works. When I step out into the main room, all my platonic French class date says is, "Ooh la la!"

We totally kiss at the dance.[93]

....

[92] Mandatory due to a city noise violation.

[93] As for Jimmy . . . three days after he dropped me off at campus, I called him and said, "Um, yeah, I'm a little sister at a fraternity now and we won't be dating anymore." What could I say? Seventeen's synonymous with fickle. Jimmy was furious and gave me the choice of dating him or dating other people. I chose other people and we never talked after that. I heard through the grapevine that he started dating a very pretty, complacent blond girl who was still in high school. They started d-o-i-n-g it days af-

Later, I have to use his chest as a pillow when we go to sleep on the floor. All I can think as I start to drift off is that my mom was right about the dress. Ridiculous.

ter they went out for the first time and she totally let him boss her around. As a result, she wasn't able to stop him when he started experimenting with drugs. She didn't fight back when he slapped her around. She did nothing when he began to break into people's houses, stealing their electronics so he could fund his habit. And she was shocked when he was finally sent to prison for robbing a home with a sawed-off shotgun. Oh, Jimmy. That's why you never choose a Marilyn.

Dying to Belong

(Gucci Bag)

One hundred sorority girls stand before me. They are blond and lovely and thin, and oddly, they all have the same nose. They spill out the front door of the mansion, shoulder to shoulder beside the whitewashed columns of the gracious old portico. They line the walkway almost to the street. And they are singing. Badly.

Exhaustion plays across their chiseled features, but their beauty isn't lessened by the lack of sleep. Rather, the delicate purple shadows that have resulted from spending the last fourteen hours affixing ten thousand tinfoil stars to the ceiling only serve to make blue eyes seem more azure. Pale skin looks porcelain, not pasty. Not having a moment to take sustenance results in bodies even more willowy than usual, a slimmer take on perfection.

Still, the girls seem tired. And cold. And let's face it, a bit pissed off at having to be tired and cold, standing in the inclement weather without benefit of coats, belting out a reworked Doobie Brothers song for the sixth time this weekend. They shake the mist out of their multihued blond manes and huddle closer together for warmth. Even under bulky sweater dresses and thick woolen kilts, there's nary a hip or bulge to be seen. *Oh, ladies*, I muse. *If only you had a little body fat.*

From where I'm standing, I see mouths curled into the kind of forced smiles that never reach the eyes. Voices reflect the strain of the weekend. Their collective utter boredom with the whole enterprise is patently obvious. To anyone who didn't know better, this would appear to be a miserable group, sharing a singularly wretched experience. A stranger would never guess she was witnessing the very apex of campus life.

And I'm here out front, being battered by sideways rain. Yesterday it was almost eighty degrees, but today it's in the low fifties with a whipping wind that feels like it's blowing right through me. Few places can boast the almost schizophrenic weather changes Indiana enjoys. My feet are soaked and I guarantee tomorrow I'll be red-nosed and watery-eyed, honking into a handkerchief during the parties. Fantastic.

My umbrella jostles into a hundred and fifty others. My group has been parading up and down Waldron Street all day, engaging in this ritual every hour on the hour. Now we've been herded together on the sidewalk in front of yet another mansion. We stand silently, listening, watching, and hoping desperately to belong.

The air inside the house is a good thirty degrees warmer thanks to a smoky fireplace that roars and crackles and fills the room with mood lighting. I'm standing in what's supposed to be *the best* sorority house on campus. I figured the inside of *the best* would be, I don't know, fancier? Better appointed? There's a haze of creosote in the air—maybe it could be better ventilated? And should there really be this many doilies in a dwelling occupied by women in their late teens and early twenties? I'm surprised at the chipped crown molding and the stained carpeting.[94] Again, a casual observer would assume this is where women live at the end of their lives, not the beginning. Or a place where teens would wait out the rest of their unplanned pregnancies, idly playing Boggle and Jenga while watching Sally Jessy Raphael on a snowy black-and-white television until birth sets them free from their lacy mauve prison. *The best?* Is yet to come, apparently.

Everyone in our rush group has been swapping rumors of the luxury that is living in one of these stately houses. There's been talk of all the gardeners and houseboys and chefs and maids sororities employ . . . but apparently interior designers are out of the question. Earlier today I went to an event up in the hills of campus. The outside of the building was gorgeous—full of interesting angles and big panes of glass, built right into the hillside. When we stepped in, I saw nothing but wicker and shag carpeting and shiny silver geometric-patterned wallpaper. All that was missing were framed paintings of butterflies and Mr. Roper jumping to the wrong conclusion as he listened in at the door. I turned to one girl in my rush group and asked, "How far are we from the

---

[94] Also, silk flowers? No.

Regal Beagle?" She shushed me, replying, "What's on the inside doesn't matter."

Interesting.

While I take in the fussy décor, one of the supermodels/members today serving as a party hostess greets me insincerely. She's got straight, waist-length white-blond hair. It's so silky I want to run my fingers through it in a nongay sort of way. Instead, I surreptitiously touch my own dark curls. Due to the humidity, it's now two inches shorter and six inches wider than it was when I left the dorm this morning. I briefly consider gathering it up into a ponytail until I realize it would look like an enormous pompom stuck to the back of my head.

The hostess demands I give her the jacket I have bunched up under my arm. I reluctantly hand it over. I'm not cold anymore—it's just that I learned far too late today that one does not wear a jean jacket to sorority rush.[95] How was I supposed to know? Our rush brochure said this was a casual round of parties. *Cas-u-al.* And denim is casual, right? Just ask Levi-Strauss. *Formal* rush doesn't start until January. What we're doing right now is supposed to be informal. I should get extra credit for following the rules to the letter.

Unfortunately for me, there's nothing informal about how the other rushees present themselves. They're all in cashmere and pencil skirts, silk blouses and high heels, which, I would like to point out again, *are not casual*. In theory, my pin-striped capri pants, knockoff Forenza sweater, and white oxford should be perfect. They aren't. And I was already slightly uncomfort-

---

[95] And what's wrong with my jean jacket? It was a huge hit when I went to Europe.

able because I dropped my tube of concealer when I was getting ready and I've got a big flesh-tone splotch that I'm hiding under my faux pearls. Then I noticed my pant cuff had come unsewn so I fixed it with a quick staple. I thought I was employing a brilliant fix at the time, but now I'm second-guessing myself. I doubt anyone else here got dressed with the aid of office supplies.

Seeing all these girls in their rush finery, I feel exactly like I did in fourth grade when everyone but me remembered to wear green on St. Patrick's Day. Even Joshua Greenblatt, renowned nose picker and former paste eater, skated through on a technicality by virtue of the alligator embroidered on his shirt. I'm worried that any minute now my very Irish principal is going to come in and tap me with a shillelagh.[96]

A different but also stunning blonde grabs the coats from the hostess and hangs them on a big metal rack in the front hallway before retreating into the kitchen. The scuttlebutt is that the ugly ones are stuck doing grunt work behind closed doors during rush. If the girl I just saw is what this house considers ugly, I may be completely out of my depth.

While I wait to be escorted further, I scan the coatrack. Yeah, I'm definitely the only one here with a jean jacket. I look at the labels inside the other coats, which are all tailored wools and muted tweeds. I see Evan-Picone, Anne Klein, and Ann Taylor—did some girls' moms get really fancy with the laundry pen when they put their daughters' names in these coats or are those actual designers? I mean, certainly I'm a fan of Guess and

---

[96] I didn't know how to spell this, so I Googled "Irish stick for hitting."

Gloria Vanderbilt but I've never heard of *these* people. Are they important? Do they matter? Does it matter that I don't know if they matter?

I've always been a huge fan of certain pieces of clothing, not because of who made them or how expensive they were but because these pieces made me feel pretty. My Girl Scout sash is among my all-time favorite items, yet it couldn't have cost more than five dollars. I'm wondering, has the equation changed? Is feeling pretty in what I'm wearing no longer enough? Does it have to have an expensive label attached to count?

We gather in the formal living room, watching overly enunciated, wooden skits about the benefits of sisterhood. Um, ladies, you do not have to sell *me* on joining. I'm in—just say the word. On this campus, Greek life is everything.

Everyone says I have to be in a sorority to have fun at this school. Sure, I'm a little sister at a fraternity and that's been a blast, but apparently until I put on my *own* letters, I don't know from fun. According to people in my dorm, it's imperative to get a bid from *the right* house. I'm told if I get into a place without the appropriate status, I may as well not even bother. But what makes a chapter *the right* house? Or *the best* house? What gives them their status? Obviously it's not the furnishings.

One of my friends joined *the wrong* house at IU; its reputation on campus is as a home to a big bunch of dogs/losers. How can that be? One of the sisters was a homecoming princess. Another was the Little 500 queen. A third became the president of Panhel, the society that governs all the sororities. How are any of these girls considered losers? Especially when I've met some of them and they could not have been more friendly or outgoing?

Still, I've seen plenty of my fraternity friends reverse their judgment of a girl based on her sorority affiliation. Sometimes the only difference between an average and an attractive girl (or vice versa) is two or three little Greek letters sewn on the back of a pair of sweatpants.

All I know is I want letters of my own.[97] I want common symbols like kites and keys and arrows to have a special meaning for me. I want secret handshakes and candlelit rituals. I want enforced study time where I have to sit with everyone at a big wooden table and tackle statistics homework. I want to wear my shortened prom dress to a dance at a midlevel hotel somewhere glamorous, like Indianapolis. I want to sip Diet Coke on a gracious old portico late at night. I want to be the pretty girl standing on a chilly porch, dreadfully tired of the whole rush ritual. *Please* let me in—I promise I'll do a good job.

Since I'm here in *the best* house, I want them to see that I'll be a quality addition. I'm trying to be as engaged and enthusiastic as I can. I want to seem like I'm really, really into the skit, but I'm sitting too close to the fire. I keep losing focus because I'm hoping my sweater doesn't melt and that I don't leave a sweaty butt-print on the tile when I stand.

Skits complete, our massive rush class is broken into smaller factions. Each group of five rushees is ushered into a different bedroom by three members. Except these aren't bedrooms because there are no beds. In big sorority houses, all the girls sleep in bunks on the top floor in what's called a cold-air dorm. The fire code requires a certain amount of fresh air when there are

---

[97] If those letters automatically up my perceived level of hotness? All the better.

that many bodies in a room, so all the windows are permanently open. Pledges are in charge of going around to wake everyone up at appointed times, but since no one really trusts notoriously flighty pledges to do it right, everyone has a plug-in alarm clock. Plus each girl sleeps with an electric blanket, so all those cords combined with all the clock cords shoved into a few outlets seems like the real fire hazard to me.[98] By the way, want to know what sorority girls *don't* like to talk about during rush? Amps and volts determination. My guess is I'm not getting into Chi Omega.

We're led up to a room a third as big as my dorm room. Even though I can tell its occupants made an effort to clean up, this place is still cramped to the point of claustrophobic. Everyone must get ready in here because it smells like the perfume counter in a department store. The closet is stuffed so full the door won't close and each of the dresser drawers appears to be bulging. How do four girls keep all their possessions in this tiny space? When sisters complained about how hard it is at the end of the semester when everyone has to swap rooms at the same time, I helpfully suggested a less-is-more approach in regard to personal belongings.

Pretty sure the Thetas aren't asking me back, either.

A couple of the rushees get to sit on the futon under the eaves, but because I'm wearing pants, I'm stuck on the ground. Again. Between the eight of us and the futon, we cover every available bit of floor.

....

[98] But what do I know? I'm just a freshman hoping to become a notoriously flighty pledge.

When I try to sit Indian-style, I notice the top of my knee-highs inching past my stapled pant cuffs. This has to be another faux pas, so I fold my legs up underneath myself, wedging my calves under the lip of the futon.

I'm approaching this rush business all wrong, I can tell. I wish I knew how to do it right. I memorized the rush brochure, but given the jean jacket fiasco, that obviously wasn't the best plan. I've since learned other girls in my rush group spent their summers getting recommendation letters from sorority alumni. Because of these letters, lots of them were invited to pre-rush bar-becues and teas, so they're going into these houses having already made valuable contacts. I haven't known one person.

Some of the rushees have the advantage of being friends with the sorority members because they met as little sisters at *the right* fraternity parties. I came close to getting a little sister bid at the prestigious Alpha Chi Rho house. They asked me back a couple of times. However, I took myself out of consideration when I had to leave the final picnic party early because I'd gotten my p-e-r-i-o-d and I was not about to participate in the wheelbarrow races.

Of course my roommate Joanna got a bid there.

And she gained major points with me when she turned it down, opting to be a little sister at *the lesser* house because they were so respectful to her.

I became a little sister at my brother's house. His is a small house with fun guys and I always have a great time there, but it's not one of *the right* houses, either. Who knew that the politics of the Greek system would be more involved than some United Nations negotiations?

Going into rush, my assumption was every sorority would throw membership at my feet because I'm cute and I have lots of activities listed on the back of my rush card. I'm kind of devastated to realize no one *cares* if I was managing editor of my high school newspaper, or that I emceed the senior talent show. And the Miss Cow Town pageant? I should get extra credit for that. I was Miss Photogenic, after all. Girls should want me in their house, looking adorable in all those group huggy-huggy pictures pinned to their French bulletin boards, yes? Regardless of whatever big-fish status I finally earned in my high school, it definitely didn't translate to college. Sorority rush has turned me into a guppy again.

Rumor has it that the more exclusive chapters like this one will only take girls whose parents are rich. Mine aren't loaded, but they aren't, like, white trash or anything. Heck, we went to Hawaii for my high school graduation and I got a pearl ring, too! Although we're only middle class, my parents can afford my dues or else I wouldn't be rushing in the first place. Why must my family be totally wealthy? And how come everyone's so curious about what Dad does for a living? Shit, *I'm* not even sure.

Polly, a sophomore from my rush group, says she roomed with a girl last year whose father was vice president at Super-Huge Investment Bank. When her roommate went to parties, she told everyone, "My dad is vice president at Super-Huge Investment Bank." She even hired a limousine to take her around during formal rush. And yet she eventually got cut by every sorority. How does that work? Maybe you're supposed to be rich but not talk about it? If you're not supposed to talk about it, then why does everyone keep asking?

We go around the room and say who we are and where we're from. The first rushee asked is perched on the arm of the futon. She's from the Chicago area. She's got flaming red hair, Cupid's bow lips, and an accent like Dan Akroyd's. She says she's from Barrington, which causes a few people to squeal and then play the hey-do-you-know? game. Another girl with streaky blond hair is from a suburb of Detroit called Grosse Pointe. Why is she so damn smug? The last rushee is from Baltimore. Other than me, not one person here is from anywhere in Indiana. I suspect I just failed another test I wasn't aware I had to take, which is not fair. This is a *state* school—it stands to reason that some of us would be from *this* state.

The sisters field everyone's queries about sorority life. Out of respect for their time, I don't chime in with my own. I've already heard the answers to every single thing anyone could ask half a dozen times at other parties today. I know what the cold-air dorm is. We *all* know what the cold-air dorm is. I could write a thesis on the goddamned cold-air dorm. Brush your teeth, wash your face, put on your jammies, then walk up the stairs to your bed. You've been doing this for eighteen years, ladies[99]—the concept is *not* that foreign.

Having exhausted any and all conversation about sleeping in a room with open windows, someone brings up the topic of fashion. Even though I read *Seventeen* and *Glamour* every month, I'm already thought of as the Jean Jacket Jackass in my rush group. I stay quiet for fear of not being a credible source.

The suburban Chicago girls are carrying plain tan purses

---

[99] Aside from making yourself more likely to get burned up in a fire.

by someone named Coach, Baltimore's got a pricey-looking leather doctor bag, and Grosse Pointe is carrying what I swear she calls a . . . Lewie? Everyone nods in awe and I can actually see her stock rising with the sisters. What's funny is Grosse Pointe's bag is all brown- and mustard-colored, covered in the initials LV. It is the opposite of pretty. And I could have sworn her name was Natasha—why would she sport someone else's monogram?

Seriously? Who the fuck is *Lewie* and why does he determine what sorority wants me? And *why was this not in the rush booklet*? I mean, everyone here seems to be following a set of rules I never saw! Did they get different books? How come I'm so unprepared? If I was supposed to be dripping in jewelry or carrying an expensive bag, couldn't someone have told me? I could have borrowed stuff or faked it or *something*. All the rush booklet said was to be myself, but clearly that is not working because no one's responded positively to the few things I've had to say. I wish my roommate Joanna was in this group with me. She's genuine and charming and always finds a way to include me.

This room is so cramped that I'm practically sitting on one of the members. When I shift, trying to get some feeling back into my feet, I accidentally tap the sister with long white-blond hair. Her face is a study in contrast because she's got black brows and piercing blue eyes, kind of like a gorgeous Siberian husky.

When I bump her, she spins her head around, whipping me with her hair. Her name is Janine and she's cut me off almost every time I've spoken. Maybe she's cranky because she's hungry? She didn't touch her ice cream cookie sandwich when we were downstairs having snacks.[100] "So . . ." She squints at my rush name tag—a construction-paper playing card with *Jen* spelled out in tiny poker chips. "Um, Jean, who made *your* purse?"

I'm carrying an awesome woven-hemp Congo bag striped in all shades of pink, tan, and brown. When I went to Boston a couple of years ago, I walked through the Harvard campus and saw tons of preppy college girls carrying their books in bags like this. I figured if it worked for them, it should work for me.[101]

"Oh, it's Jen," I tell her apologetically, like it's my fault she screwed up my name. "I'm not sure who makes it. I got it at a Marshalls in Boston." I'm so pleased to finally have a non-Indiana answer to share with the group. Boston is *way* more metropolitan than stupid old Barrington or Baltimore. "Best part? I only paid seven dollars!"

Janine's curled lip tells me everything I need to know. If Joanna were here, she'd have been socially savvy enough to stop me before I got to the Marshalls mention, but it's too late. My fate in *the best* house is sealed and my status in the room morphs from "bothersome" to "nonexistent." And I learn that in the big book of Wrong Things to Say During Sorority Rush, "I got it at Marshalls" surely ranks at the top.

My ego is so bruised from rush that when it comes time to pledge, I accept a bid at *a lesser* house. They fought to get my interest, so

---

[100] Delicious! I ate every bite.

[101] Plus it looks great with my jean jacket.

I choose them knowing I'll automatically be bestowed with big-fish status within the chapter. Yet I quietly resent my sorority for wanting me, because I didn't want them.

Even though no one at Janine's house was nice to me, I wanted the girls in *the best* house to see that I was a diamond in the rough. I wanted them to look past my jean jacket and wide hair and Indiana residency to see that I was worthy of member-ship. I wanted them to take me in and turn me into someone bet-ter. I wanted to wear their letters to show everyone on campus that I was a part of something really special and exclusive. But they didn't want me.

Joanna's sunny personality, good looks, and affable nature earn her a spot in Janine's sorority. She plasters her side of the room with arrows and angels and takes to working wine and sil-ver blue into her everyday wardrobe. She only removes her letters when we do laundry and she's forced to wear something from her life before pledgeship. We remain good friends—great friends—even though she spends more and more time at her new sorority. I pretend I'm not jealous when boys who never gave her a second glance suddenly get interested when they see what house she joined.

Due to my own poor attitude, I don't bond with any of the other pledges or sisters in my new sorority, thus all the rituals I so looked forward to feel flat and forced. When they invite me to drink Diet Coke on the portico, I decline. When they line up to study, I return to my dorm to hang out with Joanna or I call my friends Andy and Roni. I can't be bothered with my sisters' en-thusiasm and I never wear their letters unless required. And when my thoughtless yet intentionally ungrateful actions get me tossed out prior to the May initiation date, I'm relieved rather than distressed.

The object lesson I take from rush is that it's all about the right bag. Maybe it's stupid and vain, but it's the truth. So, the summer before my sophomore year, I make a vow to myself—I may not be in a sorority but damn it, I *will* return to campus with a designer bag. I will not, however, return to rush. My grades aren't great and I'm not into facing that kind of rejection again.

I apply for jobs all over town the second I return home from freshman year. I could babysit for the neighbors, but that only pays a buck an hour. (Also, I hate their children.) I need more if I'm going to make my designer purse dreams a reality.

I look for work in the malls in Fort Wayne. I so want to land a position at The Limited, because if I do I'll surely return to school with the right wardrobe. I come very close to getting hired there but the day before my final interview, I decide to trim my bangs so I'm tidier and more pulled together. Even though I've lived with curly hair for eighteen years, I didn't take shrinkage into account as I wielded my mother's sewing scissors. I showed up to my final interview with half an inch of fringe between my hairline and my forehead. Guess what? Regardless of how well she might sell Outback Red shirts, no one wants to hire Frankenstein.

My blue-collar town is full of people desperate for employment and I find myself losing out on gigs to those who can keep working come September. It takes almost a month, but eventually, with some fresh growth and bangs plastered flat by a bottle of gel, I'm hired on at a Subway franchise. In a scathing indictment of the local educational system, I get the job based on my ability to solve simple math problems on the application. No, I can't add or subtract in my head, either . . . but I *can* fit a calculator into my Congo bag.

I'm not a fan of food service and I loathe the idea of spending the summer slinging sandwiches in an airless kitchen. Even though I've got a solid work ethic, there's something particularly grueling about this job, namely, Tuna Day. Instead of my usual routine of searing off my fingerprints on a pan full of molten meatballs, scorching tender wrist skin on oven racks full of freshly baked bread, or losing a thumb tip to the meat slicer, on Tuna Day I take industrial-sized cans of StarKist and squeeze each bit of meat over and over again until every drop of oil and water is gone.

Do you *know* how much liquid there is in an industrial-sized can of tuna?

It's like a clown car, only for fish juice.

Crush and press, crush and press, extract, expel, constrict for what seems like hours on end. No matter how much I try to angle the tuna juice away from my face when I squeeze it, I always manage to end up with an eyeful and spend the rest of the day squinting at customers like Popeye.

When the oily backsplash hits my cheeks, I sometimes forget and try to wipe it away with my forearms and the juice runs directly into my armpit. Don't even get me started on trying to extract tuna-whiff from my skin. I spend two months reeking of low tide.

Even though my whole body aches after every Tuna Day, I'm confident it will be worth it when I finally run my (stinky, burnt) hands over the embossed canvas of a new bag.

Now that I understand their cache, I desperately want a Gucci, but they're too expensive. Technically, I've never actually checked the price because they're kept in a locked display case at L. S. Ayres. Anything under glass is out. In the farming community where I live, beef is king; people in Cow Town just can't handle that much tuna.

I decide that Liz Claiborne would be a more than adequate substitution for a Gucci bag and my fingers tingle in anticipation of being able to run them over the raised triangular nubs pressed into the shiny vinyl. I debate all summer over which Liz bag is the Real Me. Whenever I go to Fort Wayne, I stand in the accessories department trying on every model. Am I more of a sunflower-yellow-square girl or a big-red-feedbag kind of person? Clutch or satchel? Tote or wristlet? I finally settle on a sweet little rectangular number in turquoise, just big enough to carry a wallet, some powder, a pencil, and a fifth of peach schnapps. Adding to its glamour and cache is a zipper placket and strap trimmed in *genuine* leather.

The high point of my summer comes when I hand the Ayres cashier a wad of ever-so-slightly tuna-tinged twenties. Once purchased and back at school, I feel like a movie star every time I carry it.

I love this purse with a singular passion.

For five months.

Until Janine sails into my organizational communications class the first day of second semester sophomore year with a tiny Gucci binocular bag swinging from her shoulder.

My own new purse emboldens me. I'm good enough to talk to this girl. I'm fun and relatively smart. (Smart enough to at least do stuff like carry a calculator because I'm aware of my limitations.) More important, I'm in touch with my ability to work hard enough to turn dreams into reality. If I'm not her sister, that's *her* loss. I speak right up. "Hi, Janine," I say.

Her arched black brow practically disappears into her hairline. "Do I *know* you?"

"Yeah, you do. We met during informal rush last year and you live down the hall from my best friend Joanna. I'm Je—" I start to say.

"Jean Jacket!" she interrupts. "Of course!"

They seriously need to update those fucking rush brochures.

I'd placed my winter coat and the Liz on the empty chair next to me in the lecture hall when I got in a few minutes ago. I scramble to grab them as Janine claims the seat, but I'm not fast enough. She picks up my bag with two fingers and wrinkles her pert nose with a small moue of disapproval. "Yours? Ew."

I nod and take it from her, stuffing it under my seat. I *want* to punch her in her surgically altered nose. I want to grasp a handful of her glossy hair . . . and then yank it so hard I leave a bald patch. But I'm too stunned to act because I never realized people like this existed outside of a *Revenge of the Nerds* movie.

Why did I want *her* as a sister? This bitch is exactly why sororities get a bum rap in the first place. She's the kind of person who perpetuates the idea of *right*, *lesser*, and *best* houses.

I'd like to say I take her comments in stride, chalking up her attitude to too much peroxide and not enough calories. But my hubris has a first name . . . and it's not J-e-a-n.

◆

The attached note reads simply, *"Sending under protest—I pre-dict this is going to end badly. Love, Mom."*

Nice try, *Mom.*

I wad up the piece of floral stationery and toss it in the trash. Then I tear open the envelope to reveal the Big Kahuna, the Holy Grail, the piece de résistance. There it is, my ticket out of here. Measuring in at only 3⅛ by 2⅛ inches, this tiny jewel of a card with the winking hologram of a dove may well change my life.

I return to my room and plop down on the bottom bunk, leaning against the gray-green cinder-block wall. My roommate Lisa and I are stuck in the worst dorm on campus. I spent all of last spring assuming I'd live in my sorority house, so I never bothered with housing registration. Once I was booted, I figured I'd move into the extra room in my friend Roni's apartment across from my brother's fraternity. How convenient would that be? If the guys did something like set another couch on fire in the street or throw coffee cups at cop cars, I could be there in a minute to witness it![102]

Then, right before I returned to campus, my parents vetoed my proposed living arrangement and the only place left was the loser dorm. Lisa was assigned here because she's from Florida and didn't know any better when she filled out her form. She arrived with nothing but a trunk full of sweaters. She'd gotten the

....

[102] Sidebar? His fraternity got banned from booking dances in hotels in a two-hundred-mile radius because each place they visited had to drain the pool due to high counts of urine (and pool furniture). At their last event, my friends tore the beds off the wall and tossed a phone through a plate-glass window. How could this possibly be considered a lesser house??

book about Indiana's punishing winter, but never learned about its August heat and stifling humidity.

Lisa looks up from her homework and I tell her about Mom's note. We laugh and roll our eyes. *Moms.* They don't know *anything.*

My new credit card arrived at my parents' house a while ago but my mother refused to send it to me until she couldn't take my whining anymore. I'd applied solely because the company was giving out giant candy bars for filling out the application—Hershey's with Almonds! It never even occurred to me that a penniless college student could *get* a card, let alone have the opportunity to *abuse* one. Sure, I like spending money, but I'm used to earning it. Purchasing something on credit is a totally foreign concept to me.

For the past month, Mom's been in a lather about the potentially stupid things I might buy. For all her forbidding, she's actually the one who inadvertently planted the seed for what I'm about to do. Lisa mimics, "I predict this is going to end badly!" as I make the decision to skip all my afternoon classes. Then I slip my new VISA into my Liz bag and head out on my mission.

A thrill courses through me.

This is the greatest day of my life.

This is almost better than winning the lottery, or getting a bid from every *right* house on campus.

I feel almost *illicit* as the woman in front of me opens the display case.

Oh, yes. I'm about to join the very best sorority, the most exclusive group of girls. Nope, I won't be lording about in harps or anchors or skulls. Instead, my pledge pin will be covered in locking *G*s. That's right, I'm about to become the proud owner of a Gucci purse.

The first bag I inspect is the little binocular-case-looking one Janine has. I'd be too obvious if I came in with her exact same bag, wouldn't I?

Hey, how much did she spend on this thing anyway? I gasp when I look at the price tag and my whole body quivers. Whoa. I knew it would be a hundred—I just didn't know it would be *that many* hundred.

For the record, neither Andy nor Roni supports this little endeavor so they wouldn't come with me. Roni says there will always be mean girls ready to make others feel bad about themselves. Showing Janine I can accessorize, too, proves nothing. Andy says I should suck it up, move on, and stop skipping class. Joanna doesn't know what I'm planning, but I get the feeling she'd not be behind me, either.

If I could let my vendetta go, I would. I wish I didn't feel like Janine had everything over me—she's in *the best* sorority, she's thinner than I could ever be, she answers more questions right in class, and she's got the coloring of a purebred sled dog. I hate her and yet part of me still wants to garner her approval, if only to have the chance to be the one who does the rebuffing.[103] A Gucci purse may well be the key.

So . . . why do I feel like I'm drowning here in the middle of the accessories department at L. S. Ayres? Why can't I catch my breath?

....

[103] Except I probably wouldn't.

I picture Andy and Roni's sincere faces, imploring me to walk away. Then I imagine the surprise on Janine's face when I arrive with a better bag than hers. I'm so torn.

My ego's saying *go for it*, but my gut's telling me *this is dumb*. The worst part is I wonder if my mother wasn't on to something, because here I am, credit card an hour out of the envelope, and I'm about to spend what it would take me a whole summer of part-time minimum wage to earn. That's an ocean of tuna juice.

I look at a few other styles. I want them all so much. However, I can't bring myself to pull the trigger on this transaction. Yeah, my pride is injured but not two hundred and fifty dollars' worth.

I thank the clerk and tell her I *like* everything, but I'm not *in love*. I'm about to back away from the counter when she says, "Wait! We just got a new one in. Let me grab it." Moments later, she returns with a big white cloth bag with drawstrings and the Gucci logo in the center. "Here we go."

"It's cute," I say, examining it from all sides. "Although a white bag isn't that practical for me. I'd get it dirty pretty fast and I don't like the handles—they'd dig into my shoulder."

"Ma'am," she replies patiently, "this is the dust cover."

Okay, then.

She opens the drawstrings and pulls out a football-sized bag. Rectangular but still rounded, this is small enough to wear to a party, but big enough that I could stuff an address book and some sunglasses in it. And maybe some gin. I marvel at the buttery leather lining that's inside[104] and run my hands over the jaunty

----

[104] Leather *inside* a purse? Whoa.

green and red cloth strip dividing the two zippy pockets on the outside. The strap is long and leather and adjustable with a shiny buckle.

I stammer, "I . . . I . . . I can't."

"Want to take it for a spin?" the clerk asks.

Tossing Liz on the floor, I step over to the full-length mirror. The moment I slip the Gucci bag over my head and tuck my arm through the strap, I am transformed. I am taller. Thinner. My skin is clearer. My eyes brighter. My hair less fuzzy.

I am *magnificent*.

My mother's voice, which has been riding shotgun with me since the second I opened the mail today, suddenly disappears and all I can hear is *Do it, do it, do it.*

Seriously, I reason, *how could I not buy a bag that loops adorably over my shoulder, attractively across my chest, and rests all coy and snug against my now suddenly very narrow hips?*

And those darling little Gs? They quietly identify me as being a Person of Merit . . . they're so much better than some random Greek letters sewn on the back of my sweatpants, which would probably make my butt look big anyway.

I want this bag.

I quickly scan my wardrobe and mentally try it on with everything I own. Yep, it goes fabulously with all my favorite outfits: thick white souvenir T-shirts from fraternity dances, crisp cotton shorts in khaki and navy with knifelike pleats, and the pointy-toed Mia flats that make my legs look muscular and tan.

I want this bag.

But I can't. It costs hundreds of dollars. *Four* hundreds to be exact.

I want it.

No. No, no. Someday I'll be a grown-up and I can buy all the designer bags I want. Different bags. Better bags.[105] Now is not the time. I haven't worked to earn it and I don't deserve it.

And yet . . . how great would it be to sashay into org com with this on my shoulder?

No.

What if I got a part-time job? I'm not that busy with class. I could work and still go to school. People do it all the time.

You've had two shitty semesters in a row—is taking on a job that will distract you more than parties and boys already do your best idea?

Well . . . I guess . . . not.

I remove the bag from its rightful place on my shoulder and put it on the counter as the clerk grins expectantly at me.

I tell her, "Thank you for your time."

Somehow it comes out, "You take VISA?"

Funny thing about confidence—when it stems from *thing*s, like a new Gucci bag, rather than from a genuine place inside, it can easily turn to arrogance. Which can then turn to a sense of invincibility.

A sense of invincibility leads to bad decisions, like cutting class for weeks on end, concurrently dating three members of Phi Kappa Tau, and wearing hoop earrings the size of salad plates.

---

[105] Prada bags. And then I will carry them to the unemployment office. But that's a whole 'nother story.

The plot to avenge myself veers off course, crashing straight into hedonism.

But who cares?

I'm invincible!

Let's do shots!

❖

Which Is an Entirely
Different Chapter

❖❖❖❖❖❖❖❖❖❖❖❖❖❖❖❖❖❖

(Not Even My Yellow Argyle Sweater)

Turns out my actions actually *do* have consequences. That's why I'm here, stuck behind a cash register at a Maurices clothing store in Fort Wayne, not even at the good mall.

While I've been busy selling scrunchies and stirrup pants this week, all my friends have been moving back to campus after summer vacation. Everyone's arriving in their family station wagons packed with milk crates full of cassette tapes and St. Pauli Girl posters lovingly rubber-banded around cardboard tubes since May. The sidewalks in front of Greek houses and apartments and dorms are full of trunks, laundry baskets, and hot pots ready to fulfill a late-night ramen craving. Everyone's tan and refreshed from a summer away and their bags carry pristine notebooks and new pens and snowy white K-Swiss sneakers, tags still attached.

Tonight, all my friends are headed to a kegger at the Delta Sig house except for Joanna, who's going to a Slip 'n Slide party on the hill at the Beta house. I'm scheduled to close the store, so my plans include balancing the register, vacuuming, and if I'm lucky, not removing used tampons from the fitting rooms.[106]

Andy and Roni have apartments on opposite sides of an alley on the west side of campus this year. When they stand on their balconies, they can wave at each other. I talked to them yesterday. When I called, Andy's roommate yelled for them down at the apartment's pool, where they were browning up in anticipation of classes starting. But they came upstairs to talk to me, Andy in his new living room, Roni on the extension in Andy's bedroom. They reassured me about how sad they were that I wasn't coming back this semester. No one asked me if I flunked out, and even if they did, I couldn't tell them the truth. Shoot, if I can't admit it to myself, how am I supposed to say it to anyone else?

As a preemptive strike, I tell anyone who inquires that I'm kind of *over* school right now, and I'm just working to pay down my credit cards.[107] I say that I want to make money and I'm anxious to start my career.

Truth is, I sit in my bedroom every night after work looking at my crate of books and notebooks, still packed from when I moved out of my dorm, wondering why it was so damn hard for me to just go to class. For God's sake, I flunked *Recreation 100*. How did I manage to fail a class on leisure activities?[108]

....

[106] Why do so many people assume dressing room = restroom?

[107] Yes, plural.

[108] By being leisurely, I guess.

My parents are . . . let's just say they aren't proud. Since I failed academically and financially, they're suddenly convinced I'm twelve years old again and must be monitored constantly. They tell me when I'm having too much ice cream and listen in on my phone calls and open my mail. That's how they discovered I flunked out in the first place. I tell Dad he's violating federal law by tampering with my mail. He says until federal law starts providing me with food, shelter, and my very own pool to clean, I'll be following *his* law.

The worst part isn't being stuck on my feet full-time in the store, or even my part-time gig knee-deep in fish juice back at Subway. It's that I never even got the satisfaction of a reaction from Janine. She got one look at my new bag and then ignored me the few times I came to class the rest of the semester.

Wasn't revenge supposed to be sweeter than this? Shouldn't I feel good, not fucking awful?

The greatest irony is I didn't even keep the Gucci bag for long. I have to wear Maurices clothing when I go to work and my dad won't let me buy any. I have to sign over every paycheck I receive because he's taken over the management of my debts. I end up selling my purse to a part-time associate in order to purchase Camp Beverly Hills rugby shirts and leggings for work. My store receives a shipment of faux sorority letter shirts. I don't buy any of those.

💰

I'm busy sorting through our new collection of rhinestone jewelry. Should anyone be in the market for sparkly accessories the size of a hubcap, this is the place to get them. Earlier today a customer picked up one of the enormous chandelier-style offerings and asked, "Do those be genuine rhyme-stones?" I couldn't even begin to explain everything that was wrong with her sentence, so I simply replied, "Yes, they do be genuine."

I treat customers with the kind of forced cheerfulness our corporate office requires because I'll be fired if I get a bad review from a secret shopper. If I lose my job on top of being thrown out of college, I will never, ever be out of trouble.

A harried-looking middle-aged lady rushes in and before I can even welcome her, she barks, "I have a hold for Miller."

"Sure!" I reply in a sunny tone of voice. "Let's go get it for you." I turn around and sort through all the hanging items but there's nothing for Miller. "Hmm, it's not here. Can you tell me if you held it today?" I don't recall having seen this woman and I've been in the store since opening this morning. "We only keep items on the hold rack until the close of business, so if you held it yesterday, it would have been put back into stock."

The customer's face flushes red and she raises her voice. "Yes, it *was* today. Do you think I'm stupid? I would remember if it wasn't today."

In terms of being rude, retail customers are second only to hungry diners. I tell myself it's not really me they're mad at, but sometimes it gets hard to, you know, not kick a lung out of them. But I'm here behind this counter instead of in a classroom specifically because I let a revenge fantasy take hold. I have to learn to control myself.

I try to position my mouth into something that's not a rictus. When I do force a grin, it doesn't reach my eyes. Hey, I guess I did get something out of rush!

"Of course, of course, my mistake. Let's give this another

look-sie." I go through the rack, pulling out every garment separately. "No, I'm really sorry, I don't have a Miller here. I've got holds for Helen, for Heidi, for Marcy, and for Joan. Is it possible you gave your first name? Is one of these yours?"

The customer slams her hand on the Formica cash wrap. "No! Go look in the back." This is not a question.

Aarrgh. The back. I hate that everyone thinks what they need is in "the back." *The back* is a cramped storage area with a mini-fridge, a small picnic table, and a bunch of broken fixtures. There's a crumbling cork board with this week's schedule tacked to it, and if our cleaning crew is feeling generous, the dank employee bathroom isn't too disgusting. We don't put holds back here because the whole area is repulsive.[109]

I'm about to explain this to the customer when I notice her scrunched brows and lips pursed so hard her magenta Estée Lauder is bleeding all the way up to her nose and down to her chin. Instead, I say, "Okey-dokey! Back in two shakes!"

I go to the back, drink some of my Diet Coke, and reapply my Designer Imposter version of Poison perfume, which smells all yummy like liquefied Jolly Ranchers. I touch up my lip gloss, too. I dawdle because if I come out too soon, she won't believe I actually looked, even though there's nothing to look *at*.

"Mrs. Miller, please accept my apologies. There's no hold back there for you. Your garment must have been returned to stock. If you can tell me the size and what it looks like, I'll find it immediately."

....

[109] More important, this is not where we hide all the good stuff. Please, everyone, stop perpetuating that myth.

"Damn it, why are all you people so incompetent?"

I attempt to channel my seething rage into something resembling polite conversation. Seriously, I cannot get fired. "They were a pair of jeans, then? Acid washed, perhaps? Lycra stretch? Floral embroidered? Armpit-waisted Z. Cavaricci?"

"No! It was a sweater! It was a goddamned yellow argyle sweater with pink and green diamonds! And my daughter will have a fit if you lost it and she can't wear it on the first day of school!" The veins on Mrs. Miller's temples throb.

Must kill, I tell myself. *With kindness,* I reluctantly add. And, really, if we had a yellow argyle sweater, I'd have used my Gucci purse money to buy it for myself.

Wait. Have I seen this sweater somewhere? I can picture it so perfectly.

Slowly, it dawns on me that this lady is in the wrong store. "Mrs. Miller, I think you're talking about a sweater at Ups 'N' Downs across the hall. Which is a totally different store."

"Show me because I am not leaving this mall without that sweater."

The part-timers have quietly gathered to listen in. I shrug as I pass them in their miniskirts and maxi-bangs while Mrs. Miller and I exit, cross the courtyard, and enter Ups 'N' Downs. "Okay, here we are. In this place, which is a different store."

She yanks a sweater off a display where a half dozen of them are folded. "Aha! I told you you'd put it back! Is retail really that difficult? I don't know what's wrong with you people."

I want to tell her what's wrong with me is that I had a golden opportunity to do something with my life and I lost sight of it because of my pride. I'd like to say what's wrong is that I'm full of regret over poor choices. And that retail sucks and I'd rather die than face a future full of angry customers and synthetic sweaters.

What I actually say is, "I guess the problem is that I work in a different store. See, that's why the music, clothing, and staff are different. And it's also why we went through that big hallway past the landscaping and the Things Remembered kiosk."

Mrs. Miller thrusts her credit card and sweater at me. "Ring me up. You've wasted enough of my time."

"Alrighty, let me just find a clerk who works in *this* store, which is different from the store I work in." I spot an employee I know. "Hey, Kendra? Can you ring this up? I can't because I don't work in this store, which is different from mine."

Kendra dutifully punches the buttons on the cash register, wraps the sweater in tissue paper, and presents a charge slip. "Here you are, Mrs. Miller, please sign on the line." Transaction complete, Kendra gives Mrs. Miller her bag. "Thank you for shopping at Ups 'N' Downs!"

"And at Maurices!" I add. "Which is an entirely different store!"

What? I don't have to be polite if it's not *my* customer.

Kendra turns to me and asks, "What the hell was that?"

"That was proof that I need to get my ass back to college."

"Christ, what a d-bag."

"Welcome to retail."

Kendra looks at the hold slip she just threw in the trash. "Hey, I've got all her information here. Wanna prank her or send her a pizza or something?"

I consider her offer for a moment. "Nah. Revenge isn't really my style."

❖

I convince my university to readmit me. Never underestimate the power of contrition.[110] I enroll at a regional campus. Since I'm paying for classes myself, I have to live at home.

This is basically a commuter campus and people aren't as into meeting other students like they are on the main campus. Maybe the other students already live where all their friends are or maybe they're just too busy trying to juggle work and school and family. I'm delighted to be on the road to higher education again, but I miss the social aspect of the bigger campus. I'm not saying I have to go to a twenty-keg party, but it would be nice not to eat lunch alone.

Partway through the semester, I discover there are Greek organizations here—they even have a chapter of *the best* sorority. I decide to give rush one more shot because I'm doing it for the right reasons; I genuinely want to connect with people.

This time, I really *am* myself during parties. When I meet the members of *the best* house, I don't care what their specific combination of letters can do for me. I sincerely want *these* girls to be my sisters. I want to wear my shortened prom dress to dances *with them*. I want to line up at a big wooden table, sip Diet Coke, and be bored during rush *with these specific people.*

These are the thoughts racing through my head as I prepare for a rush party in the skeevy Maurices bathroom after my shift. My hair's a lot longer than it used to be and with careful blow-drying and patient ministrations with a wide-barrel curling iron, I can coax

---

[110] And begging.

it into bouncy strands with the hint of a flip at the bottom. Tonight's supposed to be a casual party and jeans are allowed, but I've been down that road. I select a forest green turtleneck, jodhpur-cut khakis, and a red and green plaid vest with a black backing. I'm not trying to mimic anyone else's style; I simply choose an outfit that makes me feel good.

Yet I can't help but smile when I get to the party and see members wearing jeans.

Rush continues for a few weeks and I have a blast. I love the members and I dig the other girls in my rush group. As I leave the final party, I want to slip everyone my number and say, *Even if we can't be sisters, can we at least be friends?*

Those who are invited to join the sorority are supposed to get the call between 7:00 and 9:00 p.m. I'm so anxious I call in sick to work. I spend the entire night sitting next to the phone. I keep lifting the receiver to make double sure we've got a dial tone. Minutes crawl by. I wait and wait and wait. When the phone rings, I shriek and grab it, but it's just Joanna checking on my status *again*. I practically hang up on her in my haste to clear the line.

It's nine p.m. and no one's called.

Oh, well.

I'm probably too old to pledge. Probably didn't get my grades up high enough, either.

Perhaps I shouldn't have been honest about my last sorority experience.

Maybe the real me wasn't good enough. Wasn't the right fit. Wasn't what they wanted. Maybe I laughed too hard when that one member accidentally dropped an f-bomb. Maybe I should have ignored it like the two stuffy girls in my rush group.

What a shame. I would have taken sisterhood so seriously. Too seriously because I would have appreciated it so much. I'd have worn those letters with more pride than a hundred Gucci bags, because I'd have known I'd earned them. I'd probably be one of those assholes who, even at age forty, still talked about her sorority because it was such a big deal in her life.

And then the phone rings.

They want me.

I'm in.

I'm one of them.

I *belong*.

❖

Right before pledge induction, it dawns on me that not only did I get into this campus's branch of Joanna's sorority—hence her frantic calls on Bid Night—I'm also in Janine's.

Like it or not, I'm Janine's sister. She may never know it because we're on different campuses, but I'm her brown-haired, Indiana-dwelling, middle-class-being, jean-jacket-wearing, retail-working, Congo-bag-carrying sister.

And I will be for the rest of our lives.

That's *the best* revenge of all.

Absolute Power? Absolutely!

(Gold Lavaliere, Part One)

November 9, 1988

Hey, Lisa!

Someone you know has just turned twenty-one . . . so get your fake ID ready because I'm coming down to celebrate with you next weekend!

I spent the actual big day in South Bend because that's where Carol works now that she's graduated. Andy met me up there and we went out on Notre Dame's campus. I figured it would be fun to go somewhere I hadn't already been ten jillion times illegally. Then, halfway through the night I remembered I'd been to all their bars during St. Patrick's Day back in '85. Whoops!

Anyway, now that I'm twenty-one, I'm legal to wait tables and serve drinks so my schedule will be more flexible. I'm done getting stuck with Saturday closing shifts at the mall because I got a job at an Italian restaurant!

The bad news is they have servers sing when it's someone's birthday. I'm probably going to be responsible for making an entire generation of kids afraid of spaghetti.

Later!

Jen

That Little Italian Joint, Inc.

Jennifer,

It has come to my attention that every time other servers gather to sing the birthday song, you hide in the walk-in freezer. Not only does this behavior lessen our guests' experience, but it puts a strain on the other waiters and waitresses who have to scramble to find additional singers.

I don't care if the song "Happy Birthday" "makes you itchy." This is your last formal warning to cease this behavior. Dodge your duties again and you will be fired.

Douglas Handler, Shift Manager

January 30, 1989

To All My Pledge Sisters,

Thank you so much for electing me to lead this impressive group. I promise to be the best pledge president in the history of our chapter. I'll take my role as leader very, very seriously and will work hard to help us all advance socially, academically, and morally on our path to initiation. I look forward to upholding the fine tradition of wine and silver blue with all of you.

Pi Love and Mine,

Jen Lancaster, Pledge Class President

"You can't do it," Molly declares.

"Check the bylaws," I counter.

"I *did* check the bylaws. It's not technically forbidden, but . . ."

"Then what's the problem?"

I'm currently locked in the little glass office off the Greek suite in our sorority's wing. I'm also locked in combat with Molly, the member assigned to "educate" us pledges.[111] I freaking adore everyone in my pledge class and I love all the sisters . . . except for

---

[111] Now they're called "new members." Ah, the end of an era.

Molly. I like her, but I can't seem to pry the enormous stick out of her ass. Or dislodge her sense of moral superiority.

"The problem is"—she pauses to gather her thoughts— "the problem is it's a *problem*. Some of the sisters don't like it."

"Who?" I ask.

"I'd rather not say." *So by "sisters" you mean "you." Everyone I've run it past thinks it's the best idea ever.*

I was right in the middle of a chef salad and a lovely chat with my favorite pledge sister Audra when Molly barged in, demanding she speak with me. I couldn't say no, and now Molly's been lecturing me for fifteen minutes and my patience is running on empty. Audra can see how aggravated I am so she begins to make obscene gestures[112] behind Molly's back. I have to stifle a laugh and pretend like I'm taking Molly seriously. She *is* the more senior member and I'm supposed to defer to her, even though she's wrong.

"It's not going to be an orgy, it's *a toga party*," I tell her. Molly screws her face up in confusion. "Oh, for Christ's sake, Molly, how can you be in a sorority and not know one of the most famous *Animal House* quotes ever?"

She purses her lips. "You're trying to change the subject." Actually, I'm completely *on* subject. The first time I saw *Animal House*, I felt something bordering on awe. Greek life seemed like so much goddamned fun that I couldn't imagine not being a part of it when I got to college. My standing here in front of Molly is a direct result of having fallen in love with Otter, Bluto, Eric Stratton, and the rest of the barely fictional Delta house ten years earlier.

I take a deep breath and count to five so I don't get all shouty.

....

[112] Simulating sticks and asses.

"No, I'm trying to inject some levity into the situation. Here's the deal. You *told* our pledge class we had to plan a walkout.[113] I know we normally do walkout to a sister house on another campus. Everyone I've talked to said they've had a lousy time the last few years. The walkout in Michigan blew goats, as did the trip to Ohio. I proposed something a little different, we voted on it, and there you go. Plan revised. Majority rules."

When I found out our proposed sorority walkout date was the same weekend as Purdue's Grand Prix,[114] I panicked. Attendance has been a personal tradition since I was a senior in high school and I hated the idea of not being there this year. Yet I worked so hard and waited so long to be a part of a sorority I liked that I didn't want to miss out on being with them, either.

So I got creative.

I figured if walking out to a house full of snotty girls wasn't fun, then why do it? Since Purdue runs three to one in its ratio of fraternities to sororities, I knew there'd be a bunch of places that didn't "pair" with a campus sorority for the weekend. I figured a number of them would be happy to have us come down for the night. We could go, party with cute boys,[115] and the next day I could introduce my favorite pledge sisters to my friends on campus.

A handful of calls to various fraternity social directors later, I had three houses dying for us to come.[116] I made sure they set

....

[113] Greek term meaning "Prank the members and then pack up all your shit and go drink grain alcohol punch on another campus for the weekend."

[114] Purdue's big spring go-kart race–party weekend. Way less dumb than it sounds.

[115] In the name of sisterhood, of course.

[116] That's what she said.

aside a wing of bunks in their cold-air dorms and cleaned up a private bathroom where we could shower. The whole weekend will be precisely as innocent as we want. Problem solved!

Molly argues, "You scare some of the girls because you're a little older than them."

"Bullshit. Half of them are my age." A lot of my pledge sisters went to other schools first and found themselves in situations similar to mine. Heck, that's why I connected with them in the first place.

Molly chews this over for a second. "Then maybe they didn't want to say no to you." *One* sister sees you aggressively badgering a couple of random students into buying your fund-raising Kit Kat bars, and all of a sudden *you're* the monster. Listen, the profit I made off those candy bars was going to pay for important things—like gas money to get to parties on another campus. The real monsters are the ones who didn't want to support this fine, fine organization by paying three bucks for a quality chocolate bar. (Technically everyone else was selling them for a dollar but I kind of ate a bunch of mine and I had to do *something* to make up the difference, right?)

I watch as Audra starts stealing the olives out of my salad, so I scratch my ear with my middle finger in her direction. She sees me and pretends to use my fork as toilet paper. Then she hands it to Laurie—also in our pledge class—who begins to lick it. They're obviously shaking in their boots at the thought of me.

"Molly, we're going nowhere."

"Great! Glad to hear you've come around to my way of thinking."

"No. I mean this *conversation* is going nowhere. Come on, the whole pledge class voted yes. And if everyone said yes because they were too afraid to cast a secret ballot in front of my antique ass, then it's your job to boost their confidence."

"But . . . but . . ."

The idea of losing this argument pains me but Molly's not going to get off my case if we don't compromise. "Mol, how about this? Why don't we do another vote? You can give a little speech beforehand urging everyone to vote their conscience."

Molly hesitates. "I guess that would be fair."

"Great. If you'll excuse me, I have to beat the lettuce out of Audra."

$\math令{Y}$

We vote again and it's unanimous. We're totally going.

$\math令{Y}$

All I hear from everyone the second we get back until initiation at the end of semester is, "Best walkout ever!"

I suspected as much.

Molly can suck it.

Personally, I find it almost impossible to have anything but fun around fraternity guys. There's a scene in *Animal House* when Dean Wormer is complaining about what a blight the Delta house is on campus. He goes on about how the brothers are responsible for dumping a truckload of fizzies into the pool at the swim meet and how they had the med school cadavers delivered to the alumni dinner and how every Halloween the trees fill with underpants and every spring the toilets explode, and I guarantee you there are pledge classes out there hanging on every wonderfully suggestive word.

I love fraternity guys. I love visiting their houses and seeing how they've taken pickaxes and tunneled into the turret of the building, making a supersecret party room. I love the care they take in displaying the more colorful varieties of empty liquor bottles on their windowsills. I love how they teach the house mascot, an unkempt Saint Bernard, to drink out of the water fountain. I love that no matter how tall or short or fat or thin a guy is, all of them can share the same pair of chinos and a white Ralph Lauren button-down. I love being upstairs ten minutes before the party starts and smelling the combination of steam from the showers and too much Polo cologne and the slightest tang of a now dry spilled beer coming from the hallway carpet. I love being behind them in line at the grocery store, watching them buy boxes of Count Chocula and cases of Guinness with absolutely no shame.

I have no doubt in ten years I'll be shouting when one of these kids leaves an empty bottle on my lawn and I'll seethe with rage if one of them ever chops down and steals the magnificent fir tree in my someday front yard. I'll call the police if they're too loud and I'll go to zoning meetings to see what can be done about keeping them from parking on my street.

But for now? Their kind can do no wrong, even if they might piss me off individually by breaking a date or cheating on a friend.

I absolutely plan on marrying a fraternity guy because their ability to pledge allegiance to something bigger than themselves in the name of commitment—even though it's sometimes guaranteed to suck[117]—is the exact quality I want in a husband.

---

[117] See: *Week, Hell.*

Hey, Joanna!

I'm sorry I haven't called in a couple of weeks but I've been so freaking busy with rush. I had no idea what life was like on the other side of the receiving line. I thought being a rushee was stressful, but it's nothing compared to having to learn the songs and act in the skits and plan the menu and stuff. And being forced to vote on people? That's . . . harsh.

The best news is that someone you know won the award for Best Rusher! My prize was a little gold sorority letter lavaliere with a gold arrow charm. (It looks AWESOME on me.) I was so superior at starting conversations and making people feel welcome that no one even cast a vote for anyone else. (Well, they did, but totally out of sympathy. I completely ruled.)

Regardless, I had such a great experience that I may just run for Rush Chairman next year.

Pi Love and mine,

Jen

Dear Joanna,

Exactly what is so fucking funny?

Curiously,

Jen

First She Was a Seed and Then She Was Trouble

![decorative border]

(Gold Lavaliere, Part Two)

To the Gorgeous Women of the Indiana Eta Chapter:

Ha! I totally knew that line would get your attention! I'd first like to say I'm super-excited you've selected me as your Rush Chairman. Major snaps to all of you! I promise to not disappoint, but I'd like to make the following rules clear:

Jen's Rules for a Supercool Rush

We're going to have the super-est, coolest rush ever. Live, learn, and recognize.

I can't and won't do all the work myself. Let's establish that right off the bat. I have some fab ideas that simply won't work without 100% participation. I ran for this position not only so I could plan excellent parties, but because I care about the social, academic, and moral future of our chapter. Recognize that rush isn't just about getting fun pledges. We're going to be choosing future chapter presidents and Grand Council members. The actions we take during rush will have repercussions for YEARS to come. Keep this is mind!

BEHAVE YOURSELVES ACCORDINGLY. Rushees will see you on campus. You are to uphold the principles of this sorority in public.

You WILL attend rush workshops. Rush dates are listed on the attached page. With the approval of Panhel, we'll also be able to have some informal stuff during the week. We'll discuss the details at the workshops, which you all WILL attend. No excuses!

You will join a rush interest group or I will join it for you. Once again, I need, no, REQUIRE your help getting rush together. To aid me in my quest, I've appointed a rush interest group. You know who you are. Remember to appoint your own committees to help you. Rush is everyone's responsibility and you should have no trouble finding willing volunteers. You ARE going to be a willing volunteer. Also? The rush interest group will be fun—pinky swear!

Have fun!! Rush will be a blast, especially because we'll be putting on a helluva good show for the rushees. I'll be handing out a number of awards after each party, so be on the lookout! I want all of you to ENJOY rush, not dread it. Plus, I appreciate suggestions, provided they are not stupid. (Mandy, the Little Mermaid skit is not going to happen. Get over it.)

Be positive!! I won't tolerate negativity about rush! I don't want to hear complaints that we never did it that way before. We've breaking new ground with this rush and I demand everyone have a positive attitude about it. You will be happy or I will MAKE you happy. Remember, change can be good. You will embrace it.

Thanks again for placing your trust in me. I guarantee we will have a fun and successful rush!!

Enthusiastically Yours,

Jen Lancaster, Rush Chairman

The sun is to Joanna's back, and so as she stands in front of me, all I can see is her golden outline. In a voice colored with curiosity and maybe a bit of disgust, she says, "Um . . . good morning?"

I'm sitting on the steps leading up to her off-campus apartment by the shop where they sell muffins the size of mag wheels. Since she's a fifth-year senior, she's no longer required to live at the sorority house.[118]

Good thing, too. Hers was the closest place I could think to go after I woke up. I did *not* want to be walking around campus like this. I caught a glimpse of myself in the mirror when I stopped at the muffin place. My teased hair is flat in some places and even bigger in others. Mascara is smudged so deeply under my lids I may never get it all scrubbed off. My off-the-shoulder portrait-collar black leotard now looks trashy, rather than arty, as do the big bangle bracelets I'd paired with it. And my citrus green leopard-print miniskirt? Let's just say some garments should never see the light of day. Completing the look, my gold sorority letter lavaliere and arrow charm glint in the hollow of my neck.

I stopped for a chocolate-chip muffin and hazelnut-flavored coffee, ordering them from the Mennonite lady who runs the store. She started to ask me if I needed help, then saw my necklace and gave me a wry smile. I wasn't the first morning-after girl she'd served, apparently.

Joanna knew I was coming down here this weekend. The plan was to stay with Lisa in her sorority house in the hills north of campus. The three of us were supposed to try to hook up about twelve hours ago,[119] but Harry's was beyond crowded and there was no way Joanna could have gotten back to us in the fishbowl before we left for the Wabash Yacht Club.

....

[118] Getting to live by the muffin shop is an extra bonus.

[119] I hooked up, just not with her.

There's an odd little hierarchy of desirable places to sit at Harry's, the most popular bar on campus. When I say we were in the fishbowl, I mean the big window one can only reach after heading down the long narrow part of the bar, turning the corner, and then working one's way down the west side all the way to the bay window in front. This is prime real estate because it's separated from the rest of the bar by a low wall, which can be used as seating but mostly serves to highlight who is and is not cool, at least for the evening. The glass affords the opportunity, nay the obligation, for random inebriated passers-by to thrust sweaty butt cheeks against it, to the perpetual amusement of all who are seated.

One might think this is the best seat in the house, but that's not the case. True barflies know the most desirable spot from which to see and be seen is "the fireplace seat"[120] right inside the front at the crook of the bar, no matter that it's freezing in winter and broiling anytime the air is running. Aficionados understand that this place—temperature notwithstanding—is the ideal spot to meet and greet all evening long. Plus, drink service is faster, and when the bar violates fire code—which is often—those in the good seats have an easier escape route and are far less likely to perish. So there's that.

While I sit on Joanna's steps toying with the charms on my necklace, I take in how naturally radiant she is. When we were freshmen, she'd roll out of bed, throw pants on, and go to class, whereas I'd get up an hour and a half early to shower and do my makeup. Maybe that's why I cut class all the time—too much grooming.

....

[120] Named for the long-defunct hearth that still dirties pants and coats.

Joanna's wearing a drop-waist, floral Laura Ashley dress and her hair is tucked back into a tidy ponytail. Her face is naked, save for her trademark sheer rose Clinique lip gloss. She's clutching a well-worn Bible and standing next to a cute guy with curly hair. They pulled up in his Volvo station wagon a few seconds ago.

Joanna goes to hug me, but then wrinkles her pert nose and settles for a pat on my shoulder. I may be a tad smoky. Or a tad something. Her silver arrow bracelet gets caught in my nest of hair and it takes a moment for us to untangle. "Did your party at the Playboy mansion run late?" Churchy or not, Joanna's still the master of the well-timed snarky retort.

"Let me in and give me some sweats to put on before I kill you." I turn to her companion, who's standing in stunned silence. "Hi, I'm Jen, nice to meet you." I hold out a hand adorned with chipped cherry-red nail polish.

He says, "I heard about you." Then he bids Joanna a touch-free good-bye, gets in his station wagon, and pulls away from the curb carefully but quickly.

"Who's that?" I ask as we climb her stairs.

"A guy I met at Harry's."

"Is he cool?"

She pulls a face and shrugs. "Doubtful. For our first date we went to church and then had breakfast."

I step into Joanna's bathroom to scour off a few layers of mascara and tequila. "You always say you want to date a nice guy."

She gets me a glass of water while I scrub. She sets it on the side of the sink and sits down on the edge of the tub. "He might be *too* nice, but . . . whatever. I'm more interested in what happened to you. Tell me again why you're dressed like a hooker."

"Number one, blow me. I look hot." I check myself out in the medicine cabinet mirror. Yikes. "Or rather I *looked* hot. In the dark. Now not so much."[121]

She snorts and crosses her legs. "Do go on."

"Anyway, Lisa and I were at Yacht Club then we ran into some fraternity guys and we went back to their house for an after-hours. Then we did shots. Then it all got fuzzy. Then I woke up on a pullout couch in the formal living room. And before you ask, yes, I was clothed." I take Joanna's hairbrush and try to tame my back-combed mane. A cigarette butt falls out of it as I wrestle it into an elastic band. We both pretend we don't notice while I rinse it down the sink.

Joanna talks to my reflection. "Points for being dressed. Yay, you, right?"

I glower at her. "I was sleeping next to *Dave*."

"*Dave* Dave?"

"Uh-huh."

"You *hate* Dave."

"Yeah, apparently not anymore." I snarl at my reflection. "Hey, which one of these is your toothbrush?"

She shudders. "None of them." I brush as best I can with my index finger and a squirt of Aquafresh. "You're accounted for—so what happened to Lisa?"

"Good question. She disappeared. By the way, can you drive me back to her place? All my things are there." I spit and rinse, wiping my mouth on one of Joanna's hand towels. She grabs it and stuffs it in the trash.

---

[121] I'd say I stole the look from Amy Winehouse, but she was eight at the time.

"I don't have cooties."

"You woke up next to *Dave* Dave. You might."

I consider this. "Point well taken. Anyway, can you drive me?"

"Sure. You wanna go now?"

"Nah. Let's give it a bit. Lisa lives in the Acres and it'll take her a while to do the walk of shame all the way up that hill."

"I woke up naked in a dentist's chair."

I try not to choke on my Diet Coke while I digest Lisa's statement. We're kicked back in the TV room at her sorority house on a big L-shaped couch. There are hungover girls sprawled across every surface in the room. This looks kind of like the battlefield scene from *Gone With the Wind*, except instead of Union uniforms they're all wearing Greek letters. (Also? They weren't watching MTV back then.)

After hanging out at Joanna's, I finally reconnected with Lisa around noon today. I tell her, "I woke up fully clothed next to *Dave* Dave. You win."

Lisa rakes a hand through her spiral perm. "Yeah? What's my prize?"

"Crabs?" I venture. She throws her empty plastic cup at me. "Seriously, how did you get *there*? Were you in an actual dentist's office?"

She frowns. "Jesus, no! Someone had the chair in their room at the fraternity house. Dead dentist grandfather or something along those lines."

"How did you get from just being in a room to a total state of undress?"

"How did I get *there*?" Lisa snaps. "I vaguely recall some bitch in a leopard skirt and lavaliere saying, '*Oh, come on, do another shot. What's the worst thing that could happen?*' Fortunately, Ted says it was totally platonic."

"Then what's with *the naked*?"

"He said he didn't want me to ralph on my party clothes."

"And in a fraternity full of men, not a single one had a spare T-shirt?" I ask. Lisa just shrugs. It's best not to dwell on the details.[122]

"What's the plan for the rest of the day? We gonna rally and head back to Harry's for dinner?" Lisa was a sweet, innocent math major when we first roomed together. She was just a nice kid with a penchant for big acrylic sweaters, stuffed unicorns, and Val Kilmer posters. Then I took her to her first fraternity party on Halloween. I went as a waitress and we turned her into a bunch of grapes, affixing purple balloons to a little lavender camisole and a pair of purple tap pants. Turns out when alcohol is involved, it's really fun to pop balloons and Lisa kind of ended the night in nothing but balloon shards and a skimpy set of underwear. Um . . . sorry?

Although I may not have been the world's best influence, here's the thing—you can only corrupt those who are open to corruption. Besides, her life's totally more fun now.[123]

"Nope, gotta head home. I've got my chapter meeting tonight. Hey, did I tell you I was elected rush chairman?"

....

[122] On the plus side, no one's heard of the Internet yet so no worries of photos showing up on Ted's Facebook page.

[123] Not sure her grades are so great, though.

Lisa whips around to face me and she suddenly turns quite pale. *"No!"*

"What *'No!'*? I'll be great at running rush. I've got a ton of ideas and I'm super-enthusiastic about them." Need I remind anyone I was elected Best Rusher? Unconsciously, my hand goes to touch my necklace.

Lisa lies back down and braces herself like the room suddenly got spinny. And then she mumbles, "May God have mercy on them all."

To All My Lovely Sisters!

Here's the quick and dirty on some new rush rules.

Amendment to Jen's Rules for a Supercool Rush

Yes, everyone is expected to help set up for rush. EVERYONE. Our decorations are elaborate and we need all hands on deck for the construction. If you think I'm hanging 1,000 stars from the ceiling myself, you're freaking crazy. And you haven't been paying attention.

You WILL know all the words to all the songs. There is no excuse not to know them, barring, like, a brain tumor or something. And when you're singing, you are representing your spirit in your sorority. Not knowing the words makes us look like amateurs. THERE IS NO SEX IN THE CHAMPAGNE ROOM AND THERE IS NO BAD SINGING IN

SORORITY RUSH. Feel free to practice the tunes in the shower if that's what you need to do to improve. I'll be handing out awards for the best and most enthusiastic songstress. Lyric sheets have been placed in each of your mailboxes. Understand I WILL be watching you.

Adhere to the dress code. Period. If this is problematic, borrow from your sisters. If your sisters find this problematic, talk to me.

Please pay extra-special attention to your grooming. Ideally, I'd like to see every woman in blush, mascara, and lipstick, at the bare minimum. Obviously we don't want to present ourselves as something we're not, but we do want to make the very best impression. Use of basic cosmetics will show rushees we care about looking nice for them. This isn't an outrageous request and I'll not take your flack about it.

Check your 'tude at the door. Rush is a stressful time and often tempers and patience can run short. Let's all work together to keep our bad attitudes away from rush parties. The rushees don't need to know we were all up 'til four a.m. with the selection process. As far as they're concerned, we're having pajama parties, not violent arguments.

Again, never ~~forget~~ that rush is FUN. We get to give the gift of membership to others! The rush interest group will be working to keep your spirits up with special treats and awards! Your positive attitude WILL be noticed ... and rewarded!

Pi Love and Mine,

Jen Lancaster, Rush Chairman

P.S. Never forget you are a reflection of this chapter—conduct yourselves with grace and dignity everywhere you go!

P.P.S. I expect whichever jokester glued a Hitler mustache on my composite photo will remove it IMMEDIATELY.

"Hey, Trix? It's Jen. Can you do me a quick favor? I'm going to be late to the meeting tonight and I need you to have the rush interest groups get together. . . . Yeah, yeah, rough weekend. . . . You'll die when I tell you the story. . . . Short version? A bunch of my fraternity guy friends kidnapped me and made me go on walkout with them. . . . I'm actually calling you from a pay phone somewhere between Champaign-Urbana and Fort Wayne. . . . I know, crazy, right? Totally fun. Except when I had to use the men's room. . . . Yeah, well, maybe I thought the urinals could have also been planters or something. . . . Whatever, tell them I'll be there. . . . Uh-huh, *definitely* tell them I'll be watching them. Bye!"

Ladies,

Oh, dear. Oh, dear, oh, dear, oh, dear. It pains me to
have to instruct you all this way. But after the way
our preliminary party went, I've no choice but to give
this gentle reminder about courtesy. Believe me,
you'll be saying, "Thank you, Jen!" when our next
event rolls around.

Yet Another Amendment to
Jen's Rules for a Supercool Rush

First impressions are CRUCIAL, so make them count!
Introduce your sister so you show that you are proud
of her. Perhaps try to include something the rushee
has in common during the introduction, like, "This is
Amy—she's a bio major, too!" Please never let me
hear you squeal, "Ohmigod, I think the Sig Eps are
total douchehounds, too!" There is no douchehound
in sorority rush. Say it again and fines will be as-
sessed.

Mention the rushee's name early and often. Try to
remember it so you don't have to keep looking at her
name tag. Stare at her chest too much and she'll
worry you're assessing the size of her rack. Not cool.
If you don't remember her name later (UNACCEPT-
ABLE), then just say hello. Again, do not crane your
neck to check out her tag. Be subtle.

Express an interest in your rushee's topic of conversation. She is NOT boring, she's nervous. Try to remember what it was like when you were rushing. Give her plenty of positive feedback. Smile sincerely. Again, I'll be watching.

Your rushee is your first and ONLY responsibility. Never ignore her to check out more interesting conversation in other groups.[124] Stay with your rushee as long as you are responsible for her. Pretend she's the ocean and never turn your back on her.

Maintain good eye contact. However, keep in mind there's a thin line separating a friendly, encouraging glance from the piercing glower of the psychopath. Mandy, knock it off or you WILL pull kitchen duty.

Serve the rushee first at the buffet or the table. You are the hostess. And God help you if you don't eat, too. Do NOT make them feel uncomfortable if they choose to indulge in our delish sugar cookies.

Last impressions LAST. Their last impression is just as important as the first. Give your rushee complete attention until she is out the door, which you will have escorted her to. Say good-bye with a big smile, but not so big that she worries you're glad she's gone,

---

[124] Discussing how I barfed on my date at the Screw-Your-Sister mixer does not constitute "interesting conversation."

MANDY,

Don't forget, your good attitude is contagious!

Yours in the bonds of wine and silver blue,

Jen Lancaster, Rush Chairman

P.S. My eyes are on you.

P.P.S. If I ever hear you say, "I've got to pass you off to someone else now," I will kick you so hard your babies come out naked.

Lisa,

The fact you've heard about my rush reputation in an entirely different sorority at a school a hundred miles away only serves to prove how good I am at it.

Let them all learn something from me, why don't they?

Jen

Ahem, Ladies,

Yes, did you hear that? It was the sound of me sighing. LOUDLY. I mean, really, have we all forgotten how to have a polite conversation, really? Do I have to reiterate that no matter how good our skits, songs, and décor are (major snaps to Trix!), the rushees will remember what we said the most? It's imperative that we make every word count because we've only got so much time. So here goes:

Seriously, Another Amendment to Jen's Rules for a Supercool Rush

You must effectively communicate unless you WANT to lose all our favorite girls to the Delta Gammas. You guys? They read from <u>The Velveteen Rabbit</u> at their last party. Christ, we should be able to beat them by selecting passages from the book about the babysitting Rottweiler. The bar has not been set that high! We can do this!

Be yourself! Let the rushees get to know the real you, because you don't want them to join based on the false persona you present to them. Never forget they're more nervous than you. Make it your job to put them at ease. Be natural! Remember that you're making new friends, like, for life, or at least until graduation or when you transfer back to the main campus.

Try a number of conversational topics with your rushee. Find the one she's most interested in and go from there. Ask open-ended questions, rather than yep-and-nope questions. Be sure to be an active listener! But don't be afraid of silence. Also, not every girl will make it into our house so we don't want to make them DIE for something they won't have.

Don't oversell us. We don't want to present ourselves in a false light. This sorority is a lifetime commitment and we want them to join us for who we are, not who we say we are.

Now that we've gotten that out of the way, please complete this phrase: "Now when you go up yonder to see the heavenly view / Saint Peter will run to greet us and say, 'You'll surely do! / You've sisters more who've come before _____ '"

Don't know the answer? THEN REVIEW YOUR BOOKLET OF FORMAL RUSH SONGS. (Don't you want the best songstress award?)

Pi Love and Mine,

Jen Lancaster, Rush Chairman

P.S. You know what? Introducing me as "Pol Pot" made those rushees feel really uncomfortable. They thought the Khmer Rouge was a party they'd missed. Say it again and fines will be levied.

P.P.S. I'll be awarding a gold lavaliere and arrow charm to whoever best embodies all the principles

of a successful rush. You know you want it—so work
for it.

Audra,

If you find out who started the "Free at Last, Free
at Last" chant after the final rush party, please let
me know.

Heads will roll.

Jen

Dénouement

(Gold Lavaliere, Part Three)

My eyes fly open.

What the—?

Where am I?

I reach out into the darkness and feel a wall. It's cold with smooth tiles. I try to find a place to grip, but it's too flat and glossy.

Am I in jail?

If so, then why is it pitch black? Aren't prisoners always complaining about the fluorescent lights, how they're never off? And how they provide a low-frequency buzz that quickly becomes maddening?

When I shift, I realize I'm wedged into a small space.

Am I dead?

Is this my coffin? There's something pressing down on the left side of my body. Is it the weight of the earth?

But, wait, if I were in a coffin, wouldn't someone have given me a little silk pillow at least? And why is it so cold?

And if I were dead, would my knee still hurt? And would I be . . . hungover? Did I drink so much last night that my hangover followed me into the afterlife? Is that possible?

I'll be honest, I thought my postlife would be hotter. Figured there'd be a bit more brimstone and fire. Maybe a roomful of people (mostly attorneys if all those jokes are to be believed) shoveling coal for all eternity while a red-horned guy beat them with a cat-o'-nine-tails?

But this?

Right here?

Maybe this is purgatory. Cold, dark, smooth, solid purgatory.

Although . . . I swear I hear snoring. Why would there be snoring in purgatory?

Before I can contemplate any more about the afterlife or my own demise, the whole room is suddenly flooded with light and I am blinded.

I hear my friend Suede shout, "Get out of the tub, you fucking morons!" and then the door slams.

Oh.

That makes more sense.

When my eyes adjust, I see that I'm crammed into a giant Victorian bathtub with my friend Garrison from my brother's fraternity. My shoes are missing, but other than that everything seems to be intact. I'm still wearing a sweater, walking shorts, and a pair of plaid tights. They have big holes in the middle and my knees are a bloody mess. That explains the pain.

Garrison begins to wake up. "Fuck, what *is* that?" he asks, pawing at his throat. He extracts a small gold arrow charm that has somehow gotten lodged in his neck. "Yours?"

"Thanks." I take off my necklace so I can reattach the charm to its tiny golden hoop. "Sorry about that."

"Why are we in a tub?" he asks.

"Don't know."

"Where are we?" He rubs the sleep out of his eyes and scans our surroundings.

"Maybe Suede's house?" That would explain the yelling, at least.

He nods quietly. "Huh. Hey, are you freezing?"

"Yes."

He smiles, showing the small dimple on his right cheek. "I can fix that." With one swift tug, he yanks down the shower curtain and pulls it over us like a blanket. "I'm going back to sleep. You in?"

"Um, I think I'll try to find my shoes and maybe my purse. I've got to get out of here. Good to see you though." I give him a quick kiss and extricate myself from the tub, only slightly stumbling as I get up.

"Gonna be around at Harry's later?"

"Can't—I've got a double shift tomorrow and I've got to get back for chapter tonight. I'm on a committee and we have an important meeting—"

He bolts straight up. "Oh, God, you're not still running rush are you?"

Why does everyone keep asking me that?

"No, no, that ended a while ago. Now I've got an interesting position. I didn't actually run for it—I kind of got it by default since I'm the only senior member who doesn't currently hold office."

"Yeah? What are you doing?"

"Well, I'm the chairman of our chapter's Morality Board, which means I—"

Garrison doesn't let me complete my sentence. "You? Jen Lancaster? With *Dave* Dave? Morality Board? *Chairman?*"

"Yeah, and we've had a pledge who's really been behaving badly. I've got to head to a meeting to discuss what we're—" I can't finish what I'm saying because Garrison is laughing too hard. Five minutes later, he's still sputtering and choking, slapping the sides of the tub. I turn on the faucet and run out the bathroom door.

Now, where could my shoes be?

To the Ladies of Indiana Eta,

Here's a carbon copy of the release letter we gave to our now ex-pledge Danielle this evening.

It is with great regret that we must release you from your pledgeship. Please understand when you wear our letters, you're representing every one of us. Your actions as an individual reflect on us as a group. Therefore, we've come to the consensus that your salacious comments at the Phi Kap party cannot be excused.

Please return your pin to your pledge educator. We will return this month's dues to you via mail. We

appreciate your commitment to our organization and
are deeply sorry as to how it all worked out.

With Kind Regards,

Jen Lancaster, Chairman

By the way, to all my sisters whom I love so much
and yet who continue to put me in positions of power
despite your very legitimate concerns it may go to my
head? To paraphrase Otter when Flounder found out
they wrecked his car: You fucked up. You trusted me.

XO,

Jen

Part Three

The Nineties

We Need a Montage

(A Variety of Stained Aprons)

Hey, Joanna,

Thanks for the letter of recommendation, but I'm not going to affiliate with our sorority now that I'm back on campus.[125] I'm sorry if you're bummed, but you don't even live here anymore! Plus, I'm sort of ready to move on.

Regardless, I'm delighted to be out of my parents' house and in my own apartment FINALLY. My dad said I'm foolish to waste the money living on campus when I

---

[125] Even though I'm already a member, *the best* house would have to vote on me if I wanted to live in their house.

could continue to live at home for free, but trust me, it's worth it. I don't care if I have to work full-time and can only take one class per semester; I am never living at home again.

Dad said if I wanted to return to campus, I wasn't taking one of his automobiles. So, now I'm the (not terribly) proud owner of a Toyota Tercel. Dad agreed to cosign, but he said items like radios and air-conditioning were "luxuries," so he only let me get the most basic model ever made. I don't even have a side-view mirror on the right-hand side of the car.

When the salesman took me through the car, he showed me how to work the windshield wipers and how to roll down the windows. Then he gave it a once-over and said, "Yeah. That's pretty much all it does. Oh, and drive safe. This thing'll shatter like a jelly glass if you get hit." Wow, way to earn your Salesman of the Month plaque, dude.

In other news, I switched my major to political science! Dad laughed at me and told me I'd never get a job, but I'm determined to prove him wrong.

See you at Homecoming!

Jen

Dear First Floor Back Unit,

It has come to my attention that you have installed
a dart board. I know this because you've placed it on
the wall right next to the head of my bed.

I'm asking you nicely to relocate the dart board to
an outside wall because it's very hard to sleep when
every three seconds I hear THUNK, THUNK, THUNK 'til
the wee hours of the morning.

Also, I have a number of early classes. From your
late-night darts and pot-smoking schedule, I gather
you do not. Should you not want me to crank George
Michael every morning in an effort to wake you up
before I go-go, I suggest you knock it the fuck off.

Your neighbor,

Jen

P.S. You completely suck at darts.

P.P.S. I won't narc on you. But I may kick you until
you're dead if I ever hear darts again.

CAMPUS DEVELOPMENT REALTY

February 5, 1995

Miss Lancaster,

Please remit rent for the first floor front unit on Salisbury Street immediately. This is the third time we've had to remind you to pay in a timely fashion in as many months. Should you continue to not be able to meet your obligations, we will have to take further action.

Also, when the maintenance crew had to enter your dwelling last month, they noticed there were not only cats, but also an additional person living in your apartment. Neither of these is permitted by your lease and we expect you to remedy these situations immediately.

Cordially,

Ellen Foster, Manager

Dear Campus Development Realty, Inc.,

Enclosed please find my check for March rent for the first floor front unit on Salisbury Street.

I realize it's a couple of days late but I imagine you're going to let this slide without a late fee or a lecture, considering I had to involve a television news crew last month just to get you people to provide the heat that's <u>supposed</u> to be included in my rent.

The reporter left me her card and told me to call if I had ANY other issues. I'm confident that I won't. (Did I mention I'm pretty sure she's angling for a local Emmy for investigative reporting?)

By the way, I trust that neither my frequently visiting boyfriend nor the cats who aren't listed on my lease won't be, you know, an <u>issue</u>.

Best,

Jen Lancaster

Hey, Fletch!

Didn't want to wake you before I leave for class! I forgot to tell you last night that I brought you some jambalaya and it's in the fridge. Enjoy!

By the way, a whole bunch of football players came in and sat in my section. They kept telling me how cute my legs looked in my shorts and I kind of felt like Anita Hill. Finally, I told the guys if they could clutch a ball like they clutched my butt, maybe we'd win a damn bowl game for once. They didn't laugh. (All the other waitresses did, though.)

When I complained to the owner, he was all, "If they pat you on the ass, take it as a compliment." So I totally overcharged them for beers and I made almost $200!

Dinner's on me tonight!

XO,

Jen

Mom,

Thank you for sending me <u>Brides</u> magazine . . . and <u>Modern Brides</u> . . . and <u>Elegant Brides</u> . . . and <u>Martha Stewart Weddings</u>. And thank you for dog-earing all the pages you find relevant.

As soon as I meet someone who's actually getting married, I'll be sure to pass them along to her.

Love,

Jen

P.S. <u>Brideshead Revisited</u> is not a book about wedding veils, just so you know.

You Sank My Battleship

(Navy Suit, Part One)

"You look very stylish," my mother assures me as I gaze warily at myself in the three-way mirror.

I glower, saying nothing.

She continues, growing more and more excited as she picks and pulls at me, tugging on cuffs and straightening seams. "Very professional but also quite chic. I think this is it! I think this is the one!"

I knit my brows and purse my lips. I am *not* buying what she's selling.

Perhaps I'd be quicker to believe my mother's sartorial assessment if she weren't currently clad in a peasant blouse circa 1981 and Birkenstocks paired with reinforced-toe pantyhose. Mind you, this is the woman who refuses to donate the clothes I wore in high school and college to Goodwill, insisting they're still good.

Do you know how disconcerting it is to see an almost sixty-year-old woman running around the grocery store wearing a piece of Sigma Phi Epsilon *A Roll in the Hay* barn dance swag?

Or a neon green T-shirt that reads *"I Stand on My Head for Surf Fetish"*?[126]

Don't get me wrong, I love my mom, but her fashion tips come from *Prevention* magazine. And this is the woman who wore ponchos for *years* after they went out of style. To this day, I remember when she decided her bulky hand-knit model was too hot, so she tried to pull it off while driving on the expressway. Of course it got stuck on her head and I spent thirty seconds seething over how I wasn't going to live long enough to see *Escape from Witch Mountain*.

Ponchos were her coat of choice when she'd strap me on the back of her bike and pedal us to her guitar lesson, the case of her Yamaha banging me in the head while I spat out the scratchy poncho fringe that pelted me in the mouth. One time a breeze blew the front over her head and we wiped out while flying down a huge hill on our street.

Point? Anna Wintour, she's not.[127]

At the moment I'm modeling a double-breasted navy blue suit with silver-dollar-sized brass buttons embossed with anchors. The suit is too long in the sleeves and the skirt ends at that special place about midcalf that ensures maximum stumpiness. An ancient, powder-puff-haired salesclerk has paired said suit with a

---

[126] Granted, she looks really good for her age. But come on—seeing your mom in terry-cloth, *Three's Company*-style booty shorts is just *wrong*.

[127] I still blame ponchos for my fear of motion. Acoustic guitars, too.

short-sleeve white blouse trimmed in gold piping. I look less like I'm getting ready for my first real job interview and more like I'm about to welcome a foreign dignitary onto the bridge of my aircraft carrier. All aboard the SS *Frumpy*!

"Lovely!" the salesclerk coos in agreement. When she exhales in this close little room, I can smell the menthol of her lozenge.

I spin around again, noting how the jacket completely conceals my hourglass figure. I'm cut off at the hips and I look far wider than I actually am. The skirt is too tight around my midriff and the waistband bisects my stomach into two separate rolls. The skirt has some pleats at the top and it flattens my butt completely.

No, that's not true.

I do still have a butt—but thanks to poor tailoring, it's simply been moved to the front, giving me an ass-belly. What I'm wearing right now is the mom-jeans equivalent of a skirt. The blouse is just that—blousy—and tents, rather than drapes, over my torso.

Yeah, *lovely*.

I continue to scowl, saying nothing.

"Wait!" The clerk snaps her brittle fingers. "I have the perfect touch!" She dashes out of the fitting area and returns moments later with a long scrap of fabric. Given her advanced years, I'm surprised at how quickly she moves. Before I can even blink, she's grabbed me and tied a giant plaid bow around my neck like a big, horrible birthday present.

I see the now-complete outfit, bathed in the sickly green glow of the overhead fluorescent lights.

Oh, the humanity.

"Do you love it?" my mother asks.

I'm speechless. Seriously? If this is how I have to dress to get a real job, maybe I'd rather waitress when I move to Chicago. That way if I have to put on an ugly outfit for work, people will understand I'm not doing it voluntarily. This suit makes me nostalgic for what I wore to my first job at Hardee's—a zipped brown and orange polyester tunic, matching pants, and mushroom-shaped cap. Not only did that outfit fit me, but I got to eat as many fresh-baked cookies as I could steal at that job.

"You look so elegant!" the clerk agrees.

"Why don't we ask Fletch what he thinks?" I finally suggest after a long moment of stunned silence. I exit the fitting room and find Fletch on a rigid ladder-back chair at the side of the store, reading a magazine.

Fletch and I have been together for almost two years now. We had a ton of mutual friends but didn't meet until we started working together at a new restaurant on campus. I never minded that he made terrible drinks. He felt that if customers were paying for cocktails, they should taste the liquor, not the mixer. Whenever patrons asked for an ice-cream-based drink, he'd tell them the blender was broken. No one served up a big glass of surly like Fletch.[128]

He got a kick out of how much my customers disliked me, too. In my defense, when I go out to eat, I want to hear if the onion rings are beer battered and not if my server's cat has an ear infection. My job is to get your food to the table as quickly as possible and my concern is whether or not you need more coffee, so if you want to chat? Go to a therapist.

....

[128] Of course he was in a fraternity. President and founder of his chapter!

Fletch surprised me by seamlessly integrating himself into my life. One minute I was single and happy and having a blast with my friends, and the next I was happy and having a blast with my friends, only with a really terrific guy at my side. Plus, he's nice to my cats. How people treat pets is my litmus test. I could give a shit if you bark at bar patrons, but you'd better make with the belly rubs and chin scratches the second they're demanded of you. He totally does.

Since we've been together, we've acquired two more cats.[129] My brother's super-vicious cat Bones came to stay with us while he and his wife attended a wedding. The second Bones had other cats to boss around, he became a perfect (barely biting) gentleman. A few months later Fletch spotted Ranger, an itty-bitty marmalade kitty, in a parking garage after a night class. He came home and got me and we spent an hour coaxing her out of the bushes and into our lives. I figured anyone who'd take the time to love and nurture a creature who's primarily going to hiss, scratch, and barf for no good reason is kind of my perfect match.

I'm so happy Fletch was able to tag along on this shopping expedition, coming all the way over to Fort Wayne for the day, especially given his work schedule. He graduated in December and got his first real job in February. He's been living up in the Chicago suburbs since then. The plan is for me to move in with him next month, providing I can get a job after graduation. I'm not so sure I'll ace my interview with the Great Plains HMO dressed like Admiral Halsey.

....

129 A boyfriend is the deciding factor between "compassionate about animals" and "crazy cat lady."

I approach Fletch and once I have his attention, I twirl. "What do you think? Should I burn it or bury it?"

Fletch opens his mouth, and gasps fishlike for a couple of seconds. After a telling pause, he finally replies, "Does Captain Steubing know you're not on the Lido deck right now?"

"It really *is* that bad, isn't it?" I ask flatly. What sucks is I've been shopping all day and this is the closest I've come to finding anything that fits. Size-wise, I'm somewhere in between regular and plus and nothing is cut for my shape. I need to either lose or gain twenty pounds.[130]

As soon as we're done here, Fletch and I are supposed to caravan to Chicago. I want to be up there tonight so I can do a practice run into the city tomorrow before my interview. The problem is if I don't find something appropriate to wear, I'm not going anywhere. Tears begin to well in the corner of my eyes.

Fletch jumps up and gently puts his arm around me. "No, no, we can work with this. Blue suits are classic, neutral. That's why they're a staple. Hmm . . ." He assesses me again. "Lose the bow. Tell the saleslady to return it to 1982, where it belongs. Maybe you can put some nice jewelry with the outfit to make it look more . . . *you*." He kisses me on the forehead.

For the first time today, I smile. He really does understand how to make everything better. As I sail back to the fitting room, he calls, "Please tell Isaac I'd like a piña colada."

Aarrgh.

I return to find my mother and the clerk beaming in anticipa-

---

[130] Guess which one I eventually choose?

tion. I sigh. "Fine. Wrap it up, I'll take it . . . as soon as we swap out this stupid bow for some fake pearls."

❖

Despite wearing an ill-fitting outfit and getting a little lost[131] on the way, my interview goes well. I spend close to two hours with the hiring manager asking detailed questions, although I'm still in the dark as to what the job entails. I'm concentrating so hard on sending out *Hire me!* vibes that I don't absorb everything she's saying in regard to specific job duties. Something about doctors and credentials and data entry? Who cares—it pays $24,000 and that is a fortune!

I've never had a professional interview before; this chatty, friendly, back-and-forth thing wasn't what I'd expected. For years my professors warned me about how cutthroat the business world is and how interviewers want nothing more than to trip you up by asking you trick questions all rapid-fire to determine if you can handle pressure, and of course they love hosting these interviews in a restaurant specifically to see if you do stuff like salt your food before tasting it, because that means you're impulsive and no one wants to hire an impulsive person, when honestly that's kind of bullshit, because what if you're just someone who really likes salt?

What do you suppose it means if you pepper your food first? Is that impulsive, too? Are all those guys in the fancy restaurants with the table-leg pepper grinders there solely as a way to mess with potential employees out for a meal with prospective

---

[131] Deeply, profoundly.

employers? Is the whole restaurant industry in on this evil plan? If so, why didn't anyone tell me? I'd have played along.

Honestly, this interview isn't any harder than any of the job applications I've had before now. Actually, it's easier because there's no math[132] and I don't have to remember what wine pairs best with halibut. My conversation with Jill strikes me as being more along the lines of questions you'd answer sitting on the couch with Katie Couric, not across the table from Donald Trump. (Need I remind you I've been ready for my television debut for years?)

I manage to impress Jill enough to score an interview with her staff. Woo hoo! Thankfully it's over the phone, so I don't have to put on my stupid sailor suit to talk to them.

I also won't be distracted by the view, like I was when sitting across from Jill. My potential new office is on the twentieth floor, right off the Chicago River. What would it be like to go to work every day in a giant glass skyscraper? The morning of my interview was all misty and the clouds began right above where I was standing. How surreal would it be to sit at my desk and look straight into a cloud?

How would it feel to witness a lightning storm from three hundred feet up in the air? Or, when it's clear, to watch the architectural tour boats slowly cruising out toward the lake? I bet the out-of-towners who pay to take those tours wonder who's in the big buildings. They'll catch a glimpse of someone in the window and think to themselves, *What's their story? Where'd they come from?* If I get this job, the people tourists wonder about will be

----

[132] I brought a calculator just in case.

me. I bet no one's ever curious about who their waitress is or how she got there. There's something about working with food that screams *I make bad choices.*

I want this position. I want this life. I want clouds. I want river. I want my apron neatly folded up, forgotten in a drawer in the kitchen. And I'll do my best to charm and cajole and say all the right things in my fight to get it.

I'm told I'm up against another candidate who lives in California. She flew herself out on her own dime for the interview. Honey, if you have the means to buy your own plane ticket, that simply proves you're not nearly as desperate for this job as I am. Heck, I had to borrow money from my mom to pay for parking and a full tank of gas.

My phone rings and I am *on* from the second I pick up the receiver. Everyone on the team seems funny and nice, except for one guy named Chuck, who grills me on why I'd want to work at an insurance company when I majored in political science.

Pfft. I can give you 24,000 good reasons, pal.

At no point do I mention the college placement office has no openings for political science grads. No one knows this is my only shot right now.

I do my best to demonstrate my affability[133] and my problem-solving skills. I try to smile so hard they feel it through the phone line. I pull out every stop.

An hour after my team chat, Jill calls to offer me the position. I got it!

A *real* job in a Chicago skyscraper right on the river! From my

---

[133] Shut up, I can be affable. I can be anything for $24,000.

first interview! Me, Jen Lancaster, Queen of the C students! My *Hire me* vibes worked!

I flop down on the mattress in the corner of my dingy studio apartment and try to wrap my mind around the news. I'm going to be a *professional*. The white-collar (gold-piped) world just invited me to join their ranks. I'm shocked. I'm awed. Part of me believed I'd have to wait tables for the rest of my life but I guess not.

Wow . . . no more aprons. No more black Reeboks and health-department-mandated ponytails and clear nail polish. No more balancing heavy trays full of filthy dishes on my shoulder or hitting the panic button when I get seated with four new tables at once. No more being screamed at for accidentally bringing ranch and not bleu cheese dressing because it looks exactly alike and I can't smell the difference and no one will let me stir in a drop of blue food coloring even though I guarantee it would distinguish them nicely.[134]

Sure, I won't end the day with a handful of cash. On the other hand, I won't have to play rent roulette because these checks will be consistent. How much I make won't depend on the weather or what ballgame is being played across town or if O. J. Simpson takes off in a white Bronco and my tables never turn the whole night because everyone's glued to the television you can only see in my section.[135]

I'm not going to end the workday smelling of French fries and the fish special.[136] I'll probably never have to brush bacon bits out

---

[134] I agree that no one wants to eat blue food. But blue condiments? Genius!

[135] That douche cost me about $80!

[136] Much to the cats' chagrin.

of my hair or soak my bra to remove iced tea stains again. If a co-worker propositions me, I can take it up with Human Resources. I won't have to pretend to flirt back because if I don't, he'll "forget" to cook the well-done steak for table nineteen. And I'll never have a customer accuse me of being "unfriendly" again.[137]

I'm so excited that I don't mind having to start work the Monday after my Friday graduation because my official salary is $24,500. I am going to be *so fucking rich*! It's all swimmin' pools and movie stars from here on out.

---

[137] It's not that I don't care how my customers' day has gone. It's just that I don't want to hear about it. Okay, that's a lie. I truly don't care.

Just the Fax, Ma'am

(Navy Suit, Part Two)

"*I* can't believe you're graduating. I can't believe it!" My mother has a tendency to say everything twice when she's excited, which isn't annoying at all.[138]

It's the night of my ceremony and I'm dining at the restaurant where I worked my last shift yesterday. Walking in here wearing a dress and not an apron tonight has been surreal. I'm seated at a prime table in the back with Fletch, my best friend Andy, and my parents. I specifically requested we sit as far away from the fireplace as possible. Even when it's July and eighty-five degrees outside, patrons can't see a hearth without wanting the accompanying fire, so that section is perpetually stifling. I

....

[138] At all.

tell customers, "Yeah, I can turn on the gas and light the fire, but I'm going to sweat in your food." They laugh, but I'm never kidding.

Tonight, I'm uncomfortable for an entirely different reason. Mom is all sausage-eyed on her second glass of Harveys Bristol Cream and she's already starting to gush and hold my hand. I am having none of it.

"My baby! You came out of my body! My baby! I can't believe my baby is graduating from college!" she enthuses.

For the record? I have *never* been her baby. In fact, I reject the notion of coming out of her body. I prefer to believe I was hatched, or perhaps purchased.

My father sips his Johnnie Walker Black neat and stifles an eye roll. "Well, you did have eleven years to get used to the idea, Julia."

Andy's all done up in a pastel pink T-shirt and unstructured linen jacket. Sure, it's 1996, and yes, he's totally channeling Don Johnson. Andy tends to find a look and stick with it, which I imagine makes shopping easier.[139] He nudges my dad. "That reminds me. Ron, you owe me a five spot." Dad takes the money out of the same thick brown leather wallet he's had my entire life and they shake hands.

"What was *that* for?" I ask. "You're not actually paying him for all the smokes, are you?" Andy brings a couple of extra packs of Marlboro Lights every time he visits because my father is the ultimate mooch. Dad smoked regularly until the late eighties, but none of us knew it because he never actually bought them for him-

---

[139] His George Michael phase rocked.

self. I question his rationale here. Cancer can't catch you if there's no paper trail?

"Andy won the over-under spread on your graduation date," Dad tells me.

I turn to Fletch. "Do you believe this shit?"

Fletch is all dapper in his interview suit. He shakes his head. "I don't."

I feel vindicated by his support. I can always count on Fletch. He's my rock, my fortress, my strength. "*Thank* you, honey."

Fletch places his arm around me. "Yep, I had you down for twelve."

My dining companions laugh appreciatively and before I can remind them exactly who got a 4.0 this semester,[140] my friend Meghan comes around with a whipped-cream-topped shot glass. This is the fifth round I've received tonight. My buddies in the restaurant aren't congratulating me so much as trying to see how liquored up they can get me before I cross the stage to pick up my diploma.

Oh, no. I've had eleven years to make a drunken ass out of myself on this campus. Tonight merits sobriety.

I've passed every shot to the guys. So far they've all been lemon drops or kamikazes, made with clear liquors. Neither of them wants the frothy combination of Baileys and Cool Whip comingling with their beers.

"What is that?" my mom asks, trying to focus. She's a little slurry, too. This aggravates me. How much money could I have

---

[140] Taking advanced French, philosophy, and three upper-level poli-sci courses, you assholes.

saved over the years if I'd have inherited the kind of system that got buzzed on two small girly drinks? I try to ignore her question but she pokes me and asks again.

Wearily, I reply, "It's a shot."

"What kind?"

"It's just a shot."

"Why was Meghan giggling when she brought it?" Ha, ha, ha, yes, you're hilarious, Meghan. Serve me a *b-l-o-w j-o-b* right in front of my parents, why don't you?

"Don't worry about it," I say dismissively.

"What's it called?" she persists. Sometimes it feels like my mom is a humiliation-seeking missile. She rejects the fact that I'm modest and that we're not best friends. She's always trying to nudge me outside of my comfort zone so we can be closer, but all this does is push me further away. If I had a dollar for every time she tried to engage me in a conversation about sex, I wouldn't have to worry about taking a professional job.

My friend Andy senses my discomfort at this line of questioning. And then exploits it. "It's called a blow job, Julie."

Everyone cracks up, except for me, because I'm too busy dying ten million embarrassed deaths. Eventually our entrées come and provide a needed distraction. The shot continues to sit next to my glass of iced tea, its fake whipped cream remaining erect as we eat. Or, in my mother's case, drinks and forgets to eat—as she's also wont to do when she's excited—and pesters me with questions.

"*Why* is it called a blow job?"

This? Right here? Is why I've been so anxious to move to Chicago. I hiss, "It just *is*." At this point, Meghan delivers another one. Hate.

"They call it that because of how you drink it. See, you're not allowed to use your hands; you have to use your mouth." Andy goes on to explain every intimate detail of how to deep throat the shot while I excuse myself to hit the washroom. I'm not sure why I'm surprised. He, too, enjoys watching me squirm. One time on a ski trip Andy spent half an hour engaging my mother in conversation about how porn stars keep their lipstick perfect during, um, action scenes.[141]

I stop in the bar and demand that everyone stop sending me shots, and by the time I return to my table, there are three more waiting for me.

I am getting all new friends the minute I hit Chicago.

Andy's been goading my mother to down the shot the whole time I've been yelling at bartenders. As soon as I sit down, my mother positions the glass, throws her shoulders forward and clasps her fingers behind her back, and then goes for it. Andy cheers, Fletch chokes, and my father signals for the check.

"Was it good for you, Julie?" Andy asks. I am *so* going to call Tubbs right now and we are both going to slap the Don Johnson-y stubble right off his face.

My mom wipes the excess whipped cream with a napkin. "Not bad!"

Just when I think the evening can't get any more mortifying, my mother leans in and conspiratorially whispers, "But *I've* had the real thing."

Were I to even contemplate what she may have meant by this statement, I'd curl up in the fetal position and rock back and

----

141 Lip liner.

forth for the remainder of my life. As it is, I spend the rest of my graduation night suffering from hysterical deafness.[142]

❖

Fletch works in a call center doing benefits administration for a consulting company. Much of his job entails listening to retirees call him with pension questions while they're on the toilet. Who knew seniors were such multitaskers? This isn't exactly where he pictured himself after graduation. He hates what he's doing. At least once a day he has to explain to a recent widow that her spouse elected the higher benefit rate, meaning he'd get more cash while alive, but the second he passed away, his pension ended. Fletch says at first it was heartbreaking, but four months into the job, he's just mad that none of the widows read the paperwork they had to sign when their husbands elected this option in the first place. Every time his callers flush, a piece of his compassion goes down the u-bend, too.

His shifts rotate at the call center. Sometimes he goes in at seven a.m., but this week he's on the ten a.m. crew, so he's still asleep while I get ready for my first big day. Probably a good thing, too. I've been driving him nuts for the past twenty-four hours rehashing exactly how I take the Metra commuter rail to get to the city to get to the office. I already have the train schedule memorized. I figure I live a ten-minute drive away from the station, so I plan to leave forty-five minutes early. Can't be too careful, right?

I'm so tense when I get down to my car that I'm trembling while I wipe the dew from my windshield. I adjust my mirrors and double-check everything in my *Always Prepared* tote bag—keys to

....

[142] And it's also why I begin to twitch every time I see a cap and gown.

this apartment plus the one I still have at school because I couldn't get out of my lease, two shades of lipstick, extra sunglasses, pressed powder, a tube of concealer, a book, a magazine in case I finish the book, a bagged lunch, salt and pepper in case there isn't any in the lunchroom, pepper spray, peppermints, a train schedule, a second train schedule, a third train schedule in case anything unfortunate happens to the first two train schedules, cream and black and neutral pantyhose, clear nail polish in case I run all three extra pairs, an umbrella, mittens in case of a cold snap, socks in case I lose the mittens, a sewing kit, Band-Aids, tampons, a pen, a pencil and a legal pad in case they don't have any in the office, a framed picture of my parents' dog Nixon because I love him, and one extra brass-anchor button in case anything pops off my stupid navy suit. Okay, I'm ready.

I turn on the car and drive out of our apartment complex. Then I drive back in because I realize I forgot to lock the front door. When I get back in the apartment, I notice my wallet lying on the counter next to the fruit bowl. Dumbass. How would I have paid for my train ticket without it? Spare socks? I smooth my navy skirt over my ass-belly, kiss Fletch good-bye again, and dash back to my car.

While driving toward the train station I miss my exit the first pass because I take the sign too literally. Well, what the hell am I supposed to think? It reads: *Arlington Park, Next Right.* In my mind this means: *Not This Right Right Here in Front of You, But the Right Right after It Because We Said Next Right and Not This Right, Which Is How They Would Do It in Indiana so as Not to Confuse the New Residents.*

Wrong. Stupid Illinois sign.

I double back around and get on the highway again. I only

have fifteen minutes left and my stomach is balled up in a fist of apprehension. A few minutes later, I see my train station looming in the distance. I let out a sigh of relief. All I have to do now is cross the street, park the car, and try to not walk in front of the train. Mission accomplished.

And that's when I hear an odd thunking noise.

Thunk. Thunk. Thunk thunk thunk.

This cannot be good news.

I pull into the gas station across from the train station and inspect my tires. Of course I have a flat. Of course I do.

I don't have a cell phone so I can't call Fletch. And I am not about to be late for my very first day of work. I don't want to start off my professional career being *that girl*, you know, the one who's always having some sort of crisis. Like so much so that you get weary even talking to her because something disastrous is always happening and it's never her fault and you just want to shake her and say, "Rise to the fucking occasion for once, why don't you?"

In a moment of stress-induced clarity, I realize I'm at a gas station and they probably have the know-how to fix a tire. I step inside, explain the situation, and drop off my keys. Problem solved. I even have enough time to grab a coffee and a bagel with flavored cream cheese[143] before my train comes.

I feel like such a tourist on my First Official Commute into the city. Everyone else on the train is reading or sleeping or listening to Walkmans.[144] Me? I gawp openmouthed the whole way, especially when the skyline comes into view.

....

[143] Flavored cream cheese?! Are we living in the age of miracles or what?

[144] Walkmen?

I get turned around when it's time to exit the train. Fortunately, since I've been spying on everyone, I realize the lady sitting in front of me is reading an e-mail sent from someone at my new company. We must be going to the same place, so I stick close behind her as we leave the Metra station and walk up the hill on Washington Street.

I am smack in the center of hundreds of people carrying briefcases on their way to their various office buildings. The sidewalk is full of folks in business suits . . . and some of them are even uglier than mine. Sweet.

As I stand by the revolving door to my new office, and thus new life, I can't believe I'm here.

I can't believe no one's going to yell at me today for bringing them ranch and not bleu cheese.

I can't believe I'm going to be a part of this big, bustling business world.

I can't believe how lucky I am.

I can't believe how unprepared I am.

I have eleven years of college under my blue bisecting waistband. I can detail every issue that divides the Hutus from the Tutsis. I can write a thirty-page paper on how to better involve Interpol in the fight against terrorism. I can speak in Venn diagrams. I can hold an intelligent discussion about modern playwrights from Ibsen to the absurdists. I can get a 4.0 while working full-time at a crappy restaurant. And in softer, less academic skills, I can talk three different West Lafayette police officers into not arresting me the night I run around campus in a big, borrowed, swoopy black coat pretending I'm Batman. I can buy groceries for the week on twenty dollars. I can make my cat Bones walk on a leash.

I cannot, however, send a fax.

Which is the only thing my job requires me to do at this moment.

How did I spend eleven years in academia and never learn how to use a fax machine? Or begin an e-mail? Or operate the collate feature on the Xerox machine? Or transfer a call? Or create an Excel spreadsheet?

I'm standing here eyeing the fax machine, a lump of dread roiling in my stomach alongside four foam cups of black coffee because I'm too shy to ask where they keep the cream and sugar. There are only twenty buttons or so, but there may as well be a million. What do I do here? Should I pick up the phone and then dial? And where does the paper go? Right-side up or upside down? And how will the people on the other side know I've sent them a fax? Do I call them? But how? I only have their fax number!

As I vacillate,[145] one of my coworkers comes up behind me with a stack of documents in her hands. In a flash of unexpected brilliance, I say, "You know what? I'm not quite ready. You go ahead." Then I pretend to shuffle my papers while I surreptitiously write down every step she takes.[146]

When it's my turn, I feed in the paper and push buttons, following each step to the letter and . . . success!

I faxed!

....

[145] Read panic.

[146] Later I find out she was on to me the whole time, which explains why she narrated the entire process. Bless you, Stephanie.

I am a *faxer*!

Fax this, bitches!

Feeling the warm glow of my first victory, I wander into the copy room. Someone's bound to collate something soon. And I intend to watch.

❖

After I get over my initial fear of office machines, I find the business world is different than I expected. I thought it would be all vicious and dog-eat-dog, but it's not. My professors were wrong when they said corporate America was far more challenging than academia. Sure, folks work more than three hours a day and don't get summers off, but other than that it's kind of easy.

Here people stay in the office until five, and if they don't finish their project, there's always tomorrow. No one has the sense of urgency that's been so ingrained in me from the restaurant industry. I laugh when I imagine what would happen if a customer requested ketchup and I told him I'd get it for him in the morning.

My coworkers aren't what I expected, either. Everyone (except Chuck) is laid-back and kind and more than willing to show the new kid the ropes. I can even handle Chuck. Coworkers ignore him because he's a tattletale, too concerned with minding everyone else's business.

Not long into my tenure here, I figured out Chuck doesn't really want to get others in trouble. All he wants is someone to listen to him. So I do. Ever since then, we've gotten along famously. Part of our mutual understanding is that he sees I'm ambitious. He's overloaded, so he appreciates when I ask him for extra projects when I finish my own work too quickly.

Chuck is in charge of database maintenance, whereas I do data entry. My job is to keep the provider directory current. My days are spent talking to doctors' offices to make sure I have their proper addresses, phones, and tax ID numbers. Sometimes there's a little detective work involved because physicians will move and not notify us, so I track them down and write up the new information and . . . that's it. I can't believe I needed a college degree to do a job that's 90 percent calling 411.

And I can't believe they're paying me $24,500 a year to do it!

Brass Something, Anyway

(Navy Suit, Part Three)

I can't believe how quickly I can spend $24,500.

I can't believe how much the government takes. I can't believe how much rent is and how much higher my insurance is and how expensive groceries are. Because I'm covering bills on two apartments, I'm already out of money and I don't get my check for another nine days. Looks like I'm brown-bagging it again this week.

All of my old friends want to hear about my glamorous life in Chicago. They want to know all about the trendy restaurants I visit at lunch every day. Right. Twice a month on payday I like to hit the cute Scottish place around the corner. Perhaps you've heard of it? I believe locals call it *McDonald's*.

❖

The boredom is slowly beginning to drive me crazy. It took me a month to learn the intricacies of my work and another few weeks to master it. Now that I'm six months in, I could update the directory in my sleep. I've inadvertently committed dozens of doctors' addresses and phone numbers to memory. I could even rattle off a few of their tax identification numbers. What's funny is when I have stress dreams, I don't picture myself in this job. Instead, I'm waiting tables and I have a hundred people anxiously awaiting drink orders.

I've made some friends in my department and I'm not lonely at lunchtime. Sometimes we'll do a big potluck dealie and everyone brings in their favorite treats. We have a book club and every two weeks a big group of us sits down together, discussing novels like *The English Patient* over canned soup and peanut butter sandwiches.

I've settled into a calm little groove here at work. But with this level of placidity, I feel like I'm in my fifties, not my twenties. I want some excitement. I want a challenge. Sure, I've spent years bitching about a lot of aspects of waitressing, but I can say this—it was never boring. My work life is pleasant, but I know I'm capable of so much more than what I'm doing. That's why when my boss Jill says, "I need some volunteers to—" my hand shoots up before she even gets her sentence out.

Jill's been tasked with finding people to work on the Employee Action Team, also known as EAT. Our department was tapped because we serve the least important function in the entire company. No one's actually said we're worthless—it's just my theory. But, hello? We're doing 411, not particle physics. We're so inconsequential that when a corporate merger is announced, no one in my department is worried about losing their jobs. We can't be fired if no one realizes we exist. The company we're joining doesn't even *have* people who do what we do.

EAT's sole purpose is to plan the corporate Christmas party. Everyone who'd been on EAT last year has either quit or gotten busy at their actual jobs, so the whole group needs to be restaffed. Personally, I don't know a damn thing about putting together a corporate party, but I do know that EAT-ing will get me away from my desk for a couple of hours a week. That's enticement enough.

I throw my entire self into this party. I go over every detail as meticulously as a debutante planning her dream wedding to the senator's son. The great irony is that I'm not even going to be able to attend the party because if I come downtown and spend the night in a hotel, I can't make my car payment.

I'm working with Joanne and Carmen from my department. They're both very sweet ladies but neither of them is what I'd consider a go-getter. Middle-aged and married with children and big homes in the suburbs, they aren't desperate to throw a faultless fete in hopes that someone notices their work ethic. They've already achieved their goals and right now their jobs are a means to pay for ballet lessons and math tutors and acrylic nails. And so they aren't terribly concerned when we realize we don't have the budget for a decent party.

Carmen suggests we just ask employees to contribute if they want a party, but that's so shitty to me. *Merry Christmas! Sorry you lost your job in the merger! And please enjoy having a cocktail* *with the very executives who decided your job was expendable. That'll be $50, please.*

Joanne suggests we have a bake sale to raise funds, but I'm all, What are we? Back in the sorority house? Why not just have a bikini car wash, for Christ's sake?

Our party finances make me mad. The employees here deserve a real celebration, especially if they're going to be on the unemployment line come January. If this company has $6 billion to buy a competitor, surely there are funds to pay for an extra cheese plate and some cheap champagne. I mean, I just saw an entire truckload of new Aeron chairs being delivered to the executive floor. There is cash here and it is available and we simply have to ask the right person.

I finally get Joanne and Carmen to agree we have to petition Robert Prescott Barlow III, General Manager, for more money. Carmen occasionally eats lunch with a couple of Mr. Barlow's assistants, so she manages to get one of them to squeeze us into his schedule. Joanne works on the PowerPoint we're going to show and Carmen puts together a detailed budget. I plan on tagging along for moral support.

On the day of our fund-raising appointment, I pull my navy blue suit and piped blouse out of the closet. I've been dressing much more casually for work in knit skirts and loose sweaters— people on the phone can't see me, after all—but I feel like I need to look as professional as I can today.

I'm running late this morning, and while I'm getting ready I trip over a cat and break the heel on my nice pair of pumps. Aarrgh. Falling snags my only pair of silky L'eggs, so I throw on an off-white pair of tights and some cheap navy loafers. I catch one glimpse of myself running out the door and think if I just had a bell, a bucket, and a storefront, collecting money would be no issue. Major Barbara, indeed.

When I get to the office, I find out both Carmen and Joanne have called in sick.

Fucking cowards.

I don't know what else to do, so I decide to take the meeting myself.

I quickly research the general manager and learn he came up through the sales department and figure that he appreciates self-confidence. No one buys from a timid sales guy, right? I also find out his peers call him Bob, even though everyone else at my level simply calls him *Mr. Barlow* or *Sir.*[147]

Even though I'm the most junior person in the least important department on the entire corporate totem pole (and I'm practically sharting myself in fright), I make sure to walk into his office like I belong there. I try not to look around too much, because if I calculate the size-of-this-room-to-my-cubicle comparison, I'll probably wuss out myself. I sneak a peek at Waterford tchotchkes and framed pictures of him on the cover of various health care magazines and oh, shit, I think I'm going to barf and—

Knock it off! Eyes straight ahead, I tell myself.

I sit down in front of him, making a conscious effort to look relaxed as I ease my way into a plush leather chair across from him. I figure if I want to gain, I have to venture, so I take a deep breath and open the meeting.

....

[147] Unless they're too chickenshit to come into work, in which case they don't call him anything. Yeah, I'm apparently still mad about that.

"Bob," I say, "we've got ourselves a morale problem."

Bob is all polished with his hair combed into perfect grooves, a grown-up version of a Ken doll. I bet he and his wife (CEO Barbie) have a standing tennis date every Saturday morning. Then they eat a brunch made up of something topped with hollandaise and they stop at a farmers' market before tooling home to their Dream House in a giant plastic convertible, where they drink wine from their last trip to Napa. (At no point do they ever open their Chinese curio cabinet to watch television.)

Ken—I mean *Bob*—tents his hands and rests his sculpted chin on his fingertips. He's deeply tan and I can tell it's come from the actual sun. He must have just returned from somewhere tropical. Heck, I just wish I had the funds to hit the tanning booth.

Bob's straight white teeth look even more dramatic against his golden skin. He's smiling at me, like my presence amuses him.

Or maybe he's smiling because I'm dressed like Cap'n Crunch.

"A morale problem? How so, um . . . Jennifer, is it?"

"It's Jen. And the problem is we're merging with the other HMO. Everyone's afraid they're going to lose their jobs." I (purposefully) languidly cross my legs, shift back in the chair, and lock his gaze.

Bob brushes a bit of nonexistent lint from his jacket. The real buttonholes on its cuffs mean his suit cost more than I make in an entire quarter. The contrast of his outfit to mine makes me feel like I'm clad not in a starter business suit but a shower curtain plucked from the Salvation Army bin. Still, I continue to look him right in the eye. What choice do I have?

"We are *not* laying anyone off, Jen. We've been crystal clear about that."[148]

"Sure, you say that, but no one believes you." Bob starts to interrupt, but I give him my most charming[149] grin and raise my hand. "Bup, bup, bup, in this case perception *is* reality. It's almost Christmas and people think they're going to be unemployed. They are freaking the—can I say 'hell' in here?—they are freaking the hell out."

Suddenly Bob is a lot less charmed. "I assure you *nothing—*"

I continue, speaking as fast as I did on days when I was triple-seated and had to spit out all the evening's specials. "Hear me out, Bob. The employees are scared. They're unhappy. You know what they need? They need a gesture. They need the equivalent of a big, warm corporate hug. They need a—pardon my French—they need a *kick-ass* Christmas party. And they need you to pay for it."

Bob sits there and stares a hole through me and my navy wool for what seems like an hour.

Oh, shit, I think, *he's going to have me killed, just like all those evil insurance executives John Grisham always writes about.*

Then he begins to laugh and his whole face softens. "How much more do you need?"

Without skipping a beat I say, "Five thousand."

He snorts. "Not happening. We're in a budget crunch. How about five hundred?"

---

[148] By the way? *Bullshit.* The company lays more than a quarter of its workforce off within the next two months. And I was right—my department isn't touched.

[149] Read desperate.

I fold my arms over my shiny buttons. "Bob, it's *Christmas*. Four thousand."

"Six hundred."

"You're killing me, Bob." *Please don't kill me, Bob.*

"Seven hundred."

"Can you really put a price on happy employees?" I oh-so-casually begin to finger my faux pearls.

He considers my statement for a moment. "Yes. Yes, I can. Fifteen hundred, final offer."

I pretend to mull it over. In reality, we'd hoped to walk out of there with a couple of hundred extra bucks. But I gambled and I won. I lean across his enormous mahogany desk to shake his hand. "You've got yourself a deal. Thank you very much for your time and for giving us enough money to throw a great party. Correction, a *healing* party." I stand up and head toward his big glass office door.

"Excuse me, Jen?" he calls, right as I'm about to exit.

"Yes?"

"I have a quick question."

"Shoot." I make a finger gun at him. Okay, now I'm really pushing it.

"Why aren't you negotiating for us?"

I think about it for a moment. "Dunno, Bob. You tell me." Then I spin on the heel of my sensible loafer and I run to the elevator as soon as I'm out of his line of sight because I'll probably never get the chance to give such a perfect exit line again.

I'm jumping up and down by the time the doors slide open and I can barely punch the button to return to my little cubicle on the non-executive-level floor. Don't know how, exactly, but

I'll wager the cost of his suit that I just changed my career trajectory.

I can't wait to tell everyone about my meeting! Fletch is going to be so proud. My mom will want to celebrate with a drink, after which she'll tell me the story of my conception.

Maybe I'll hold off on calling her.

By the way, the Christmas party is a smash hit. More important, Bob doesn't forget me, and when a contract negotiator's position opens up a few weeks later, he personally gives HR the recommendation. I won't make any more base salary, but I'll earn small quarterly bonuses and I'll be far away from data entry.

I get the job.

And then I live happily ever after and never have to consider being a waitress again . . . right?

Worst Movie Ever

◆◆◆◆◆◆◆◆◆◆◆◆◆◆◆◆◆◆◆◆◆◆◆◆◆◆◆

(Canvas Book Bag)

The screaming isn't even what bothers me most.

It wouldn't be so bad if it was just one voice raised in anguish, but there are so many. I could deal with it if it only happened on occasion. But it's every day.

The voices, my God, the voices are so shrill.

So sharp.

An aural attack.

The howling resonates and echoes. The shrieking curdles my blood. Screams pierce my eardrums, assaulting all my senses. The keening is so loud I taste it on my tongue. I feel the collective grief in my chest. I smell the fear. This is the noise rabbits make when they realize too late they've stumbled into a coyote's den. It's the noise that results from the losing battle between flesh and metal and velocity.

And it's coming from the exam rooms in this particular pediatrician's office.

I grit my teeth when I hear the latest round of Dip/Tet-related wailing and shift in my tiny throne. There's a whole array of half-sized, primary-colored seats here in the waiting room, conceivably meant to match the giant Crayolas painted inexpertly on the physician's walls. Walls that also boast some creepy Bambi, Barney, and Sleeping Beauty murals that make me wonder if anyone cares about this doctor's blatant disregard for copyright and intellectual property.[150]

I'm sitting in a wee blue chair and the pharmaceutical sales rep across from me is wedged into a bite-sized yellow one. Yes. This makes perfect sense. Since no adult-sized people would ever accompany their children to checkups, why should the good doctor worry about providing a reasonable place for them to sit?

At least I'm empty-handed, save for the battered old canvas book bag I use as a purse. The poor Merck rep is anchored to her chair under an enormous satchel of samples. Plus, she has three pizzas rapidly congealing and leaking grease on her lap and a whole tray full of drippy sodas. She's trapped. I see her stiffen during the next bout of screaming and I watch as she catches herself, swapping out pursed lips for a toothy but insincere grin.

The office is especially chaotic because it's the last Friday before Christmas. I guess all the suburban soccer moms in this wealthy North Shore suburb want to be sure their kids are healthy for their upcoming holiday cruises.

I should have known better than to come here today, but it's

....

[150] My guess is no.

the end of the quarter and I'm ambitious.[151] Even though I already met my goal, I'm eligible for bonuses. After reaching my minimum recruitment number, I get a hundred dollars for each new physician I bring into the HMO. And I get two hundred bucks if the doctor is a pediatrician, so I've been hitting these loud, teeny-chaired places every day. I figure if I can get a couple more peds in-network this quarter, my bonus will be sweet and I'll *finally* start a new year not being flat broke.

While I wait—trying not to cringe at every yelp and holler—I root through my bag to find my bottle of hand sanitizer.[152] The Merck rep wistfully gazes at my antibacterial gel. I'd share, but her hands are buried.

A towheaded kid in expensive ski pants toddles over to the chair next to the Merck girl. He smells like spilled milk and bubble-gum shampoo. Clutching a little toy hammer as he approaches, the kid has a vicious green crust going under his nose. If experience serves me right, he's too young to have discovered a proper regard for cold-and-flu etiquette.

Technically, this child isn't unsupervised. However, his mom has been on her mobile the entire time, too deep in conversation about how St. Bart's is *"so last year"* to notice her child contaminating everyone within a twenty-foot radius. This mom is so emaciated I'd swear she was from one of the war-torn, drought-suffering countries NPR's always droning on about. I mean, if she weren't wearing a diamond the size of a donut hole. Her donut-diamond (in a platinum and pave setting, naturally) spins around her bony

---

[151] Read desperate.

[152] After getting the flu seven goddamned times last year, I finally smartened up.

finger like the Showcase Showdown wheel every time she gestures, as does her twenty-carat tennis bracelet. Her phone is wedged up against her ear and the more she talks, the looser her enormous ruby earring becomes.

The second one of those jewels hits the floor, I'm diving for it.

I see women like this all the time up here. They flounce into the doctors' offices and throw their fur coats across most of the available seats. After briefly stopping to tell the receptionist they do *not* expect to be kept waiting long, they whip a phone out of their Dior bag the second they sit, ignoring the sick kids who are the reason they're here in the first place. I loathe them almost as much as I do the screaming.

Shouldn't this mom be snuggling the towhead toddler or, like, patting him on the head or using Kleenex and mom juice to clear away some of the crud under his nose? Instead, she keeps talking while the child lurches toward us, who, despite his stuffy nose, is drawn to the aroma of the pizza.

Merck girl and I lock eyes. We both know what's next.

A second later, the child drops his sticky hammer on the rep's pizza boxes and sneezes directly into her hair. The word "juicy" comes to mind, but it doesn't aptly describe the tsunami of *awful* now clinging to the rep's neatly arranged Rachel-from-*Friends* cut. I silently empathize as she does her best to only exhale and then I divert my attention. Sorry, honey. It's every germaphobe for herself in here.

To avoid meeting her gaze, and thus laughing myself out of the waiting room, I pick up the first non-*Highlights* magazine I can find. My appointment with Dr. Bronner was supposed to be half an hour ago. Most likely I won't see him until he's done enjoying his Merck-provided (hot zone) pizza luncheon, so I've got plenty of time to read.

I tab past all the advertisements for sexy, strappy shoes. Wish I could get away with *those* at work. My sartorial choices at this time of year are limited to whatever kind of pantsuit best covers up the utilitarian waterproof boots I'm forced to wear while trudging through a million snowy parking lots every day.[153] If the sidewalk salt didn't destroy them, surely I'd lose a toe to frostbite.

Yet I can't complain because I've got a ton of freedom as a recruiter, as opposed to my early days here at Great Plaines HMO when I was shackled to my desk. The only time I left my cube was for lunch, but I was even more financially tapped out then and had to brown-bag it every day, so I never got to explore the city. I had no idea where to find a decent restaurant, but I could absolutely tell you which lunchroom microwave was the best.[154]

I'm on my third position here at the HMO. Technically, this job isn't much different from being a negotiator, but my new bonus structure is a *lot* more motivating. That's why I'm here, enduring an hour of screaming—and possibly catching tuberculosis—for an extra two hundred bones.

When I was a negotiator, I didn't go off-site nearly as much as I do now. Sure, I attended the occasional hospital meeting, but they were hardly every day. Since I became a recruiter, I'm practically a vapor trail. We recruiters are out in the field so much we

....

[153] Why don't any of you bastards pay for people to shovel past the sidewalk?

[154] Second shelf, second unit.

don't even have our own desks. We have to share them,[155] which is only a problem during our staff meetings on Wednesdays when everyone's in-house. Lately it's become a contest to see who can get there the earliest to stake out the prime real estate next to the copy machine. Last week my two work best friends (David and Tim) and I all arrived before six fifteen a.m. After Christmas vacation, you can bet your ass I'll be there by six a.m.

The receptionist calls Merck girl to the back and she bolts away from Towhead and his Ski Pants of Death. His mom remains completely unaware of anyone else's presence because, damn it, Maria Elena is just *not* scouring the grout like she used to and this *will* affect[156] her holiday bonus. I continue to peruse my magazine because it's going to be a few more minutes. Also, the doctor's a lot less likely to join my network if I start administering diamond suppositories to his patients' parents.

Towhead's mom gives her phone companion an icy laugh before murmuring, "Maria Elena isn't smart enough to know she's making less than minimum wage."

Flipping pages keeps me from balling my hands into fists.

Flip, flip, flip.

I like the pocketbook ads because they inspire me to work harder. I spend a lot of time daydreaming about what kind of purse I'll buy once I get my first big bonus. The canvas bag I'm carrying has seen better days, plus it makes me look like a college student. I need something more professional to be taken more seriously.

....

[155] The sharing is called "hotel-ing." I call it "company is too cheap to spring for another half floor in our office building."

[156] Read eliminate.

All the seasoned recruiters have Coach bags, so they figure prominently into my fantasies. Coach is good because their bags aren't *so* fancy that the doctors notice them and resent the "big money" we make at the insurance company.

Swear to God, if one more physician bitches about how "rich" I'm getting, I'll probably start swinging. Last week I had an ob-gyn crying to me about how our reimbursement rates were bankrupting him. Then I watched him drive away in his brand-new S-class Mercedes with personalized plates while I climbed into my old Toyota Tercel with the dent I can't afford to repair.

I always want to tell these doctors, *Listen up, I make $26,000 a year, and 80 percent of that goes to rent and transportation. Every month I do the reverse-bill lottery, figuring out which payment I can get away with skipping. For heaven's sake, I'm carrying a bag I got free at a trade show! If anyone at the insurance company is making big money, it ain't me.*

Shoot, half the furniture in my apartment came from the alley in my neighborhood. And earlier this spring, I specifically scheduled an appointment to coincide with the town's heavy trash day. My friend David and I Dumpster-dove in front of the homes of the very doctors with whom we'd just met. Bet they'd change their tune if they spotted us snapping up their old cross-country skis and worn luggage.

I continue to idly browse until I see an automobile advertisement. The car doesn't interest me—the Tercel[157] is okay—but there's something about the copy that intrigues me. If I remember

----

[157] It's so gas efficient that I actually make money on my mileage. That's why I'm able to buy groceries.

my college Italian, one phrase means "To live life like you're in the movies."

Huh. What would *that* be like?

The movie version of my life definitely doesn't include inhaling lunch from the dollar menu while trying to navigate a stick shift through rush-hour traffic to get to my next appointment. Or sitting around a shouty, disease-ridden office in unventilated boots and damp polyester pants, hoping to score enough cash to bring the gas bill current.

Do they make movies about people who work 'til nine every night?[158] And who have so much paperwork in their tiny dining room–home office that they have to put all their beloved books in storage so the stacks can be housed on the shelves instead? Who's camping out in line to see *that*?

I *want* to live my life like it's a movie, but I have no idea how. The closest I've come so far is the time last spring when Fletch and I ditched work and went to a ballgame at Wrigley Field. I remember I got a really cute army green Cubs bucket hat that day when I applied for a credit card. Too bad I didn't catch a pop fly like in *Ferris Bueller's Day Off*. That'd be movielike, right? I didn't cruise up Lake Shore Drive in a convertible, chiffon scarf floating in the breeze like in *My Best Friend's Wedding*, nor did I plow through Daley Plaza all Jake and Elwood–style like in *The Blues Brothers*. Actually, I didn't do anything else exciting that day and as soon as the game was over, I went home and did more work because I felt so guilty.

Come to think of it, I didn't even get approved for the credit card.

....

[158] Who aren't Gordon Gekko?

Damn.

I bet the skinny soccer mom lives *her* life like a movie, only she's not the heroine. She'd be the one making coats out of puppy fur or causing Sandra Bullock to cry over her lack of grout-scrubbing prowess.

I shrug and close the magazine. Wouldn't matter if I knew how to live my life like a movie because I couldn't even afford a ticket for admission.

Pretty (Average) Woman

(Utilitarian Snow Boots)

Jim, David, and I are on our way to the Starbucks on the other side of the Randolph Street Bridge. It's Wednesday and we've already claimed our desks. Since no one else will be in the office for another two hours, we figure we can spare the time to grab a coffee.

The bridge is steel and it's made up of thousands of tiny metal grids. I like being on it in the summer because I can see straight down to the very river that made me want to work at this company. (The great irony is I didn't discover access to the grassy area adjacent to the water until I was too busy to consider taking my lunch down there.)

I always get a walking-on-air vibe when I go over this bridge. Little different story in the winter, though. The grids prevent ice from forming, but the unfortunate side effect is that when the wind blows, it has nowhere to go except directly up my skirt. My feet are warmed because they're protected by thick, ugly boots, but my thighs are freezing. It only takes us a minute to cross the bridge, but by the time we reach Starbucks, I'm a total Jen-cicle.[159]

Tim and David both get cups of drip coffee. They add sugar and cream at the condiment bar while I wait at the service counter for my mocha. My boots squeak on the floor as I shift my weight from one leg to the other in an attempt to defrost myself from the waist down while the hyper-caffeinated barista grills everyone in line about their New Year's resolutions. When he gets to me, I grit my teeth before saying I resolve to drink more Starbucks. He laughs and moves on.

As soon as we leave, I kind of explode. "I hate that so much!"

Tim is puzzled. "Then why'd you order it?"

"No, not my mocha, dummy. The barista—did you hear him? He asked me about my New Year's resolution," I huff.

"What of it?" David asks, slurping the excess coffee off his lid.

"Doesn't that irritate you?" I demand.

David and Tim exchange one of their Jen's-got-PMS-again glances. "Should it?" David, the mellower of the two, asks.

"Hell, yes! I've never even met that guy. I could understand him asking that if I had, but I haven't."

Tim nods and takes a giant step away from me. "I see your point." David nods vigorously.

....

[159] If we'd been on the bridge one more second, I'd have frozen in place, like Jack Nicholson at the end of *The Shining*. Yes, I want to live life like it's a movie, but not *that* movie.

"Both of you stop patronizing me. Let me put it like this—say your job is to bag my groceries, or ensure the check I deposit gets credited to the right account, or make my coffee, then my resolutions are none of your goddamned business and are certainly not small-talk fodder."

David turns to Tim. "How was your Christmas?"

"Don't change the subject; I'm serious! This line of questioning is a violation of the social contract."

"Clearly," Tim replies. He and David begin to walk faster.

I chug along behind them, trying to catch up. "The thing is, resolutions are rarely about what we already find kind of awesome about ourselves, like, *I resolve to continue to be a great parent* or *I resolve to keep visiting my senile grandma in the nursing home as often as I do* or—"

David interrupts, "Or I resolve to not garbage pick."

"I resolve to stop drinking coffee with certifiably insane people," Tim supplies.

"My point is resolutions generally have to do with what we don't like about ourselves, as in *I want to lose weight (because I'm too fat)* or *I pledge to get organized (because my life is a huge mess)* or *I'm going to save money (because my spending is out of control)*. Therefore, when *you*, a perfect stranger, ask me about my resolutions, you're basically asking me to lay all my flaws bare and it's incredibly presumptive and rude, especially when the person asking is in no position to help me achieve whatever it is I resolve to do."

As usual, Tim argues the counterpoint. "You answered his question. By giving him an answer, aren't you part of the problem by encouraging him to do the one thing you hate?" We get to our building's revolving glass door. David steps aside so I can go through first. Once in, we stamp all the slush off our boots. We go up the escalator to get to the main floor and then select the bank of elevators to take us to fifteen.

"I answered because I didn't want him spitting in my mocha. And I didn't want to give the tired old *I resolve not to make any resolutions, yuck, yuck, yuck* response. Not everything has to be a fight with me, you know."

David and Tim both clear their throats and look at the ceiling.

"It doesn't! I don't fight with any of my doctors, now do I?" I challenge.

At the same time, David and Tim both answer, "Yet."

I sigh. "You are two enormous bags of douche. I'm going to start calling you Massengill"—I point at Tim— "and Summer's Eve."

"Okay, okay," David concedes. "Then riddle me this, Batman—the next time the cashier at the grocery store asks you about your resolutions, what are you going to say?"

I consider this for a moment while Tim pulls out his magnetic card to unlock the door. We all pass through and I finally reply, "I'm going to say *I resolve to be cognizant enough to spot potential problems within myself and to begin to work on them immediately, without making a public declaration or waiting to start the improvements on an arbitrary date. And yes, I* would *like my milk in a bag.*"

We're arranging ourselves in adjacent desks and booting up our laptops by the time I thaw from our trip across the bridge. "Hey, Jen," Tim asks, "what are you thinking about doing with your bonus when it finally comes?"

"Umm . . . probably take care of some bills, buy a real purse, maybe pay off my car note? Why?"

He replies, "You ought to consider taking a vacation. Like, a *long* vacation. To a happy place."

I roll my eyes. "Maybe I'll do just that, Massengill."

We're well into spring now, but I can't get the idea of living life like it's a movie out of my head. And even though I hate when strangers ask about my resolutions, I believe in the power of making them.

Here goes—even though I'm a few months late—I resolve to live my life like a movie for the remainder of this year.

Now . . . how do I go about accomplishing this?

People in movies seem to live better lives when they get makeovers. I bet I need an image overhaul. Fortunately, I don't have to have sex with Richard Gere for money to start the process. I have a secret weapon I've inadvertently been saving for a special occasion—my corporate American Express card.

I've had this card since I went to Philly last year for a month of intensive training. I've never bought anything on it not directly related to a business travel expense, even though I'm allowed to use it. The numbers on it are still black because I've pulled it out of my wallet so few times. I'm not afraid to touch it, but this is a card I have to pay in full each month or else I'd get in trouble with both Amex *and* my employer. Luckily, I get my bonus in a few weeks, so if I want to use it? I can.

I assess myself in the mirror hanging on the outside of my bathroom door.

Hair? Blackish, curly, sort of coarse,[160] with a few too many grays to ignore. (How did I manage to go straight from campus to corrective color?) I don't take care of it like I used to. When I was in school and I had a profitable night waiting tables, I'd splurge on the fancy salon across town. Sometimes I'd get a gloss put in my hair and sometimes I'd have it straightened and I'd always buy the very best product to put in it. Except when it was jammed back in a mandatory ponytail, my hair was down to my elbows, silky and beautifully layered.

For now, my cut is unremarkable. I've been going to Great Clips exclusively since graduation and it shows. (Being salaried has meant no profitable nights and very little splurging.) I went really short once I started working because I thought that would give me some professional gravitas. Instead, I just looked like a gym teacher. I've grown it back to a shoulder-length bob but it's shapeless, except for whenever it's humid out. Then it turns into a giant wedge of pizza.

My grocery store hair dye has done me no favors, either. There was a *purple* incident a couple of months ago when I opted for the sale brand. (Let us not speak of it again.) I've been running dark rinses through it lately. The gray's gone . . . but so's all the shine and depth. The color is as flat and black as if I went over it with a Sharpie.

My flat black hair only serves to highlight how pasty I am. I haven't been to a tanning bed for ages and my skin's practically translucent, except for where I've broken out since I used up all my Clinique products and replaced them with stuff from the

---

[160] Cheap conditioner.

drugstore. Upon closer inspection I can confirm it: my cosmetics give me the appearance of being neither wet nor wild. (Got a bit of a vampire vibe going on, though.)

I swing open the ratty folding doors in my microscopic bedroom and I feel sad at the sight of all my stuff. My closet is where ill-fitting suit jackets and cheaply cut trousers go to die. There's not one item in here that quickens my pulse, making me excited to get dressed.

Back in school I could dress casually every day. Although I'd occasionally embrace a trend—e.g., leopard print—I always defaulted to wearing preppy items . . . nicely cut khakis, ice-creamy-colored polos, striped rugby shirts, argyle sweaters, loafers, etc. These items made me happy because I felt good when I wore them.

Clean, simple lines flatter my figure most. However, since I graduated I've eschewed fit for price. Discount stores like Marshalls and TJ Maxx and Stein Mart have been my main source of staples and I'm seeing what a mistake that's been. I've gone for quantity over quality. I've screwed up by buying three cheap acrylic sweaters rather than one well-crafted twinset. I no longer buy the item that makes me feel the prettiest—I just get whatever has been marked down the most. This has to stop.

I glance at the floor. All my shoes are boxy, flat, and ugly, which makes perfect sense because they pair so nicely with my dowdy wardrobe. I see my big black snow boots taking up valuable floor real estate. They represent everything that's wrong with my wardrobe, and ergo, my life right now. There's no color, there's no style, there's just utility.

But I feel a change coming on—winter's over and I realize I

don't have to wear what's practical. Going forward, I should opt for pointy, heeled, and pretty. Maybe it's time for style to trump comfort.

A makeover will likely help my career because if I feel better about myself, it will translate into my job. And if this were a movie, I'd start the process the second the thought occurred to me.

"Hey, Fletch?" I call. He's in our living room, busily engaged in his own non-movielike activity: folding towels. "Grab your coat, we're heading down to Michigan Ave."

❖

This is where I'd put the *Pretty Woman*-style shopping montage if I were making a movie. I'd show myself at the salon, in the tanning bed, at the Prescriptives counter, going in and out of boutiques, and trying on strappy shoes.

Except in this film, all the clerks are happy to help me when I hand them my American Express.

Or maybe it's just because I'm not a prostitute?

My Kind of Town

(Cubs Bucket Hat)

*F*eedback from my reinvention has been overwhelmingly positive. Everyone's noticed the changes I've made. With a professional cut and color, well-tailored clothes, and cute shoes, I'm way more self-assured in my negotiations. My recruitment numbers reflect this bounce in confidence.

So how come I'm still in my boring old workaholic life and crappy apartment? The only difference is now I stuff better brands of shoes into my tiny closet.

I want to feel like I'm living in a movie and maybe a makeover's only part of the equation. Maybe some kind of cool hobby would make my life seem more ready for the big screen? But what should I do? Back in college, I used to take horseback riding lessons. That's as good a place to start as any.

So, Fletch and I take my Tercel to the stables in the southern suburbs a few times. Given the expense of the activity and my inability to walk for *days* after each ride, turns out I'd rather use that money to buy pony-skin shoes.

I hearken back to my childhood again when I decide to take up ice skating. I sign up for adult lessons, and every Tuesday for a month I leave work by five to drive to the rink in the northern suburbs.[161] I enjoy the skating but my classmates are a bummer. I find out they're all nannies who've been tasked by their employers to learn to skate in order to keep up with their charges. My classmates are always freezing and quietly cursing in Spanish about having to be there. The sessions become less about gliding effortlessly across the ice and more about class struggle. Granted, I do feel like I'm living in a movie . . . made by Michael Moore.

When I get stuck at work on the fifth Tuesday and I miss my lesson, I'm not so upset. I miss it the sixth week and then I kind of forget about ever going again. (The added bonus is David and Tim stop calling me Peggy Fleming.)

I don't want to give up on my quest, though. Fletch says I should look for something that gives me an endorphin rush, but I'm not about to start robbing banks like the adrenaline junkies in *Point Blank*. I have no desire to become a Navy SEAL à la *G.I. Jane*,[162] nor do I want to skydive like in *The Drop Zone*. Shoot, I don't even like to fly commercially. The very thought of being on a plane makes my pulse race and my breathing shallow and—

Hey . . . I may be on to something.

....

[161] If I live in one of the biggest cities in the world, how come I have to drive out of town to do anything fun?

[162] Or get that haircut.

Conquering a fear—you see *that* all the time in the movies. And surely it speaks to my self-awareness that I realize this is a problem, right? Really, no one's more scared of flying than me. I was on a plane coming back from corporate training that almost went down last year and ever since then air travel—which had never caused me any distress before—suddenly petrifies me. What if I booked a flight and made myself take it?

This could work. I've got the money from my bonus and I have plenty of accrued time off because our bosses wouldn't let us use any vacation days during the busy recontracting season over the past few months.

Where should I go?

❖

Luckily, my movie boyfriend Vince Vaughn has the answer—I'm going to Vegas, baby!

❖

If I wanted an adrenaline rush, I've got it. My plane has been stuck on the tarmac for-freaking-ever during this enormous May thunderstorm. The captain came on the loudspeaker and said something about losing our window and having to wait, but he mentioned *nothing* about it taking multiple hours.

Just being strapped into this confining seat has been enough to kick my adrenal glands into overdrive. The top I'm wearing is drenched in frightened perspiration. I'm in one of my favorite old Lacoste shirts paired with khaki shorts because I wanted to be comfortable. What I didn't count on was sitting here perspiring so hard that I'd even wreck my 'do. I had to grab my Cubs bucket hat out of my carry-on about an hour ago just to keep the sopping strands up off my neck.

The worst part is I'm by myself. Fletch had some mandatory training come up this week and he wasn't able to join me. Now I get to conquer my fear of being on vacation alone, too.

I sit on the tarmac for four hours, terror-sweating in a middle seat, sandwiched between a compulsive throat clearer and a harried mom holding a colicky baby. We finally take off, and the flight is so bumpy I spend the entire time white-knuckling the armrests and bargaining with God.

When we finally land safely on terra firma,[163] I find out my luggage decided to vacation in *La Guardia* (airport code LGA), not *Las Vegas* (airport code LAS). The airline baggage clerk apologizes profusely and assures me I'll have my things back soon.[164] Although I'm relieved all my bags aren't gone forever, I'm daunted by the prospect of spending the rest of my vacation in this sweaty polo.

It's one a.m. when I finally arrive at the hotel. After getting lost on the way to the Strip,[165] the cab drops me off at the wrong door for registration. I drag my carry-on the length of ten football fields until I find the main reception desk. Normally the combination of flashing lights, clanging coins, and euphoric gamblers makes my heart smile. However, at the moment I'm ready to go Donald Rumsfeld all over the next person who squeals in celebration. All I want to do is take a bath and go to bed.

....

[163] Great, now I'm obligated to work with orphans.

[164] No worries, everything arrives the next day.

[165] How fucking hard is it to find a forty-story pyramid?

I'm staying in the new Luxor tower, so it doesn't have the weird slanted walls or the creepy sideways elevator of the main pyramid. I had a room there the first time I visited Vegas when I went with my waitressing buddy Fiona Fleur. Over the course of that trip she stole forty dollars out of my purse and a handful of quarters out of my Harrah's bucket. I also discovered she was bulimic and, more disturbing, that she'd been trying (unsuccessfully) to put the moves on Fletch. We parted ways as soon as we left the airport and never talked again. (Honestly, I should have figured our friendship would end badly. I'd met her years earlier when we were in the same dorm freshman year. She was in my rush group and when we were formally introduced, I said, "Fiona Fleur— what a pretty name!" to which she replied, "I know.")

My second trip out here was marginally better, at least until my friend strong-armed me into putting all my slot machine winnings toward prime seats at what she promised to be "the most fan-tabulous event in live theater!!" I'd wanted to get the gorgeous pearl bracelet I'd been eyeing in the Forum Shops at Caesars Palace, but she was so sure I'd love the show that eventually I capitulated.

We ended up front row center at a *fucking* Andrew Lloyd Webber musical about *fucking* trains that took place on *fucking* roller skates. Every time the actors whizzed by within an inch of my face, my fury grew. My anger deepened when I then couldn't get the stupid "One Rock and Roll Too Many" song out of my head for days.

Now that I think about it, I'm struck by the fact that being here alone isn't such a bad thing. Everybody says this is the greatest vacation city in the world, but every time I come, I end up mad at my friends. Inauspicious start notwithstanding, I figure if I don't have a good time on this trip, then the problem is me and not Las Vegas.

When I get to my room and open the door, I'm blissful for the first time today. Sweet setup! I've got super-soft linens,[166] a big squashy bed with tons of pillows, a bigger TV, and a bathroom that hosts a separate shower and a large Jacuzzi tub. Vegas, baby!

The air-conditioning everywhere in this city is set on "polar freeze" and I can't wait to get out of my damp travel clothing and into a warm bath. I stop up the tub and run the water. When it's halfway full, I turn on the jets and pour in a capful of my pear-scented Victoria's Secret body wash, then go to unpack my carry-on. I don't have a change of clothes, but at least I have the essentials—grooming supplies, pajamas, underwear, and a bathing suit. I finish up and stretch out on the lovely bed, anticipating how amazing that bath is going to feel . . . which reminds me, I'd better turn off the water.

I notice some foamy stuff spilling out from under the door, but the full impact of what I've accidentally wrought doesn't hit me until I enter the bathroom and walk into the wall-o-bubbles.

Not only is the entire floor covered in a foot of pear-scented suds, but the bubbles have climbed so far up the wall they're spilling into the detached shower stall.

I appear to be hosting my very own foam party.

I have to dive into the center of the heaving, sudsy mass to shut down the jets and turn off the water. This is exactly what I'd

---

[166] Egyptian?

hoped would happen years ago when my mom would put me in a bath with a bottle of Palmolive dish detergent.[167] I'd sit in my tub, kicking my feet and splashing my arms, wishing I could generate results like this. Now that I've finally achieved such an august goal, I find that it's not so great, actually.

I'm sliding all over the marble floor as I open the door to the shower. I try to gather up the froth in my arms, but it squishes out and trails down my legs, making my trajectory even more hazardous. I need some kind of scooping tool, so I go into the main room to grab the ice bucket, leaving a dozen cotton-foam footprints in my wake.

Fifty buckets, twenty minutes, and four towels later my bathroom stops looking like the dance floor at Senor Frog's during spring break.

Finally—it's bath time! I throw my wet clothes on the floor next to the bed and slide back into the bathroom. I dip one toe in—ahhh, *nice*. I decide to make use of the facilities before I get into the tub.

Business complete, I flush.

This quick foray onto the toilet has been no different an endeavor than any other time I've used the restroom in my adult life. Try then to imagine my surprise when instead of the waste going down the u-bend like the thousands of times previous, the bowl's contents go not gentle into that good night.

Instead, they shoot directly up at me . . . at approximately 80 miles an hour.

As I leap backward, slamming into the glass shower door, the

....

[167] I'm soaking in it!

only thought going through my now-banged head is, *When did I eat corn?*

I'm well versed in the four principles/forces of gravity,[168] so I find myself vaguely surprised when, flushing again, I get the same results.

Twice.

As I look around my sodden and befouled bathroom, I long for the salad days of twenty minutes ago when my only problem was suds. Fluffy, effervescent, sanitary suds.

The screams that inadvertently escape my lips far rival anything Jennifer Love Hewitt produced in *I Know What You Did Last Summer*. And I realize I'm not living a movie so much as an episode of *I Love Lucy*.

I care not to speak of the specifics of what happened with the ice bucket next. Please know I gave it a hero's burial, first tying it in one and then another plastic laundry bag before depositing it deep within the bowels of a casino Dumpster.

The universe is telling me I may as well gamble because I can't be any more unlucky. I call the front desk, loudly describing the problem using words like "geyser," "horrific," and "corn on the cob." After giving my shirt a quick once-over with the hotel hair drier, I smooth on some Clinique blush, adjust my Cubs hat, and head down to play nickel poker so I don't have to endure the shame of facing maintenance when they arrive to fix the toilet.

---

[168] Pressure, density, temperature, and vertical component of magnetism. Thank you, Dino Kraspedon, for explaining it all so neatly.

By three a.m., I assume they've had ample opportunity to adjust my toilet's flush direction. Yet when I return to my room, I find that absolutely nothing has changed.

I may or may not scream again.

Or cry.

I'm exhausted, I'm freezing, I'm damp, and I'm pretty sure I touched a biohazard.[169] I haul my bedraggled self back down to the front desk. Too drained to tap into my usual level of vitriol, I simply tell the clerk I can't wait for maintenance anymore. I'm cold and pooped[170] and just want to sleep.

"Can you give me another room?" I beg. "Please?"

"Yes, yes, of course," the clerk replies. As she works her keyboard, she glances back at me. "You came in from Chicago?" She gestures at my hat.

I scrub at my eyes and stifle a yawn. "Yeah, although I'll be honest. I'm not a Cubs fan so much as I am a fan of going to Wrigley Field."

"I'm with you! There's nothing like spending a summer day with a brat and a beer, being a bleacher bum!"

"Hmm," I reply noncommittally. Less talky, more change room-y, please. The clerk beams at me, so I feel obligated to continue. "You've been to a Cubs game?" I resignedly ask.

"Of course! I'm from Chicago, too!" she exclaims.

Oh, good. We're apparently girlfriends now. Let's have a long, boring, keep-me-out-of-bed conversation, shall we? "Then why are you here?"

....

[169] To be fair, I am up seven dollars.

[170] Pun intended.

"Well, Chicago's a great city, but I couldn't take the weather anymore. I used to work at Michigan and Wacker and every time I crossed over the river in the winter, I swore I'd be blown into the water."

Great, *now* she's gotten me engaged. "I work on Riverside Plaza and I know exactly what you mean," I volunteer. "I always give the railing a death grip on windy days. In fact, I may still be frozen from the waist down from this winter."

She looks me up and down one more time and then types a couple more notes into the computer. Change complete, she hands me a fresh set of electronic key cards. "Here you go, neighbor. This room's going to be more to your liking," she assures me.

"As long as the toilet doesn't explode, I'll be happy. Thanks."

Since I only have to pack up my overnight bag, I'm quickly out of the sullied room. I leave a big tip on the vanity as well as a note stating simply *I am so, so sorry.*

My new room is only a couple of floors up and I get there in no time. When I open the door, I notice a weird echo as I grope for the lights. Huh. I've never been in a hotel room that echoed before. I hit the switch and suddenly realize why—it's because I've never been in a room this big before.

In an instant, I'm fully awake again. I drop my bag and wander past all the cool King Tut–themed art. This is amazing! There's an entire wet bar in here, all trimmed in granite. A wet bar! I should get some booze! And a dining area! I should get some food! And a whole living room![171] Before I wonder which of the deluxe couches might be the pullout bed, I realize this isn't a room; it's a *suite.*

---

[171] I should get a life!

Whoa. If I got this just for wearing a Cubs hat, imagine what might have happened if I'd actually been *nice*.

My floor-to-ceiling windows display the majesty of the entire Strip and the view takes my breath away. There are no obstructions from here to the Space Needle and I see every single twinkling light. In my last room, all I could see were the air-conditioning units.[172]

The master bedroom is equally elaborate and the bed could fit me and everyone I know. The bathroom is the size of my apartment with a tub I could literally swim in.

This is the greatest hotel room to ever exist.

Or . . . wait.

I walk back to the separate WC and give it a test flush. Its contents disappear immediately.

Okay, *now* it's the greatest room to ever exist. And it's all mine for $79 a night.

Fletch suggested I pamper myself on this trip so I decide to give the spa a whirl. I've never actually had any spa services done before. Once I had fake nails put on by this German lady at school but she'd just finished cosmetology school and kind of didn't know what she was doing. Her application was so sloppy my fingers looked like I'd dipped them in candle wax. I figured out how to do acrylic fills myself after that and kept the fake nails until I realized there was mold growing between the fill and my nail bed.

---

[172] Which I thought was problematic until I learned what problematic really looked like.

I tore them off immediately and was so grossed out I haven't had anyone touch my hands since.

I lie on my big bed and study the spa services menu. I can't figure out which option I'd like and which would entail me showing strangers my underpants, so I decide to ask in person. I throw on my shorts and my now-dry polo and head downstairs.

I enter a quietly dim and serene waiting area. Soft music plays and I catch a whiff of something wonderful. Because I am an urban, suave sophisticate, the first words out of my mouth are, "Hey, what smells in here?"

The girl behind the desk answers me. "I believe you're referring to our eucalyptus steam room."

"Woo, I could huff that all day. It's like a jar of Vick's Vapo-Rub, only better."

"If you're interested in some services, the eucalyptus steam room will be at your disposal." When she smiles, I notice she has no pores on her face. None. Whatever she's selling? I want.

"Neat! What do you suggest?"

She explains a variety of different options and I decide on a manicure, pedicure, and facial. I'm given a robe and I change in a lovely locker room before going to relax in a lounge filled with all kinds of beverages.

An esthetician named Dottie takes me into the steam room first and I can feel the polluted physician's office air releasing from my lungs and sinuses. Once I'm good and steamy, Dottie brings me to a comfortable private room, where she begins the extraction process.

By the way, "extraction process" means someone gets rid of your blackheads for you! I'm equal parts repulsed and fascinated. Is this what it's like to be rich, paying people to squeeze your zits and scrub your grout and ice skate with your kids? I kind of want to know.

Twenty minutes later, the ugly pores on my nose have gone from deep to nonexistent. Dottie finishes up with some serious lotion slathering. I return to the lounge to wait before I'm retrieved for my mani-pedi.

A manicurist works on my cuticles while another technician attacks my feet. There's scrubbing and pushing and filing and clipping. I feel like Tom Hanks in that scene in *Joe Versus the Volcano*, except no one's hitting me with a fish.

A girl could get used to this.

The spa provides free bottles of juice, water, and fruit to patrons, so later, when I'm poolside, I'm allowed to go back and help myself. The spa has a bunch of showers and each one is filled with a set of different scent-themed products. As I'm not fully recovered from the horror of last night, the notion of a powerful rain cleanse sounds pretty damn good. I avail myself of the showers rather frequently. By the time I return to my room, I've tried all eight deliciously different stalls.

I buy a bottle of Cinzano Asti from the gift shop and spend the evening in, curled up on one of my many couches, watching the *Seinfeld* finale.[173] I may not be living a movie, but I'm too relaxed to worry about it.

My dad calls the next morning and breaks my reverie when he shares the tragic news. Sometime during the night, my idol Frank

---

[173] I prefer my bubbles in a glass where I can control them, thanks.

Sinatra passed away. If I were at home when I heard this, I'd be devastated because his songs have been a part of my life ever since I could remember. His was the one kind of music upon which everyone—Fletch, my parents, my friends, my elderly relatives, my coworkers, even strangers in a bar—could agree. Just last week Fletch and I were out with David and his wife and Tim and we all sang along when "My Kind of Town" played on the jukebox.

I'm sitting on my lush linens in my sweet suite in the town that ol' Francis Albert built and I'm actually happy in a bittersweet way. I feel like I'm in the one place on earth where I can properly pay tribute.

The second Sinatra's death is announced, people begin to pour into the city and the entire atmosphere becomes electric as everyone gears up to watch the lights go out. They've only darkened the Strip a couple of times before and what we're about to witness is history.

I make my way down the Strip, but before I go outside to join the masses, I stop at a quiet bar in a remote part of Caesars Palace to have a Jack Daniel's. Normally, I hate the stuff, but it was Frank's favorite. My cocktail goes down surprisingly smoothly. I tip my Cubs hat in silent salute. After all, Chicago was *his* kind of town.

When I finish, I find a spot on Flamingo Boulevard with thousands of others. The noise is almost unbearable with all the laughing and shouting. But the minute the lights go out, everyone goes quiet. Even traffic stops. We all stand silently, watching as one by one the casinos fade into the night. In the distance, I can hear fans start an a cappella version of "That's Life," and that's when tears start streaming down my cheeks.

I'm not crying because I'm sad. I mean, what right do *I* have to mourn? I'm not Nancy Sinatra or Mia Farrow. I only ever knew Frank Sinatra through his music and films. I'm not family, I'm not a friend, and I can still have him in my life any time I turn on the TV or put in a CD. But this here? Right now? Surrounded by a handful of the millions of lives he touched? I'm filled with such hope and happiness and love for everyone and these emotions manifest themselves in tears. Then this enormous crowd of strangers begins to spontaneously hug one another.

I feel like I'm part of a religious experience.

I feel like I'm a piece of something that's so much greater than myself.

I feel like . . . I feel like *I'm in a movie.*

Yeah, in a couple of days I'll get on a plane and I'll freak out all the way home. Then I'll go back to my shitty apartment and my difficult job and I'll be broke again because I spent all my money coming here. And when I run across my fellow man, particularly in my doctors' offices, I'll want to punch, not hug, them.

But right now, for this one tiny moment, I want to toss my Cubs hat in the air all Mary Tyler Moore style. And I want to shout.

With joy.

❖

Carrie Bradshaw Made Me Do It

(Not Manolos—But Close)

Every Sunday night, I worship at the altar of Sarah Jessica Parker.

Okay, that's not quite true. Every Sunday night, I change into my jammies, microwave some popcorn, and close the bedroom door to watch *Sex and the City*.

I haven't had a lot of female relationships since I left college. I'm so used to being surrounded by sorority sisters and roommates and other waitresses at work that it's weird that I don't know more girls. All my friends at work are guys, and sure it's fun when Fletch and I go to dinner with David and his wife or Tim and his gal du jour, but it's not the same. I miss hanging out with a big group of girls, so I've made Charlotte, Carrie, Miranda, and Samantha my friends for the time being.

I always watch in the bedroom because the show kind of

repulses Fletch. He says it's totally unrealistic, which, fine, he's got me there. I mean, I've certainly never frequented a swanky club . . . or even been to a party that isn't full of Natural Light keg beer and shag carpeting. I've never gotten a chemical peel from an aggressive Swede named Inga or paid more than twenty dollars for brunch.[174]

Fletch came up with a term for the *SATC* ladies—misoGuynistic[175]—and says SJP has a foot for a face. I disagree. I think Sarah Jessica's an unconventional beauty. Plus, she's totally been my patron saint ever since I was a kid because the roles she's chosen have been such a great guide to life. In *Square Pegs* she proved it was fine to be a socially awkward junior high school student.[176] She made me feel like everyone had a big-glasses-and-frizzy-hair-and-oh-God-please-like-me phase. *Girls Just Want to Have Fun* taught me how to rebel without breaking *too* many rules. I love what a free spirit she was in *LA Story*. (And I'm still jealous that she dated John-John and married Ferris Bueller.)

Actually, I dig *Sex and the City* not just because of the friendships and despite the bedroom antics. (Frankly, these ladies would benefit from keeping their pants on a little more often.) I admire how they conduct their respective businesses. They all have so much professional confidence. Carrie's column is doing great, Samantha's at the top of her field in PR, and Miranda and Charlotte completely rock their jobs. I get the feeling none of these characters ever agonized over how to operate a fax machine, nor did they

....

[174] I'm totally open to it, though.

[175] Meaning they hate men but want to have sex with them.

[176] Although I'm still in pink puffy heart love with how Muffy Tepperman dressed. Argyle socks and saddle shoes! Swoon!

shart themselves every time they were tasked to transfer a call. Sure they may suck at relationships, but they rule at being strong, smart businesswomen and their passion for their careers is enviable. Plus, they get together every week and actually *eat* at brunch; I like how they send the message that it's okay to digest.

The only downside of my Sunday night *SATC* habit is that as soon as the show's over, I'm hit with a huge Sunday night anxiety attack. I dread Monday mornings so much. Each week I pray I'll come down with something daunting but nonfatal, like mono. I always dash to the mirror when the show's over to see if there are any spots in my throat or if I have swollen glands, and I never do, damn it.

I remember when I couldn't wait for Mondays. I guess I've lost my passion for what I do. Or maybe I've just had it shouted out of me? The problem is that even though I'm a recruiter for the HMO now, I still have to deal with existing providers' issues. If anything, I'm even more deeply involved because most doctors I'm assigned to recruit are already part of an established practice. Often, they won't join unless I fix whatever compensation troubles are plaguing their partners.

My company has an entire division that's supposed to deal with this stuff, yet I feel like I'm always haggling with adjusters trying to get claims processed and paid. While my bonus is based on who I can bring in, sometimes I wonder if everyone else is encouraged to find ways *not* to pay the very doctors I worked so hard to land.[177]

What complicates matters is these doctors gossip more than

---

[177] Note I said "I wonder if," not "I know." No need to murder me John Grisham–style, thanks.

Carrie & Co. over brunch. They're contractually forbidden to discuss their reimbursement arrangements with each other, but our repeated warnings carry about as much heft as jaywalking laws. So if I cut a particularly sweet deal with one doctor because we need him, every other guy with a stethoscope in a ten-mile radius demands the exact same thing. Then I'm stuck having an uncomfortable conversation where I have to dance around the fact that the company values[178] degrees from Harvard above those from Hollywood Upstairs Medical School.

Most of my doctors practice on the tony North Shore of Chicago, so the normal physician level of arrogance is multiplied by ten. Regardless of their superior skills and credentials, sometimes I have trouble explaining that even though they may have once treated Michael Jordan, we're not going to pay them like they *are* Michael Jordan.

Today I'm supposed to be having a one-on-one meeting with a practice manager, a lovely gal named Pat. Instead, my casual conversation over coffee has turned into yet another ambush where I have to defend my company's practices to an entire hospital board. Five different gray-suited old men take turns shouting at me in something I can only describe as a verbal gang bang.

I try to pretend I'm Miranda while they bluster and blow. There's no way Miranda would lose her cool if she were in, say, a courtroom situation. She'd stay steadily calm and wouldn't allow opposing council to detect any emotion.[179] Even though I want to

....

[178] Read compensates.

[179] Though she might b-a-n-g opposing council in a broom closet afterward. Again, this is where we differ.

go hide in my car, I cross my arms over my chest, lean back in my chair, and attempt to appear nonplussed. I don't even flinch when someone sprays me with shout spittle.

If anyone deserves an Emmy here, it's me.

❖

"This has to be a mistake!"

I accidentally say this out loud and then quickly clamp my hand over my mouth. Shit! Did anyone hear me? I'm on a covert mission and I almost blew it.

I pull out my compact and wipe the excess powder from the mirror. Then I use it to peek around one corner and then the other. I don't see anyone. Because I have army training[180] I know that threats can come from any angle. I surreptitiously look up. The sky, or rather the dropped acoustical tile ceiling, is clear. I bend over to check below because I can't be too careful. I see nothing but a broken plastic hanger, a few menacing dust bunnies, and a butterscotch wrapper. There's no one lurking, waiting to steal my great prize. All clear.

I'm being ultra-careful because I've got to keep this unbelievable find to myself . . . at least until I get out of the store.

Having recently upgraded to buying well-fitting clothes from better retailers like Bloomingdale's, Saks, and Nordstrom, I vowed to never shop at discount places like TJ Maxx again. However, I kicked myself in the ankle with a chunky heel just to keep from erupting in today's meeting with the hospital board and

....

[180] I can hear Fletch watching military programming through the bedroom door on Sunday nights. That totally counts as training.

ended up ripping my trouser sock. Usually I keep a couple of spare pairs in my bag, but I've been kicking myself a lot lately and I've burned through them all.

Since I was on my way home, I figured I might as well pop into the Maxx and stock up, stashing some in my work bag and the rest in my glove compartment.[181]

I headed right to the hosiery department and pawed through the cream-colored knee-highs on the rack. I located a few acceptable, non-factory-second pairs and began to take my purchase to the register when I spied something desperately out of place in my peripheral vision.

I sidled up to the items that caught my eye, afraid that if I gazed at them dead-on, they'd prove to be a mirage. I exercised the same intentional nonchalance needed to approach my cat Bones prior to stuffing him in a carrier to bring him, hissing and clawing and spitting, to the vet.

Finally, as soon as I was within reach, I snaked my hand out and grabbed. I had the items clutched to my chest in less than a second. Eventually, I loosened my grip and held them out for inspection.

Could they be real?

Did I dare believe?

I verified their authenticity by looking inside, and then I flipped them over and went all Forrest Gump for a moment. *Mama says they was my magic shoes. They could take me anywhere.*

And that's when I shouted.

I'm standing here—big mouth agape—wondering how on

---

[181] Heh. I could call it my sock compartment.

earth a pair of couture crocodile-skin pumps ends up on the sale rack in the ghetto TJ Maxx between all the defective Nikes and last year's off-white, size-twelve Steve Maddens. The original price tag is over four hundred dollars, but now they're marked down to fifty.

I decide I'm buying them long before it occurs to me to try them on. I kick off my snaggy-heeled loafer in preparation to slip on the pump.

The shoes are a rich, mellow golden brown that will coordinate nicely with practically my entire wardrobe. Casual enough to pair with jeans[182] and dressy enough to go with my best Jones New York suit, these may well be the world's most versatile shoes. The toes taper slightly and the three-inch real wooden stacked heel is thick enough to balance on, yet thin enough to elongate the legs. The actual skin is textured and the tiny bumps and markings make each shoe slightly different, but in this case, perfect symmetry would look fake and cheap.

Tentatively, I slip one torn-trouser-socked foot inside. Suddenly, a choir of angels starts singing.

Or maybe it's just a Michael Bolton song playing on the store's sound system.

Whatever, the fit is so right that if this were a Brothers Grimm story, I'd currently be saying sayonara to two bitchy stepsisters and a life of cleaning out fireplaces. I slide my left foot in with the same result. Perfection!

This is kismet!

This is fate!

....

[182] That is, if I wore jeans anymore.

This is divine intervention!

This is a problem.

I only have about sixty bucks to my name and I'm supposed to use it to pay my electric bill.

I'm about to set these little treasures down and walk away when the curly-haired, tutu-wearing, unfortunate-nosed devil on my shoulder asks, *What would Carrie Bradshaw do?*

Carrie would live by candlelight for a couple of days if she had to in order to possess these shoes.

Oh, Carrie Bradshaw, Thy will be done.

She Gets a Long Letter, Sends Back a Postcard (Times Are Hard)

(Silver Tiffany Ring)

" *I*t's like I'm stuck in *Groundhog Day*." Two cosmos and half a caprese salad into dinner, I still can't shake off my frustration.

Fletch dips a piece of focaccia into a little plate of olive oil and parmesan. "How so?"

Fletch is kind of like my Mr. Big, although he's always nice to me. Also, he shows up when he says he will.

And he's not cold or distant.

Nor is he a commitment-phobic douchehound.

Fine, so he's nothing like Mr. Big except that he's picking up the check tonight.[183] We're having dinner at Cucina Bella, the twee Italian place around the corner.

....

[183] Mr. Big's best trait!

Normally I love it here. The atmosphere is wonderful—they're always playing Sinatra, which makes me feel like I'm sitting in my Auntie Virginia's kitchen in the middle of the party. The food is hearty and delicious, but it's presented with a sense of humor— like the wine might be served in a jelly jar and the appetizer on an antique washboard.

I should be delighted Fletch's calamari comes in an old colander, but I can't appreciate the kitsch because I'm still too wound up from work. I'm so anxious about my job, I've picked up the habit of spinning my big silver ring. I bought this ring for myself on my thirtieth birthday. And truly, it is gorgeous. There's a thick silver band that goes around the back of the finger and then it comes up on either side, where ribbed gold pieces hold a center silver loop. It's classy and equestrian-looking, and I get a million compliments on it. (Were there a diamond in the middle, this would be the perfect style of engagement ring, *hint, hint.*)

The heft of the metal on my hand is comforting, but it's so heavy it tends to shift a tiny bit. Because it's already predisposed to movement, I tend to spin it around when I get anxious. This nervous tic makes me crazy, yet I can't seem to stop.

Spin, spin, spin.

"Every time my goddamned phone rings, it's an office manager named Pat or Kathy or Linda—they're all named Pat, Kathy, or Linda, by the way—and they're always calling to yell at me because their doctor isn't in-network yet. Each time I have to tell them he's not because he won't fill out the form to disclose his malpractice history."

"Why? Do they all have major lawsuits against them?" Fletch asks. "Too many watches left where the gallbladder used to go?"

"No, most of my guys are on the North Shore and they're all really good. Although I did once see an application from a doctor in the city who kept operating on the right side of his patients instead of the left. I had to laugh when I read his file because I thought he'd greatly benefit by tattooing *Ralphie* and *Louie* on his wrists."[184]

"Then what's the problem?"

Spin, spin.

"The problem is they're determined to make me prematurely gray." Fletch gives me a pointed look over the rim of his martini glass.[185] I shrug. "Seventy-five percent of the time whatever suit's been brought against them has proved to be bogus. Or it's settled out of court for a pittance because their liability people say it's the easiest thing." I stab a piece of buffalo mozzarella and chew violently. My job puts me in a perpetual state of anger. "The issue is these physicians are unwilling to tell our medical director about it one hundred percent of the time."

"Doesn't he need the info to decide if the doctor gets in or not?"

I gesture at him with my fork. "See? You get it and you don't even work in the industry. Here's what makes me want to pull my hair out—the doctors know we can't approve their application without disclosure, but I have to fight with them for disclosure. Then they get furious at how long the approval process takes, which is entirely their own fault because they won't disclose. It's a vicious cycle of stupid."

....
[184] Yeah, we didn't let him in.

[185] Stoli up, dry, twist of lemon and God have mercy on you if you don't shake it long enough.

Ever the problem solver, Fletch suggests, "Work for a different HMO, then."

"If it were only that easy. I'd still be dealing with the same assholes. And the thing is, doctors say they hate *us* the most, but I'm
friends with people at a couple of different payers and it's the same
old mouthwash just swished to a different side. I was in Dr. Dickweed's[186] office last week and I could hear him shouting at the
Humana rep for twenty minutes, telling her they were the worst
company out there. And then when it was my turn, he said the
same exact thing."

"You wanted me to violate *his* entryway, right?" Last time we
were at the mall doing Christmas shopping, I begged Fletch to
pee on the doctor's office door, which is located in the professional services building across the street. He wouldn't do it because he has no sense of adventure. Or maybe because it was ten
degrees out. Or something.[187]

"That's the guy." I motion to the waiter as he passes by and
order another cosmo.[188] I hand my salad plate over to Fletch.
"Wanna finish this? I don't have much of an appetite."

"Thanks." He neatly slices the salad so he gets an equal ratio
of cheese, tomato, and basil in every bite. He chews carefully and
deliberately. "Are you still considering quitting?"

"Pfft. Only every second of every minute of every day. What
would I do, though? I've had a Monster search with a *political*

....

186 Not his real name. But it should be.

187 I wonder if Mr. Big would whiz on a knob for Carrie? Doubtful.

188 BTW, whoever came up with pink drinks? *Is genius.*

science keyword for six months and it hasn't turned up one listing."

He guffaws. "Bet your philosophy minor keywords aren't helping either." I glower and Fletch lays his fork down. "Listen, I don't know how many times I have to say this. The tech industry is exploding right now. Go do sales for a dot com. Everyone's hiring. I've been slammed with all the business I'm getting from these start-ups because they've got a ton of VC. You've got the tenacity and you know how to negotiate—you'd make a shitload of money."

I mull over his suggestion. There may be something to this dot-com business. I've been noticing subtle changes in the general population every time I go to my office in the Loop. The cars have gotten a lot nicer lately. I was so proud of myself when I earned the privilege of driving a company car and I got to upgrade from my Tercel to a brand-new Dodge Stratus. The car only had thirteen miles on it when I got it! Now it seems like everyone's in a Beemer or a Land Rover and suddenly my gleaming gold Stratus feels gaudy and cheap.

I see people wearing a lot more designer sunglasses when they stroll past me, too. They no longer carry briefcases—instead they've got weathered computer bags with whatever-dot-com logos on them. And they aren't stuck in suits anymore—they're clad in jeans and cargo pants and dirty khakis. An occasional tattoo peeks out of a sleeve or a wrinkled collar. When I started my job three years ago, no professionals ever showed their ink, let alone went to work unshowered or unshaved. I still have to stick a Band-Aid over my tiny sorority ankle tattoo any time I'm wearing pantyhose.

I bet if I were friends with Charlotte, she'd agree with my dis-approval of casual business wear.[189] Regardless, something big is going on out there, but I'm not quite sure what.

The vibe on the streets is almost euphoric, like everyone's so damn excited about their jobs and their companies. I can't re-member the last time I enjoyed what I do for a living. I can't imag-ine what it would be like to leave work on a Friday and not spend the entire weekend dreading Monday. Or what it'd be like to have a spittle-free client conversation.

Yet I'm not quite ready to make a change. "I don't want to stay, but I can't leave because then I'd be admitting defeat." I spin my ring so much that Fletch finally places his hand over mine to stop me.

"That's your problem right there. You won't concede the game, yet you can't justify why you're playing it in the first place."

"Touché." I exhale loudly and drain my cosmo. He's not wrong. "At the moment, the path of least resistance is just giving this job some more time."

"That's nothing but a short-term solution."

"Well, maybe Mexico will be just what I need to improve my attitude." I'm leaving for a vacation in Cancun with my folks at the end of the month. You know what I just realized? You never hear the *SATC* girls talk about their families. That's odd.

"Yes," he quickly agrees, "I'm sure that after a week with your parents, your work problems will seem insignificant."

....

[189] There's nothing more appealing than a good suit on a man. Fletch's making money now and he's been shopping at Brooks Brothers. He looks *amazing*.

I nod and dunk a piece of bread in some homemade marinara sauce before glancing over at him. Why's he's smirking?

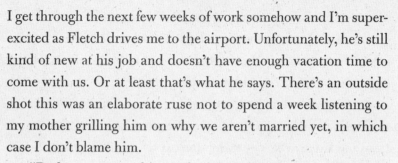

I get through the next few weeks of work somehow and I'm super-excited as Fletch drives me to the airport. Unfortunately, he's still kind of new at his job and doesn't have enough vacation time to come with us. Or at least that's what he says. There's an outside shot this was an elaborate ruse not to spend a week listening to my mother grilling him on why we aren't married yet, in which case I don't blame him.

"Dad says to meet him at the international terminal." I navigate while Fletch drives.

Fletch shakes his head. "Your ticket says terminal three."

"But Dad said this is an international flight so I have to go to the international terminal. I'm supposed to meet them there."

"Your father is wrong. Your ticket is right," Fletch argues.

"But he said—"

"Jen, do you want to go to the correct terminal or do you want to listen to the same man who once led a convoy of sixteen hundred marines *to the wrong country* because he refused to ask for directions?"

"Terminal three, please." We have to take another lap around the periphery of O'Hare to get to the right terminal.

Fletch helps me with my bags, hugs and kisses me good-bye, and then I'm off. I cruise through security and grab a coffee and scone before proceeding to my gate. My parents are already there. My mother lunges to hug me and kisses me on the neck, *which I hate.*

"Please never do that again," I say, wiping off her kiss. I should be kissed on the neck by my boyfriend, not my mother.

"Oh, don't be ridiculous," she replies.

"Jennifer, you're late. We were going to leave for Mexico without you," my father tells me.

"You said to meet you in the *international terminal. This* is not the international terminal. *This* is terminal three. Had I listened to you, I could have missed the flight."

Refusing to admit he was wrong, he merely shrugs. "This isn't the international one? Oh, well, you figured it out. Hey"—he gestures toward my coffee— "why don't you go get me one of those? Two sugars and four Sweet'N Lows." My father prides himself on never having retrieved his own coffee in his entire professional career. He's retired now, but old habits die hard.

"Let me see your hand first," my mother singsongs. She grabs me by the wrist and inspects what would be my wedding ring finger. "This? What is this?" She taps the thick silver band. She raises her voice with rabid excitement. "Is this what I think it is?"

I grit my teeth. "Mom, if you think this is the Tiffany ring I bought myself, *which I already showed you at Thanksgiving*, then yes. Yes it is."

"Jennifer?"

"Yeah, Dad?" Thank God for my dad. He'll run interference between me and my mother's ever-growing wedding obsession.

"I'm ready for my coffee now. Run, run, run, we have a plane to catch."

As I walk back to Starbucks, I realize why Fletch was smirking.

We arrive at our hotel in Cancun and my mother and I sit in the lobby while my father checks us in. As we wait, I'm growing skeptical of our accommodations. We're staying at the very beginning of Cancun's main drag. According to the cabdriver, this is the least nice section of the beach and all the good stuff is a couple of miles away. As I take in the scene, I notice the paint is peeling and the couches in here are threadbare. And the bar? Yeah, Studio 54 called and they want their chrome and mirrors back.

Aarrggh, again.

You know what? I have to stop all this unconstructive thinking—it's not getting me anything except a smooth spot on my finger from all the spinning. I need to channel my inner *SATC* girl. Samantha's a testament to the power of positive thinking. Carrie doesn't dwell on the negative. Charlotte's so upbeat she practically has bluebirds flying out of her ass. So . . . screw it. I'm here in Mexico, a whole country away from my hateful job. No one's going to call me a parasite because of the industry I work in. Nobody's going to tell me *I'm* the incompetent one when *they* refuse/forget to hand in paperwork. Best of all, I can't receive a phone call from an angry physician demanding I swing by their office on a weekend because my cell phone is two thousand miles away. Suck on that, Dr. I-Don't-Care-If-It's-Saturday Dickweed.

I'm going to sit here and have a good attitude. I'm sure the shoddy lobby is no reflection of the accommodations and that the rooms will be great. After all, I wrote my dad a huge check to pay for my third of this trip back in October. For that price, my room can't *not* be luxurious, right?

I spent my whole bonus from last quarter on this trip, but it's worth it because I'm finally independent enough to pay my own way . . . although I'd have had plenty of money left over if the company hadn't just revised our bonus structure. However, I'm not thinking about that because I'm trying to have a good attitude. I'm thinking about bluebirds. Happy, chirpy bluebirds. Bluebirds who know how to fucking compensate you for your fifteen-hour days.

The one positive thing I should focus on right now is that we aren't going to be parents and child on this trip; we're going to be three grown adults sharing a pleasant vacation in separate rooms. We're going to each pay for our own meals and activities and I'm delighted at the prospect. Our old family vacations where we kids had zero say in any matter[190] are now a thing of the past. Going forward, we are equals!

My dad strolls back from registration carrying keys and one margarita. For himself. "We're all set. Jennifer?" He points to his carry-on. "My bag."

I throw it over my shoulder, schlepping it along with my own stuff. I guess the equality will begin after I get to my own room, then.

We arrive at a room on the seventeenth floor and open the door. This room is . . . big. It's not nice, or pretty, or for that mat-

----

[190] E.g., driving to fucking Knoxville.

ter all that clean, but it's big.[191] There's a kitchen, a table with a couple of spindly chairs, a sitting area with a ratty old couch, and a bedroom with a small attached bath. The literature in the lobby said the hotel was undergoing renovations and the suites weren't yet done. But that doesn't matter—all the single rooms are complete so mine should be better. Bluebirds! Bluebirds!

"We're here!" My mother claps her hands as she enters the room. "This is great; I love it!"

"Okay, I would like to go to the beach," I say. "Please give me my keys so I can go to my room and put on my suit. See you down on the sand in ten minutes?"

Suddenly, no one else in my party can meet my eye. "Um, hello? Keys?" Still nothing. "You guys, I need my keys to get into my room." I look at each of my parents' guilty expressions and I get the overwhelming feeling that there are no keys.

Dad says, "Your mother has something to tell you," and then he runs off to the bedroom, closing the door behind him.

"Mom?"

"Isn't this beautiful? Look at that view!"

"Mom?"

"There's a whole kitchen! We can cook if we want to!"[192]

"Mom."

She will not even glance in my direction. Instead, she focuses on inspecting every leaf on the plastic, dust-covered palm tree by the rickety sliding glass door.

My dad peeks his head out and in one giant breath blurts,

....

[191] Big is the new black?

[192] Yes, I spent $2,000 to go to Mexico specifically so I could cook my own meals.

"Your mother thought you'd be afraid to stay in a room by yourself so we got the only hotel with an available suite and you're sleeping out here on the couch and that's why we're staying in a lousy hotel instead of a nicer one down the beach and I told her you wouldn't want this but she didn't listen." Then he closes the door again and I can hear him shut and lock the bathroom door, too.

I am dumbfounded. Surely this can't be true, because I'm thirty years old and I have my own apartment in the middle of the third largest city in the country. And why do I suddenly feel like we just drove two hours for a lobster?

After a few frantic calls to the front desk (and to neighboring properties), where I try to compensate for only speaking English by talking louder, I find there's no room at any other inn. I am stuck.

My mother's response to the whole situation? "This will be fun!"

Sure, if sleeping in the living room with no privacy and a hide-a-bed bar digging into your back and finding your parents' partial dentures soaking in every cup in the entire suite and learning the meaning of one Spanish word—el Niño—is what you consider fun, then yes, it's a goddamn blast.

On the bright side, I've stopped obsessing about work.

And I've figured out why Carrie never talks about her parents.

❖

"I wouldn't hire you."

"Thanks, Dad. What a tremendous vote of confidence that is."

My parents and I are having lunch in a thatched hut by the

water in Xcaret, a Cancun nature conservatory. When we arrived this morning, we saw ten thousand signs begging guests not to wear any kind of mass-produced sunscreen. The conservators are emphatic about this because patrons can swim in all the hidden ponds and lagoons on the property and there are ingredients in commercial sunscreen that could mess up the delicate ecosystem here. Naturally my mother refuses to part with the pesos necessary to purchase the environmentally sound stuff sold in the gift shop and she's slathering herself liberally with something sure to kill every tree frog within a two-mile radius. (And correct me if I'm wrong, but I'm pretty sure a thatched roof has an SPF of at least 100.)

"You should listen to your father, he's usually right," she agrees.

Of course he is, Slathery McFrogkiller.[193]

"Dad, can't you agree that it's possible the business world may have changed since you were in your prime?" I ask. He retired a few years ago, yet still takes a tremendous amount of pride in having never once sent an e-mail. This reminds me of when I was a kid and it looked like the metric system was going to catch on—Dad pledged he'd paint over every thermometer because he refused to accept the concept of Celsius.

Lasciviously, my mother waggles her eyebrows and suggests, "He's still in his prime." I do not acknowledge this statement, yet I find myself unconsciously scrubbing at my hands with my napkin.

....

[193] Do I even need to mention this week has been a long one? I've pretty much worn all the skin off my finger.

"I'm just saying that quitting a job without having one lined up is not necessarily the kiss of death in this economy," I argue. "The dot-com market is exploding and it sounds like tons of places are hiring."

My father simply sips his cerveza before replying, "Pfft. Not relevant. The business world is a constant."

I consider this for a moment. "Wait a minute . . . you've told me stories about having so many martinis in the middle of the day that Mom had to pick you up from the restaurant and drive you home."

"Jennifer, that only happened a few times," my mom chides.

"If that happened even once in the professional world right now, you wouldn't be sent home to sleep it off; you'd be sent to rehab. At the very least, you'd get a huge HR write-up."

"Our HR guy used to come with us. If I recall, Bob didn't drink martinis," my dad muses. "He preferred red wine."

I may as well be having this conversation with the dead tree frogs right now for all the headway I'm making.

Resigned, I defer to my father's flawed logic. "Okay, Dad, you win. I won't quit."

"Good girl."

And then I wrench my ring so hard I practically break my knuckle.

The End of the Beginning

(Crocodile-Skin Pumps)

Tim, David, and I are lunching at the food court in the Citibank building. They're both chowing down on some kind of tuna-based sushi, while I have my usual chicken teriyaki bowl.

Can I be honest here? I kind of don't understand sushi. Like, what's the draw of raw fish? Especially raw fish wrapped in seaweed? And, really? *Seaweed?* Who came up with the idea to eat this? Was someone all, *"Hey, you know that disgusting green algae? I'm talking about the crap that gets stuck to our oars when we row the boat and ruins our nets and makes our hair all slimy when we dive in? And that washes up on the sand and reeks like an ocean full of dead fish? Yeah, we should totally have that with dinner."*

In my opinion, sushi is less a meal and more a game of truth or dare gone horribly wrong. Yes, I appreciate the aesthetics of a big plate of sushi, but I also dig how pretty my couture crocodile shoes are and you don't see me dipping them in soy sauce. (Shoot, I practically encase them in Lucite.)

I shudder as Tim and David shovel the glistening pink bits into their mouths. I try not to gag imagining the raw texture on my tongue.

"I can't believe they picked you," Tim says. "Why would they pick you? You hate everything about this company."

I've been selected to represent my department as part of a company-wide quality-improvement task force. Because of this, I'm one of the people set to meet with the president of the company later today. My work friends are astounded I was asked because they think I complain all the time.

"No," I correct him, "I don't *hate* the company; I hate its lack of innovation. I hate that the applications to join the network are thirty pieces of repetitive paperwork when a Web-based tool would be ten billion times more efficient. I hate that we merged almost three years ago to capitalize on another company's technology and yet we never integrated their systems. I hate that there's no centralized database that stores all the relevant information."

"So . . . what you're saying is you hate everything about the way they do business, not to be confused with your actually hating *them*," Tim says. Sometimes these boys are too blunt, even if they are right. I bet *SATC* Charlotte would occasionally if not sugarcoat reality, then at least wrap it up in a pretty plaid bow.

I frown and gesture toward his plate. "Finish your sushi."

"Are you nervous?" David asks.

"No . . . I'm more excited than anything. I usually feel like I'm pissing in the wind every time I broach a problem with management. So I'm psyched that someone with the power to actually make changes wants to hear what I have to say."

The day we went to Xcaret, I stood on the balcony after my parents went to bed and spun my ring and promised myself *this* is the year I'm going to make it happen. I started my career being bold and outspoken but lately I've done nothing but go along with the status quo. Going along to get along has been safe but it's made me miserable. I've allowed these physicians to bully me. And I don't like bullies.

I've let management steamroll me, like when I stayed mute when I found out my bonus was being slashed. That's not me. I think that's why I continue to identify with the *Sex and the City* girls. They aren't corporate drones. They aren't living their lives like a Dilbert cartoon. They're who I was and who I can probably be again.

Today I have the opportunity to set things right.

Today I'll make sure I've been heard and I can't wait.

I'm dressed for the part, too. I look like I've just walked out of a Jones New York catalog. I splurged on a fitted cranberry suit coat with a slight peplum at the bottom and a long, matching pencil skirt. The crisp white blouse with pointy collars makes me look extra professional. I pulled my crocs[194] out of their protective casing and they complete the whole outfit.

David glances at his watch. "T minus fifteen minutes. You guys ready to roll?"

We pick up our trays and gather up dirty napkins, dumping the trash in the big cans on the periphery of the food court. We

---

[194] Crocs—isn't that an awesome nickname for a pair of shoes?

cut through the train station to avoid as much of the slushy streets as possible. My shoes are completely waterproofed but I like to steer clear of what hazards I can. When I first got them and it was warm enough to go without trouser socks, I'd take them off and carry them rather than allow them to touch the sidewalk. The guys always laughed at me, but I bet Carrie Bradshaw would totally understand.

Back in the office, I fix my lipstick and run a quick brush through my hair. Then I grab my notebook and my Mont Blanc[195] pen and head toward the conference room. David and Tim are both sitting at David's desk. "Knock 'em dead, tiger!" David calls.

"Come tell us what happened when you're done," Tim adds.

I already know what's going to happen; I'm going to rock this meeting.

An hour later, I'm back at David's desk. I stand there until he looks up from his spreadsheet and notices me.

"Hey, how'd it go?" he asks.

"Okay, *now* I hate the company," I tell him.

"Why? What happened?"

I flop into his visitor's seat and I wave for Tim to come join us. As Tim ambles our way, David tells him, "*Now* she hates the company."

"Shocker." They both laugh.

I shoot daggers at both of them. "Do you want to hear this or not?"

....
[195] Fake.

Sheepishly, Tim says, "Sorry, go on."

"We're in there and after we chat for a bit, the president goes around the table and begins to ask everyone what they need to do their jobs better. The first three morons are all, *'Oh, we're so happy, don't change a thing!'* Then he gets to me and I present a clear, concise list of ideas on how technology could really change our business. I mean, I have an actual vision for how much better everything could be. I can see his eyes light up like, *Hey, this girl might be on to something.*"

"Good for you!" Tim claps me on the back.

"Hold your praise. Then the jackass sitting next to me tells the president that she's having trouble getting another employee to return her calls and can he please make them talk to her? Then the original three morons jump in and tell him about how they need stupid shit like sturdier file folders because the ones they use rip too easily." I take a deep breath and continue but I'm almost too disgusted. "And here's the kicker—instead of him saying, *Listen up you ass-tards, I'm the president of this company and I could totally have you killed and—*"

"Why would he threaten to kill them?" David's brows knit in confusion.

Tim replies, "She's been reading too much Grisham."

"*Anyway*, instead of telling the group that we should really focus on the macro, he whips out a pen and begins taking requests for office supplies and phone messages. Then it hits me like a ton of bricks—none of the higher-ups actually want change. They just want to create the *appearance* of change so we shut the hell up already."

David nods sadly. "Jen, I could have told you that."

Tim loosens his tie and leans way back in the other visitor's chair. "What's your contingency plan? You want to stay here and make the best of it, or do you want to try something else?"

"That's a really good question."

And I'm going to find the answer.

❖

I'm sitting in my Stratus a couple of days later giving myself a pep talk. *Listen, as soon as you're done here you can cross the parking lot and go to the mall. And you can buy makeup at the Prescriptives counter and ogle the David Yurman jewelry and pretend like you can afford a Prada bag. I'm giving you permission to play hooky from your job for an hour. All you have to do is get through this.*

This is when I wish I carried a bottle of Jameson in my car.[196] A shot of liquid courage would sure soothe my nerves. My hands are trembling and the butterflies in my stomach keep crashing into my heart. I'd totally vomit right now, except I'm afraid I might hit my crocs.

I've been summoned to Dr. Dickweed's office to discuss[197] more unpaid claims. His partner has finally been admitted to our network, so now dealing with this abusive man is in no way, shape, or form any part of my job . . . yet my boss said I had to come anyway. Apparently Dr. Dickweed is "a crucial member of our provider network" and he specifically asked for my assistance.

I'm stunned this guy is able to maintain a thriving practice.

----

[196] Even though I'm not sure how I'd mesh the whole Irish whiskey–driving home conundrum. My mom isn't driving three hours to get me.

[197] Read be screamed at about.

He yells at his patients the same way he yells at me. Seriously, he bellows with everything he's got. He even opens his mouth so wide I can see his uvula vibrate. (It's gross.) And his office staff—oh, God, do I pity those poor people. Whereas I only have to deal with his bullshit every couple of weeks, they endure the full brunt of his rage forty hours a week. His staffers scuttle along right next to the walls and never make eye contact.

I check the time on my dashboard clock. It's 11:53 a.m. If I wait a few more minutes, it will be twelve p.m., our scheduled appointment time. Yet if I stroll in at twelve p.m., I will be "late" according to Dr. Dickweed, and then he'll tack on another fifteen minutes of bluster explaining how valuable his time is.[198] I unfold myself from the driver's seat, grab my bag, and with great resignation traverse the sidewalk to his office.

Kathy behind the desk pulls a compassionate face when she tells me. She says the doctor is ready to see me *right now* and sends me directly back to his private office. As I retreat down the hallway, I hear her whisper more to herself than to anyone else, "Good luck."

I stand at his open door for a moment before I knock. The doctor has his back to me. The fluorescent lighting highlights the liver spots on his bald patch. He's hunkered over his computer and he appears bony and delicate. Middle age has stooped his shoulders, slimming his limbs and thickening his waist. From this angle, he almost looks frail. Weak. Scrawny. Possibly in need of a hot bowl of soup and a bear hug. I'm almost feeling sympathetic when he spins around in his chair and spots me.

....

[198] Someday he'll see the irony here.

"Well, you took your goddamned time getting here, didn't you?"

It is 11:55 a.m.

I plaster on a smile. "Good morning, Doctor, I understand you have some claims you'd like me to address?"

He stalks over to a filing cabinet, pulls out a stack, and literally flings the whole pile at me. The space in front of my face goes white for a second before all the pieces of paper drift to various locations on the floor.

I'm very quiet for a moment while I figure out my next move. If I punch him—*oh, God, do I want to punch him really hard with my big silver ring*—I'll end up in jail. If I scream back at him, I'll get fired. I bet Samantha would seduce him and then totally destroy him, but I'd rather eat roofing tar.

I decide my best bet is to do nothing at all. "Looks like you dropped something!" I say sweetly. I don't make a move from where I'm standing.

I've spent so much time apologizing to this man over issues that aren't my fault, it takes him a second to realize I'm holding my ground. I can actually feel the balance of power tipping as he crouches down to retrieve the papers. "I'm happy to take these back to my office and get them all figured out for you," I tell him.

"Come with me," he says brusquely. I follow him down the hall. I'm almost always seated when I meet with him, so I never realized that in my crocs, I'm just as tall as he is. We get to a little storage closet at the end of a hallway, filled with boxes and a makeshift desk.

Before I even realize what's going on, the doctor jumps out

from behind me and shuts the door. From the other side, he shouts, "You can come out when you've resolved my claims issues."

I grab the door knob and try to turn it.

That crazy old bastard actually locked me in here.

This? This is a new one. Can't say I've ever been kidnapped before. I try the door handle again. Yep, still locked. I walk to the tiny window over the desk. It's just a pane of glass and doesn't open. Okay, I would have stayed a journalism major and taken the Beirut beat if I had any interest at all in being kidnapped.

I sit in an old office chair and weigh my options. I could try to break the door down except I think that's one of those things that looks way easier on TV. I shove up against it a little bit—*ow*—and realize I'm right.

Samantha would throw the chair through the window and jump out except it's little and I might not fit.[199]

Charlotte would call the police except I'm pretty sure no one would believe me.

Miranda would be the most levelheaded. I follow her lead and decide to use my cell phone to call my director. After I explain the situation (and she finishes snickering[200]), she tells me not to do any of the above. Her suggestion is to just sit there and work on the claims. She doesn't want me to make any trouble because we really need this doctor in our network.

Miranda would never take this kind of shit.

So I use my phone to dial Kathy in reception. I tell her the

---

[199] Also, there's snow outside and I don't want to get my shoes wet.

[200] Because felony kidnapping? Is a total laugh riot.

doctor has locked me in the storage room. Strangely, she isn't that surprised. I demand she come let me out. When she opens the door, I hand her the stack of claims, saying, "These belong to you."

"What are they?"

I stand up straight and pull my shoulders back. "They're what I like to call *the last straw*."

❖

I go home with every intention of writing up a letter of resignation. But before I can even boot up my laptop, my Sunday fantasy comes true and I break into a cold sweat. I alternate between broiling and freezing and I begin to cough my lungs out. I'm stricken with the worst flu of the decade.

I'm so exhausted that I can't even stay awake to see *SATC*. And I barely have the energy to change my voice mail at work, but I do anyway because I have to make sure the Pats, Kathys, and Lindas have the number of my backup.

An entire week later, I'm finally well enough to return to the office. I've changed my mind about tending my resignation. Yes, I hate this job, but I can't just quit. It's too dicey. I can't get my dad's words out of my head.[201]

I get to my desk after stopping to say hello to David and Tim. They both remark that they've never seen me so pale. (Girls would mention the five pounds I've lost.)

I throw my purse in a drawer and slide my laptop into the

---

[201] He also told me I made lousy coffee and could therefore not be his secretary, either. I'm thinking he just doesn't know what coffee without spit in it tastes like.

docking station. As I settle in, I notice my voice-mail light blinking. I can't have too many messages because my greeting instructed callers to talk to my backup for urgent matters, and to e-mail me whatever wasn't.

I pick up the receiver and punch in my password. I cradle the phone on my shoulder while I log in to the computer. I have ten new e-mails but none of them are pressing. Sweet! And then I hear my voice mail kick in.

Welcome to the Audix Network. You have one hundred and three new messages.

Eighty of these are from Dr. Dickweed.

None of them is apologetic.

All of them are apoplectic.

As I listen and transcribe, I notice I'm sinking lower and lower in my seat. I'm practically cowering by the end, and I'm shaking all the way to my shoes. I kick them off in case my feet start terror-sweating.

Then I step outside myself and really examine the situation.

Hold on, this isn't who I am.

I'm not a coward.

I'm not a patsy.

I'm certainly not a punching bag, even if the blows are only verbal.

I will not be bullied.

I look down at what I've written in quivery handwriting and I decide I've reached my limit. That's enough.

I wad up the paper, then put my shoes back on and stomp on it before tossing it in the trash. Then I open a Word document and begin to type.

Dear Human Resources,
It is with regret that I'm tendering my resignation. . . .

❖

You know what, Dad?

You're wrong.

Plenty of companies will hire me if I'm not employed. And if I go into my interview with a good attitude, a solid résumé, and some killer crocodile shoes? They'll even give me a better salary.

❖

"Where are we going?" I'm almost completely out of breath and starting to fall behind.

Someone in the group assures me that we're almost there.

"Yeah, you said that, but where are we *going*?" I'm trying to keep up but three-inch crocodile shoes aren't exactly the best choice for climbing the hills of San Francisco, especially on a slippery sidewalk. I could take them off for better traction, but the street's cold and wet.

"Here," says the girl with the spiky red hair. I think she's from San Diego. "We're going here."

I eye the exterior sign dubiously. "This looks like a sushi bar."

"That's because it is," replies the girl from Boston.

Okay, did *no one* listen to me in the getting-to-know-you part of our training session earlier today? My "one interesting fact about you" was that I hated sushi.

I'm here in San Francisco as part of corporate training. I quit the HMO, telling them I'd rather be waiting tables again than spend any more time in health care. Fortunately, the universe did not call my bluff and I was quickly snapped up by an information technology recruiting firm. My new job entails developing relationships with companies and providing them with IT consultants when needed.

I've been on staff for a few months now and realize this isn't exactly my dream career. However, they gave me an extra couple grand just for walking in the door and it's super-easy to earn commission. Plus, I should learn enough about technology to land a better dot-com job when the opportunity arises. Also? No one's yelled at me once, even when one of the contractors I placed sexually harassed a secretary.[202]

"Yeah, I heard you. You can't say you hate sushi if you've never tried it," Boston argues.

Pfft. "Of course I can."

Boston stares me down as the rest of our group files into the restaurant. "No. Don't do that. Don't be that way."

"What do you mean?"

"Don't be outspoken and ballsy in class and then not even have the courage to try something you can buy in the grocery store."

I take a step back. "*Ouch*. That was straight to the heart."

She grins. "Did it work?"

I pause for a long moment. "Yes."

"Then let's go." Boston holds the door open and I enter in front of her. The rest of our group is already seated around the bar. As I sit, I notice there's a channel full of water between the chef and us. I'm going to be honest—I'm kind of a sucker for anything with a moat.

....
[202] I don't advocate his behavior. But I do advocate calm, rational customers.

"What is this? How does it work?" The other girls from my class explain how the chef continually puts together new combinations of fish and rice and then sets them adrift on a floating plate. They sail around the bar and if you want something, you take it. Each plate is coded, so when the waitress collects them, she knows how much to charge.

I sit still as fish bits packaged like pretty little Christmas presents float by. San Diego shows no hesitation, grabbing three plates in quick succession. She wolfs down each piece after covering it with wasabi and pickled ginger.

Boston carefully selects one of the pink things that I always used to see David and Tim eating. She douses it with a little soy and eats it in two bites.

"You're not eating," she says. "Here. Try this. If you don't like it, I'll buy you some chicken fingers once we've finished. You can eat them with ketchup." She hands me a little boat with something green, white, and black on it. I stare at it and make no motion toward it. "Oh, my God, you're worse than a *child*. My eight-year-old son eats sushi. You really want to be bested by a second grader?"

"No." *Maybe.*

I hold the piece up to my mouth and give it a tentative sniff. I smell . . . nothing. That's a relief. If it smelled fishy, I really would have barfed on my shoes. I hold the roll against the very tip of my tongue . . . and my head surprises me by not exploding. Then I take my first mouse-sized nibble and then another. And another.

"You like it, don't you?"

"I can neither confirm nor deny your allegations."

"You're an asshole. Try this." She picks up what she calls

hamachi and sets it in front of me. My reaction time is quicker and I clean my plate in a couple of bites.

I go on to try snapper, scallops, and squid. I do spit the salmon out into my napkin, but I never cared for it cooked, either.

Over the course of dinner, all of the girls from my training class laugh and talk and tell stories for hours and it's just like a *Sex and the City* brunch only with more business and less b-l-o-w j-o-b chatter.

I also have something like ten cups of sake, which is why I don't blame the sushi when I do eventually vomit in the vicinity of my feet.

But you know what? I wiped off my shoes in the morning and they're fine.

They're a lot more resilient than I ever expected.

❖

Today is by far the high point in my professional career. When I look at all the reasons I might have had in becoming a writer, what I'm about to do ranks in the top five. I've known this was a possibility for an entire month, yet I didn't dare to dream it could actually happen.

Where am I?

In the car, on my way to meet one of my all-time favorite authors, Candace Bushnell!

I'm so keyed up that the truffle oil fries I inhaled at lunch roil in my stomach. Or possibly it's all the cupcakes.[208] A while back I wrote a blog post on cupcakes and I got more feedback from it than anything else I've written in my site's five-year lifespan. Seriously, our nation is never going to be on the same page on issues like gun control, welfare, the economy, the environment, etc. I doubt we'll ever come to terms on tastes great or less filling and hybrids versus Hummers, and there will always be Yankees fans and Red Sox fans, and never the 'twain shall meet. Fortunately, all it takes for us to be of one mind is some buttercream frosting.

Because of this, a number of people in cities with great bakeries wrote and offered to bring treats to my events. My response? *"Cupcake up, bitches!"*

After my overly enthusiastic reply, I began to have second thoughts. I mean, for God's sake, I'm beyond neurotic when it comes to issues like "safety" and *The Gift of Fear* is like my personal user's manual. Do I not have Homeland Security on speed

---

[208] I am the *fail whale* of diet-book-tour healthy eating.

Epilogue

Back(Fat) to the Future

◆◆◆◆◆◆◆◆◆◆◆◆◆◆◆◆◆◆◆◆

I got rich during the dot-com era.

Then I went broke.

Then I got fat. I guess my mom was right about all that sugar and butter.[203]

So I wrote a book about my experiences called *Bitter Is the New Black*. People liked it, so I wrote another one called *Bright Lights, Big Ass*. People liked that one, too. So I wrote a third book called *Such a Pretty Fat*.

I've since married Fletch, adopted a pit bull named Maisy, and my trainer Barbie got me to run my first mile in thirty years.[204]

....

[203] My brother is still a jerk, though.

[204] Please feel free to buy all these books if you'd like the complete story.

I guess that brings us up to now, the night before I leave for my cross-country book tour.

❖

What I said—"Please give me a loose, casual, messy updo."

What the stylist heard—"Please fashion my locks into a giant, impenetrable hair bullet."

What I said—"I'd like my makeup to be light, polished, and natural."

What the makeup artist heard—"I would like fifteen shades of lavender eye shadow. And boob glitter. Lots and lots of boob glitter."

Finished in the salon, I sit in the car and stare at myself in the rearview mirror. I look like a Russian mobster's girlfriend. Yes. This is exactly what I was going for when I forked over three hundred dollars.

I tried to prevent the problem with the hair, telling the stylist it wasn't what I wanted while she was in the middle of doing it. To compensate, she scrunched the enormous dome she'd created on my head a couple of times to loosen it up. Now I have one piece solid with hairspray, and because of the rumpling, it keeps swinging open on the side like a broken garden gate.

I pull out of the parking garage, doing my best not to mow down innocent pedestrians in my cosmetic distress. I attempt to mellow out by telling myself when I get home I can *probably* turn the dome into a bouncy retro ponytail. And I can likely remove fourteen of the fifteen layers of eye shadow . . . right?

I catch another glimpse of myself at a stoplight. The eyelashes . . . they may be a problem. I asked the makeup artist to supplement my own stubby, thin lash line with some false pieces. She said it would be fifteen dollars for the case of loose lashes and another twenty for the application. Sure, I said. If that's what it costs, that's what it costs.

At no point did I realize she'd apply every single last lash in the box in an effort to give me my money's worth. I couldn't see what was happening, so I made the (wrong) assumption to trust her judgment.

If I happened to bump into a Vegas showgirl right now, she'd be all, *"Bit much, doncha think?"* Plus, the lashes aren't even on straight. On my right eye, half of them are facing west, the other half facing east. They come together in the center of my lid in a hairy little teepee. Also? I appear to be cross-eyed.

As I turn off of Michigan Ave and onto Chicago, the rogue bit of hair swings out to the left, hits me in the eye, and gets stuck in the forest of lashes. When I attempt to detangle it all, I almost lose control of the car and narrowly avoid plowing into a family of tourists wearing Navy Pier sweatshirts.[205]

On the bright side, maybe no one will show up tonight and there won't be any witnesses to me in all my Moscow Mafia-doll glory.

In her book *Save Karyn*, the author Karyn Bosnak writes about spotting Stevie Wonder in front of a New York restaurant. She's so starstruck it doesn't even occur to her that Stevie won't see her when she waves.

....

[205] Chicago—Come for the shopping; stay for the vehicular manslaughter.

Save Karyn is one of my favorite books. I've read it half a dozen times, and I particularly love the Stevie Wonder story. So you'd think that when I run smack into Stevie and his entourage in the Admirals Club at O'Hare, I'd have the sense not to wave at him.

You'd think that, anyway.

Since I arrived at the airport two solid hours before my flight, I have plenty of time to call my friend Angie to report on my dumb-assedness.

"How many times did you walk by him and wave?" Angie asks. "More than once?"

I hesitantly admit, "Yes."

"More than twice?"

I exhale. "Yes."

"More than five times?" I clear my throat. What? The Admirals Club is very dry. By they way, I can thank my author friend Stacey Ballis for clueing me in on the Admirals Club in the airport. She explained that I didn't have to be an *actual* admiral to join; I only had to have four hundred dollars. "Jen? You still there?"

"I can't help it if his seat's on the way to the bathroom. I paid a lot for this membership and I'm absolutely going to make that up in mini-muffins and hot beverages."

"How many free coffees have you had so far?"

"Also more than five."

"Is his entourage concerned you're starting to stalk him?"

"If I pee one more time, then probably. For now, I'm okay."[206]

....

[206] Although I'm tempted to beg him to never let the less-talented kids on *American Idol* sing his songs ever again. I've yet to recover from Kevin Covais's version of "Part-Time Lover."

I hear pans rattling in the background. Angie has the ability to whip up a four-course, five-star, nutritionally complete breakfast for her kids using nothing but spray cheese and tub margarine. She'd be running the world right now if it didn't interfere with her PTA meetings. "Tell me about last night. Nice turnout at your Chicago reading?"

"Thank God, yes. Great crowd, lots of enthusiasm, and they didn't laugh at my hair or makeup too much. The only hitch of the whole night is now my face hurts from smiling."

"Aww . . . you were that happy?"

"Yes . . . but also I got too much Botox."

Right before the first draft of *Such a Pretty Fat* was due, my editor and I began to talk about author photos for the back page. The pictures on my first two books are a bit posed for my liking. Stacey suggested I should have one that showed my personality more, so I thought it would be funny to print a more informal shot.

Considering how many stories there are in that book about getting high on Ambien and ordering Barbie merchandise, I figured posing with my life-sized Barbie hairstyling head would be hysterical. I took my digital camera and did some arms-out, MySpace-type test shots. Since I can never be alone in any room of this house, my dogs Maisy and Loki tagged along to my impromptu photo shoot, staying close while I tried out various angles.

When I uploaded the photos, the first thing I realized was that posing with a Barbie head and tousled hair and two dogs wrestling in the background makes one look less "upbeat" and "iconoclastic" and more "bugfuck, batshit, ham-sandwich crazy."

On closer inspection, I noticed how awful my skin looked:

leathery, spotty, and in need of some serious ironing. I kept staring at the shots and telling myself, *Oh, honey, the sun is not your friend anymore*. I briefly considered printing out my photos and bringing them to grade schools to Scare Kids Straight into Sunscreen.

Despite my glaring lack of time management skills, I managed to finish the book and couldn't dwell on what was happening above my shoulders. Shortly after that, my manuscript came back for editing and I got immersed again in work. When I finished the revisions, I found myself with nothing but time.

And a mirror.

And an approaching fortieth birthday. I'm not ashamed of my age, but I kick myself for eschewing sunscreen for all those years. Plus I'm still kind of emotionally immature and I decided I'd be better off if my outside matched my inside.

I began to seek solutions. When I found out procedures like Botox and microdermabrasion cost less than a good pair of boots or one night in a nice hotel, I said *Sign. Me. Up.*

I started getting injections right after my birthday and I've been thrilled with the results. The only problem is I went overboard this last session because I figured if a few poisonous facial injections are good, then more must be *more* good.

Again, not so much.

Now if I grin too broadly, my forehead offers resistance and my face aches. The sensation is wholly unpleasant. Yet I've got skin like a baby's ass, so you can see my dilemma.

Angie laughs at me. "You're kind of a moron."

"Well aware of that, thanks."

A quick series of beeps goes off on the other end of the line. I assume it's Angie's dryer, but she may be initiating a launch sequence. All bets are off with her. "You all stressy about your flight?"

"I'm actually calm. I bought an iTouch and downloaded a bunch of episodes of *Gossip Girl*. I figure if I'm concentrating on whether or not Blair and Chuck will work it out, I won't worry so much about being airborne."

"Then forgive me, I take back calling you a moron."

"I appreciate that. Listen, I've got to scoot."

"Oh, are you boarding already?"

"No, but I *am* about to wet my pants. I've got to go find a bathroom in the terminal so Stevie doesn't sic his security team on me. Talk to you soon!"

I arrive in New York for my first official tour event and it goes well. I'd say the evening is perfect, until the next morning when I start receiving photos on my BlackBerry. I wore a great yellow and white dress. Although this garment is a bit lower-cut than I'd normally choose, it's so flattering that I couldn't *not* wear it. I love how it hugs my chest and emphasizes my newfound waistline,[207] and then the fabric cascades out gracefully all the way to a tea-length swirl. This dress hides a multitude of sins.

Except I never tried it on while sitting down.

I'm casually elegant in all the photos where I'm standing at my lectern. Unfortunately, I had no idea that when I sit, the dress gaps and so the top two inches of my black bra showed in *every seated shot*.

....

[207] Thank you, Barbie.

Despite my foundation garments being documented for posterity, I take some comfort in the fact that it's a top-of-the-line bra. Right before the tour, I went in for my first professional fitting. I found out I was six inches and two cup sizes off! (Who knew everything up there was rolling around like a couple of honeydew melons in the trunk?) I didn't care for the fitting itself because it entailed a stranger moving my b-r-e-a-s-t-s around like a shell game for thirty minutes, but I forgave her when I discovered the right fit trims twenty pounds off immediately.

The irony of having shown the entire audience my bra is how reluctant I was to putting a bra on the cover of the book in the first place. *Oh, no!* I argued with my publisher. *I can't have underwear on the cover! I'm too modest!* Fortunately, my gaffe at the reading will be a one-time mistake. Before my lunch meeting today, I'm going right out to buy fashion tape.

Hey, guess what I didn't know about fashion tape? Apparently the double-stick stuff *will* keep the neckline of my garment from gaping. However, if I peel my dress back even once to readjust, I'll ruin the sticky bond, thus not only showing a generous swath of underwear but also large, mangled bits of tape. And this will happen when I'm shaking the hands of important people at my publisher's office.

Then, if I buy stronger tape, it will be *too* strong, and when I peel it off I'll take an entire layer of skin with it, leaving me with enormous tape hickeys.

I have one word for my next tour: *turtlenecks.*

dial? And live in a city where all the 911 operators recognize my voice?

Were I not temporarily made insane by the idea of a box of treats with my name on it, I'd have never agreed to people bringing me cupcakes. I asked myself, *"Really? You're going to eat food from a stranger? Really? No."*

Then I received cupcakes last night at my event.

Um . . . guess what?

I totally *will* eat food from strangers.[209]

Right now, though, I'm probably feeling sick because Candace is about to interview me on her Sirius radio show. I'm about to have an actual conversation with my idol. Other writers dream of making bestseller lists, but me? I dream of meeting the inspiration behind Carrie Bradshaw.

Even though Carrie and her friends got me through a few rough patches early in my career, I must admit I stopped watching *Sex and the City* a few years before it went off the air. I got tired of hearing other women try to figure out which character they were, e.g., *"Oh! I'm a Charlotte because I'm a good girl!"* or *"I'm an attorney so I am all about Miranda!"* or *"I'm a Carrie because I write!"* (Rarely do I hear anyone say, *"I'm a whore so I'm a Samantha."*) And their romantic insecurities? I'd had enough.

The thing is, there are plenty of gals out there who have healthy self-esteem and solid relationships and they don't waste all their energy fixating on whether or not he's going to call. Rather, they're of the mind-set that *"Of course he'll call. Why? Because he knows*

---

[209] Later in Dallas I eat three cupcakes and have half a bottle of wine and then throw up in the wet bar's sink. I believe this is the universe's way of telling me how not to eat on a diet-book tour.

he's fucking lucky to have me." These women don't trawl the town every night. Sometimes they enjoy sitting at home with a partner (or they're content to be alone), watching reality TV in their sock-monkey pajamas and good jewelry, drinking wine.

Point? Maybe you aren't a Carrie or a Samantha or a Charlotte or a Miranda.

Maybe you're just *you*.

Regardless, I've already decided that Candace and I will be BFFs by the time we're finished with our interview because I'll be a breath of fresh air. I'll be different from all her New Yorky friends because I was raised in Indiana and because I have a pit bull named Maisy and because I get into fights with people at Target. She'll appreciate my middle-class status and will consider me all brave and avant-garde because I buy my own groceries and spy on my neighbors for fun. I'll call her Candy and she'll still call me Jen because I have no other nicknames.

We'll become thick as thieves and I'll get to hang out at her summer house with movie stars and she'll come and stay with me in my guest room and won't mind when Maisy the love monster insists on sleeping under the covers with her and she'll pretend to enjoy my husband's cooking because she's kind.

Of course, I'm pretty anxious to make a positive impression and I'm concerned I may freeze up on the air and lead to long moments of awkward silence on her show. She might not like me if I come in all panicky and wigged out. What if my mad respect for her causes me to make an ass out of myself? What if she hates boob tape?

I'm afraid I'm going to break into a *Wayne's World* "we're not worthy" at her feet the second we meet. Oh, God, what if I accidentally try to be funny and adopt a cornpone accent and tell her, "Ah've seen your stuff on the tee-vee!" After all, turning into a babbling idiot is what I do when I meet people I admire. I was at a book fair a few years ago and Augusten Burroughs was giving autographs. When it was my turn to say hello, I completely lost my shit. There I was in my twinset and pearls and pleated skirt and the one thing I could think to say to him was, "Ha, ha, I'm from Indiana, where everyone likes NASCAR! Wouldn't it be funny if I asked you to autograph my boob? Like at a NASCAR event? Ha, ha!"

Three years have passed and I'm still cringing.

What if I accidentally manage to hold it together and she hates me anyway? Or what if I get to the studios and her producers say, "Yeah, we made a mistake. We don't actually want you on the show."

Normally I wouldn't have so much insecurity and I'd be all, *She's lucky to get to meet* me. But come on—this is Candace Bushnell. The regular rules don't apply.

These thoughts race through my mind while I pass through the security checkpoints at the Sirius studio. I'm cleared at each level, so at least I can be sure that if I've been booted from the show, the producers haven't yet spread the word. I find this oddly comforting.

My editor, publicist, and I are standing in front of the little pod where Candace is doing her broadcast. I can't believe this is real. We just passed the studio where Howard Stern records his show and we're catty-corner from Opie and Anthony's broadcast hub. How on earth am *I* here?

I make Kara, my editor, confirm again that I'm well put

together, but I'm not sure I believe her. Seriously, do you know how fucking daunting it is to pick out an outfit Candace Bushnell will see? The woman is known *worldwide* for her taste. (I end up wearing a gauzy purple dress embellished with little silver balls and a white cardigan. Unfortunately I terror-sweated all the style out of my do. I wedge a pair of sunglasses on top of my head so my messy hair looks intentional.)

The producers wave to us on the other side of the glass and motion that they're about to wrap it up with the guest before me. While waiting, I toy with my buttons and chew all the lipstick off my bottom lip. I'm just about to hyperventilate when the door opens and a gorgeous black woman walks out. She smiles at me and says I can go in.

Hey.

I *know* her.

How do I know her?

Is she my cousin?

No, dumbass, you think every person who looks familiar is your cousin. I'm surprised you can even watch television without making Fletch crazy.

Television . . . television . . . wait! That's right! Oh, my God, that's Fatima from *America's Next Top Model*!

My thoughts are spinning. Fatima! That's so cool! I'm totally rooting for her! I love her even if she did make me do a terrible Google search when she discussed her ritual genital mutilation with Miss Tyra Banks.[210]

....

[210] I didn't know what it meant. Note: if you're curious, do not search images. That's something you can't un-see.

No, wait, that's not Fatima. Can't be. Her season is still running. I know this because I've got it loaded on my iTouch. Whether Fatima wins or loses, she's probably not allowed to do any media yet. So, if she's not Fatima, then how do I know this woman?

Wait a second . . . holy crap! That's *Iman*! As in CEO of *Iman* Cosmetics! As in global ambassador for Keep a Child Alive! As in *Mrs. David Bowie!* I'm here standing face-to-face with a world-famous supermodel![211] And I'm about to sit in *the very seat Iman just vacated.*

I wonder if she thinks my dress is cute?

Does she notice my tape hickeys?

I wave good-bye to Iman. (At least *this celebrity* can see me wave.) And now it's showtime. I steel myself and pretend to be calm when I enter the studio. *Come on, Jen. This is the big time,* I tell myself. *Save the squealing fangirl stuff for when you get back into the car. No one wants to be BFF with someone screamy.*

I say hello and am warmly welcomed by Candace and her producers. Then someone offers me a glass of wine in a paper cup.

Oh, thank God there's liquor here.

I sip my wine and adjust my headphones and, just like that, we begin to chat. We speak naturally and normally, even though I sort of blank out on the first ten minutes while we're discussing my book. I'm totally overwhelmed that Candace Bushnell has actually read it. That's like the Pope mentioning he saw you give mass. Or Frank Lloyd Wright remarking on the clean lines on the doghouse you built.

....

[211] Who has seen David Bowie naked!

As our conversation progresses and I snap out of my haze, I ask Candace if she's got anything coming out soon. She says yes, and I accidentally squeal. So much for my cool, collected demeanor.

"What else are you reading?" I ask. My hopes are she'll say *Bringing Home the Birkin*, which I just read, and we'll both agree on how much we loved it and we'll have our first (of many) bonding moment(s).

Candace tells me she's been all wrapped up in Baudelaire lately. I nod in agreement, vowing to Google "Baudelaire" on my BlackBerry the second this thing is over. Seriously, should I know this? Is Baudelaire a book? Is it a guy? Is he on *The Hills*? I have no idea. When she asks what I read, I agree that classics are best. I fail to elaborate that I consider anything by Helen Fielding to be a classic.[212]

Somehow our conversation turns to wedding rings and Candace mentions she hasn't been wearing hers because she's having a missing diamond replaced. She tells me it's okay since her husband still wears his. "After all," she says, "my husband's ten years younger than me, he's a principal dancer with the American Ballet Theatre, and everyone wants to sleep with him."

My response?

"Really? My husband's thirty-nine, he works for the phone company, and no one wants to sleep with him." Candace laughs for the first time during our interview.

We chat and drink more wine and before I can even catch my breath, we're done. Candace graciously allows photos (and hugs!)

....

[212] If Bridget Jones didn't change her life, too, we might not be able to be friends.

and then I'm back in the car, headed for the train station so I can take the Amtrak to Philly.

I take big gulps of air as I digest the whole interview. How am I this lucky? I just spent an hour with the *real* Carrie Bradshaw, the one who's ten thousand times more colorful in person. And she was wonderful.

I realize we probably won't become best friends. There likely will be no trips to her beach house and she'll never snuggle my pit bull. We live in entirely different universes. She's never going to shop at Lane Bryant, and I'm never going to go on a spree at Hermès. But you know what? I made my idol snicker a couple of times and that feels like a little miracle.

I can't manage to get the goofy grin off my face even as I board the train. I arrange my luggage next to me and settle into my seat for the short trip to Philadelphia. The lights on the train are all the way up for boarding so I can't really see out the window. I can, however, see my own reflection.

And I realize if we were truly destined to be BFF, she'd have told me I had lipstick on my teeth.

The tour has gone on for what seems like months, but I'm only in the second week. I'm exhausted from the travel and have taken to turning my ringer off during downtimes, which is why I miss Fletch's urgent call stating, "The cat barfed in the cleaning lady's shoe. What do I do?"

My phone starts to vibrate again and again. I ignore it because if he can't figure out to tip her extra, I can't help him. My room phone rings and I'm aggravated when I pick up. Seriously, can I not nap without being disturbed? Except it's not Fletch. It's my agent, editor and publicist. And they're calling because I just made the *New York Times* bestseller list.

❖

How can this be? I can't have made the list. Obviously the *New York Times* screwed up its reporting. Yes, my events are going well and the tour audience has been great, but I can't be on the *NYT* best-seller list. I don't write those kinds of books. I write stories about my dogs and about my husband's unfortunate attempts at cooking. I write about fighting with my mother and shopping at Trader Joe's.

Right now, if the list is right—which it isn't—I'm on the same list with two books by Barack Obama. He's going to be *the president* come November. I can't be on a list with the president. That's insanity. And I can't be on the same list as Elizabeth Gilbert and her spiritual awakening. She crossed the globe to discover a true relationship with God. I crossed the kitchen to discover the TwinkWich.[213]

Seriously, I'm just a big girl with a big mouth, cute shoes, and positive self-esteem who wrote a book about being a big girl with a big mouth, cute shoes, and positive self-esteem. The book ends with me being slightly less big, slightly more healthy, with the same amount of self-esteem . . . and maybe a few more pair of shoes.

I've always considered myself the sum of all my parts. I'm not just a manifestation of my mental and physical self. Personal style

....

[213] A sandwich consisting of a Twinkie and Ding Dong. It's a beautiful thing.

and proper wardrobe have been a part of making me who I am ever since I can remember. I've spent my whole life trying to accessorize in a way that would help me gain acceptance, so the idea of an entire audience liking me for my words alone is almost too much to comprehend.

Therefore the *Times* is wrong.

Obviously.

On the list that comes out a week later I'm no longer at number twenty.

Now I'm at number fourteen.

Seriously, your readers are not going to put up with these constant errors, *New York Times*. Get your shit together already. Same goes for you, *USA Today*.

I'm on the plane coming home from the West Coast leg of my tour. I've still got half a dozen more places to go in the next few weeks and the added pressure of writing an entirely new book[214] in the next two months. I feel like I'm at the end of my rope. I'm craving a couple of days where I can be home and make spaghetti and sit and watch TV with my husband, dogs curled up on either side of me, and not have to worry about repacking my suitcase.

It's beginning to look like the *New York Times* and *USA Today* aren't going to have to print retractions. Making these lists is the real deal, but at the same time celebrating these victories alone in

---

[214] Which you're totally reading right now!

strange cities feels hollow and fake. I want to be there to hug my husband when I get good news and not just get cursory congratulations from the cabdriver who happens to hear me when I take the call.

I want to share a pink champagne toast with Stacey, rather than have a glass (or four) of minibar wine in a sterile hotel room.

I want to run on the treadmill while yelling at my trainer Barbie, as opposed to doing nothing. Success doesn't mean nearly as much without anyone around to share it with me.

I was in such a haze this morning that I don't even remember showering or leaving the hotel. I just want to be home. I'm so tired. Even though I've been upgraded, I still have to sit here on this stupid plane for the next four hours next to a snoring jackass before I can kiss my husband and hug my dogs and pet my cats. I want to shut my eyes, so I decide to play some music rather than watch the *Survivor* finale.

The first song that comes on is Eminem's "Lose Yourself." I had this on constant rotation when I was in the throes of training. When Eminem sang about having one shot to seize everything he ever wanted, I'd get enough of a boost to run an extra quarter mile or to lift a few more pounds. *I want to capture this moment,* I'd think. *I won't just let it slip away.*

What always choked me up was where he sings about how success is his only (motherfucking) option, failure's not. More than anything, this is what drove me to work harder, live better, and put my entire self on the page in the third book.

Striving to be my personal best has always been a constant in my life, way before I ever heard the song. It's what kept me sane when Fletch and I were almost evicted and nearly had to move home with my parents. This quest taught me to fight to have my writing read and gave me the strength to plug along through a series of degrading and ridiculous jobs while trying desperately to get a tiny bit of notice in the publishing world.

So why am I feeling sorry for myself because *I'm tired and I miss my dogs?*

Here I am, on the *New York Times* bestsellers list, practically the greatest barometer for success an author could ever hope to achieve. And I got here by telling *my* story *my* way.

Me. A nobody from Indiana. A random girl with a bunch of sorority dance T-shirts and old Jordache jeans stored in her mom's attic. Nothing remarkable about her except an unvarying yearning to be better . . . and maybe an unhealthy fascination with cupcakes.

I did it.

I made it.

That's *my* name on the list.

But I recognize that I'm here right now living my dream because my audience connects with me, not because I'm carrying a Prada bag, but because we all have the same fears, insecurities, and joys. Thus, *they're* the ones who motivate me to be better. And the notion of having an audience pull for me *because I'm one of them* is far more daunting than making a list ever could be.

As I listen to the lyrics, I come to realize I have the ability to work toward other successes in my life. Maybe there'll be a screenplay or a sitcom or some kind of award in my future. Provided I try hard enough, there *will* be other shining moments in my career . . . and I won't always be alone when I get the good news about them.

This right here, this tour, this book, this very second . . . this is unique. Finally accepting that I earned a spot on the *New York Times* list for the very first time will never happen again.

When I look back on today years from now, I'll forever remember as the tipping point the second when everything I've ever worked for came together, and exactly when I realized my life had been permanently changed for the better.

But I might not remember what I was wearing.

A·C·K·N·O·W·L·E·D·G·M·E·N·T·S

❖

First, much love and thanks to Fletch, who totally deserves better but sticks around anyway. You make me smile about the past and look forward to the future.

Extra-special thanks and recognition go to my editor and friend (frienditor? edifriend?) Kara Cesare of NAL, along with Kara Welsh, Claire Zion, Craig Burke, Sharon Gamboa, Lindsay Nouis, sales and marketing, art, and production. Y'all are the Cadillac of publishers.

Big fat thanks to Kate Garrick for always having my back. (And to Brian DeFiore and Melissa Moy for having hers.) Four more years! Four more years! (I don't actually know what this means, but I just made myself laugh and that's key.)

Stacey Ballis, Angie Felton, Carol Kohrs, Wendy, Poppy, Jen, and Blackbird, the next hundred rounds are on me. Kristin "Kristabella" Johnson, Gina Bee, Shayla, Jolene Siana, Caprice Crane, Stephanie Klein, Kristi Reasons and the rest of the Avanti girls, Jess Riley, Eileen Cook, Stephanie Elliot, Melissa C. Morris and Allison Winn Scotch, you're invited, too. (Don't worry. Fletch will drive us. He's good like that.)

Finally, thanks to Shannon, Karen, Karl, Dave and Dave, Marnie, and Dean. I'm a better me for having known you.

Photo by J. B. Fletcher

Jen Lancaster is the author of four bestselling memoirs. She's appeared on NPR's *All Things Considered* and written for *Women's Health* and *Cosmopolitan UK*. She resides in Chicago with her husband and their ever-expanding menagerie of ill-behaved pets. Despite a heavy writing and appearance schedule, she still finds time to spy on her neighbors. Visit her blog at www.jennsylvania. com.

*S*ipping wine out of a paper cup, I'm perched on a tall stool across from my literary idol, Candace Bushnell, who's interviewing me for her Sirius radio show.

This is the single greatest day of my life.

I've managed to keep myself together enough to avoid (a) bursting into creepy fan-girl tears, (b) asking if I can please, please braid her pretty, pretty hair, or (c) shrieking, "OMFG, you're the real Carrie Bradshaw!" but it hasn't been without heroic effort. I'm mostly holding my own in the interview until Candace tells me she's totally into Bow da Lair.

Beaux de l'air?

Botta-layer?

Baudelaire?

I have no idea what she's talking about. Baudelaire—what is that, a kind of sushi? Some superstretchy Pilates move? This season's must-have stiletto? I am without a single clue. Yet I quickly confirm that I'm *absolutely* into Baudelaire, too, and then change topics with the grace and dexterity of a veteran White House press secretary.[1]

As I try to keep myself from breaking into terror sweat, it occurs to me that I don't know who Baudelaire is because I've become a little bit dumb.

What prompts this epiphany isn't my dearth of knowledge of All Things Baudelaire. Plenty of smart people are unfamiliar with Baudelaire.[2]

What gives me pause is the ease with which I cover up my ignorance. I'm confident I used to be smart, but when I got laid off from an executive position post-9/11, I was no longer tasked to use my critical-thinking skills. On top of that, while I searched in vain for a new job, reality television went from being an occasional guilty pleasure to a full-time source of solace. I mean, sure, I was unemployed and broke and I'd totally lost what defined me, but at least I wasn't one of those idiots attempting to get *Married by America*. And I never had to ask my friend Nicole Richie if Walmart was the place that sold walls. Reality television gave me an amazing feeling of moral and intellectual superiority without actually requiring any effort past moving the dogs to find the remote.

Although my life eventually improved,[3] I never weaned myself off of reality television once I started writing. And at this point I'm so used to not having much interest outside of what's happening with *The Real Housewives of Orange County* and in the

---

[1] Or a Lohan family publicist.

[2] Right?

[3] As evidenced by today's sit-down with Candace.

Rock of Love mansion that I've become an expert in faking most other knowledge. Lying about what I don't know has become my lazy but elegant solution to not acquiring the basic facts in the first place. Because I no longer report to a boss, I never have to take on hard or boring tasks, thus traveling outside of my comfort zone is a rarity, and most likely involuntary.

Frankly, my steady diet of sloth and avoidance has served me well, and I will see no reason to change things . . . until the unthinkable happens next week, and I inadvertently end up on the *New York Times* bestseller list.

Ten times.

Dude.

What gets me is the sneaking suspicion that I'd be a better writer if my first thought at this unexpected windfall wasn't *"Dude."* So I grudgingly admit that broadening my horizons is something I should work on, but I've got to get through this book tour first.

Anyway, our interview eventually draws to a close, and I leave the studio with no idea if Baudelaire is some kind of yogic breathing technique or French-Vietnamese cuisine.

But I do know if I want to be more like Candace Bushnell, perhaps I should make an effort to find out.